Shadow Economies in Turkic Republics

"This timely volume, edited by Elshan Bagirzadeh and Omer Gokcekus, sheds light on one of the most persistent and complex economic development challenges facing the modern Turkic World. By rigorously documenting the scope and consequences of shadow economies, this book not only advances our understanding of this economic problem but also underscores the broader importance of science and scholarship in shaping the sustainable futures of the Turkic Republics. It is especially encouraging to see these analyses produced by scholars from the region itself, demonstrating the growing strength and maturity of Turkic economic studies. Similar collaborative efforts will be invaluable if they continue and expand in the years to come. For societies seeking to combine economic development with social equity and environmental responsibility, this book may be a valuable and much-needed guide."

—Aziz Sancar, *Nobel Prize winner in Chemistry, University of North Carolina at Chapel Hill*

"The Turkic heritage nations share cultural commonalities but differ greatly in economic structure and recent development. A common thread, however, is the presence of large shadow economies—often exceeding 40 percent of GDP—that undermine transparency, rule of law, and governance, and hinder economic growth. The Bagirzadeh & Gokcekus volume is the first to identify both core challenges and the uniqueness of individual countries, offering a foundation for policies to contain the shadow economy and strengthen government effectiveness, thereby fostering economic growth. The book also highlights the region's heterogeneity, noting that while some countries have advanced in digitalization and formalization, others are only beginning to take steps in that direction. The case studies enrich this analysis and cover a wide range of topics. They represent the frontier of modern development economics – unimaginably different from what the founders of the discipline had in mind, and focusing on policy decisions in a digital era that lead to vastly different outcomes."

—Charles M. Becker, *Duke University*

"A significant scholarly contribution to the field, this volume delivers a cohesive and authoritative study of the shadow economy across the diverse and growing economies of the Turkic world."

—Nigar Hashimzade, *Brunel University of London*

"This edited volume brings together an outstanding collection of studies on shadow economies in the Turkic republics. By focusing on the Turkic republics, it enriches our understanding of how informality evolves in a region marked by both rapid economic growth and institutional diversity. I can highly recommend this fascinating work to anyone seeking to gain deeper insights into the shadow economy."

—Friedrich Schneider, *Johannes Kepler University of Linz*

Elshan Bagirzadeh · Omer Gokcekus
Editors

Shadow Economies in Turkic Republics

Governance, Institutions, Trust, and Policy Responses

palgrave
macmillan

Editors
Elshan Bagirzadeh
Department of Economics
Azerbaijan State University
of Economics
Baku, Azerbaijan

Omer Gokcekus
School of Diplomacy
and International Relations
Seton Hall University
South Orange, NJ, USA

ISBN 978-3-032-12871-3 ISBN 978-3-032-12872-0 (eBook)
https://doi.org/10.1007/978-3-032-12872-0

This Palgrave Macmillan imprint is published by the registered company Springer Nature Switzerland AG
The registered company address is: Gewerbestrasse 11, 6330 Cham, Switzerland

To our parents, for always instilling in us honesty and fairness

Foreword

The shadow economy, that vast realm of economic activity operating beyond the reach of official statistics and government oversight, has long challenged economists, policymakers, and development practitioners alike. While its existence is universally acknowledged, measuring its true scope and understanding its complex dynamics remain among the most formidable tasks in modern economics. This collection of studies on shadow economies in the Turkic republics represents a significant contribution to our understanding of informality in one of the world's most economically dynamic yet institutionally diverse regions.

This volume could not be timelier. As the Organization of Turkic States (OTS) strengthens its economic cooperation framework through the "Turkic World Vision 2040," understanding the informal dimensions of these economies becomes increasingly critical for crafting effective regional policies. The Turkic republics—Azerbaijan, Kazakhstan, Kyrgyzstan, Türkiye, Uzbekistan, and the Turkish Republic of Northern Cyprus—share linguistic and cultural heritage but exhibit remarkably different institutional trajectories. This diversity provides a natural laboratory for examining how varying historical experiences, from Soviet central planning to market capitalism, shape contemporary patterns of informality.Informal activity is not a curiosity at the margins of these economies; it is part of how they actually work. What this volume does especially well is to show that, across the Turkic republics, informality is patterned, not random, and that those patterns move when institutions move. The comparative chapter, using a consistent MIMIC framework, shows that between **1993** and **2020** the OTS group's average shadow economy eased from **46.7%** to **42.2%** of GDP, with Türkiye the persistent low outlier and Azerbaijan the high one. In **2020**, Türkiye sits at *32.2%* while Azerbaijan remains at **53.1%**, a spread large enough to demand country-specific explanations rather than one-size policies.

Readers will also notice that the editors keep the cross-country comparisons coherent (MIMIC throughout) yet make room for methodological innovation where the data allow it. The Uzbekistan chapter, for example, leverages an electricity-consumption model on high-frequency power data and, after correcting for efficiency trends, traces a steady decline toward the **35–40%** range by **2023**. That sits well beside the MIMIC series and gives policymakers a second lens on progress.

Some of the most instructive pages are where numbers meet behavior. In Northern Cyprus, a newly extended MIMIC series puts the average shadow-to-GDP ratio around **31%** for **2011–2023**, but the chapter also documents striking income underreporting, **64%** on labor income in a 2015 microdataset, and locates it in low institutional trust and weak accountability. We learn as much about enforcement credibility as about measurement.

A few themes recur across the country chapters. Digitalization now matters: Türkiye's move to integrated digital registers and online tax systems, and Kazakhstan's use of digital tools as state-capacity levers, both appear to narrow room for off-the-books transactions. Trust, its presence or absence, does a lot of work in explaining the persistence of undeclared employment. And the labor market, self-employment especially, acts as a pressure valve when formal absorption is weak. These are not abstract generalities; they are patterns that surface again and again in the data and the narratives here.

The region's recent policy coordination under the **OTS** makes these findings more than academic. As OTS economies align development agendas, the book's evidence offers a shared empirical baseline while still respecting national context. Notably, Turkmenistan is absent for data reasons, a useful reminder that measurement itself is a policy capacity.

I have spent much of my own work thinking about measurement, incentives, and the institutional drivers of informality; what surprised me here was how consistently **trust** and **digital state capacity** travel across such different political economies. That is an actionable insight. The policy lesson is not simply "enforce more," but "make formality the low-friction default," via clearer rules, credible social protection, and digital rails that reduce the everyday costs of being formal.

To sum up, I honestly believe that this book gives policymakers something precious: not just a number to quote, but a map to follow. It represents a significant milestone in shadow economy research, combining rigorous empirical analysis with deep institutional understanding to produce insights that will be valuable to academics, policymakers, and development practitioners for years to come. It stands as a testament to the power of collaborative research in illuminating the hidden dimensions of economic life.

Ceyhun Elgin
Bogaziçi University
Istanbul, Türkiye

Preface

This volume grew out of a shared recognition that the shadow economy remains one of the most persistent and underexplored challenges facing the Turkic republics. While the phenomenon has long attracted attention in both policy and academic debates, no systematic comparative study existed that placed the region's diverse experiences side by side.

To address this gap, we brought together a group of researchers from across the Turkic republics, each of whom contributed a country-focused study following a common structure. This approach ensures both comparability across cases and the integration of country-specific insights. The result is a volume that combines regional perspective with national depth, and which we hope will serve as a reference point for both scholars and policymakers.

We are grateful to our contributors for their dedication and to the institutions that supported this collaborative effort. It is our hope that the analyses presented here will stimulate further research and provide a solid empirical basis for policy discussions on informality in the region.

Baku, Azerbaijan — Elshan Bagirzadeh
South Orange, USA — Omer Gokcekus

Acknowledgments

Working with colleagues from across the Turkic republics on this volume has been a truly rewarding experience. It has provided us with the opportunity to collaborate with a diverse group of scholars, whose perspectives and expertise have greatly enriched this work. It has also allowed us to deepen our understanding of the shadow economy in these countries, both through comparative analysis and through engagement with local contexts and data.

Omer Gokcekus wishes to thank Seton Hall University for granting him sabbatical leave and the Azerbaijan State University of Economics (UNEC), which generously hosted him in Baku for one month during this period. This visit was instrumental in advancing the progress of the book. He is also grateful to his family members for their continuous encouragement and support, and in particular to his wife, Rumeysa Gokcekus, whose understanding and patience made it possible for him to devote himself fully to this project.

Elshan Bagirzadeh extends his sincere appreciation to his family, especially his wife, Nurana Amirova, and his daughter, Seljan Bagirzadeh, for their unwavering support and patience during the preparation of this volume. He also wishes to acknowledge the valuable insights and constructive exchanges with numerous colleagues and experts, whose contributions, though too many to name individually, have enriched this work.

Together, as co-editors, we extend our thanks to all chapter authors for their valuable contributions and to all contributors whose professionalism and commitment ensured that the process proceeded smoothly and productively. We also wish to thank Ceyhun Elgin for kindly writing the preface to the volume and Aziz Sancar, Friedrich Schneider, Nigar Hashimzadeh, and Charles M. Becker for their valuable insights regarding the book.

Finally, we are grateful to Geetha Chockalingam and Bronwyn Geyer at Palgrave Macmillan for their guidance and support throughout the preparation of this book.

Elshan Bagirzadeh
Omer Gokcekus

Contents

List of Figures

Chapter 1

Chapter 2

Chapter 3

Chapter 5

Chapter 6

Chapter 7

Chapter 8

List of Tables

CHAPTER 1

Introduction: Comparative Analyses of Shadow Economies of Turkic Republics

Elshan Bagirzadeh and Omer Gokcekus

1 Why This Book

Located in a strategically important geography—a kind of center of Eurasia—the Turkic Republics are increasingly recognized as pivotal players in global economic development, with their natural resources (especially energy and rare earth elements), human capital, and transport and communication corridors. Their role has been increasing and becoming more concrete in recent years as they have come together under the umbrella of the Organization of Turkic States (OTS) and have sought to align their economic development policies (OTS, 2021). The OTS, of which Azerbaijan, Kazakhstan, Kyrgyzstan, Türkiye, and Uzbekistan are permanent members and Hungary, Northern Cyprus, and Turkmenistan

E. Bagirzadeh (✉)
Department of Economics, Azerbaijan State University of Economics, Baku, Azerbaijan
e-mail: elshan.bagirzadeh@unec.edu.az

O. Gokcekus
Seton Hall University, South Orange, USA
e-mail: gokcekom@shu.edu

E. Bagirzadeh and O. Gokcekus (eds.), *Shadow Economies in Turkic Republics*, https://doi.org/10.1007/978-3-032-12872-0_1

are observer members, has further strengthened its position on the path to becoming a regional economic group by recently accepting the Economic Cooperation Organization (ECO) as an observer. In this regard, the economic development issues of the Turkic Republics are increasingly becoming the focus of attention of academic circles, and the number of works on the subject in bibliometric databases has increased significantly in recent years.

Although the population of the Turkic Republics shares the same ancestry and culture, the socialist heritage of Azerbaijan, Kazakhstan, Kyrgyzstan, Uzbekistan, and Turkmenistan, and the capitalist heritage of Türkiye and Northern Cyprus, has in many cases led to their different economic problems. However, these republics also have many similar economic problems, one of the most important of which is the shadow economy. Numerous international studies show that the share of shadow GDP in official GDP in these countries, although it has decreased relatively in recent years, is still significant (ACCA, 2017; Medina & Schneider, 2018; Elgin et al., 2021; EY, 2025; World Economics, 2025). The existence of such a significant shadow economy can be considered one of the factors undermining the sustainability of the economic development of these countries. Thus, the problem mentioned in these countries limits the tax sources of public budget revenues, prevents the establishment of a reliable pension system, worsens income distribution, disrupts healthy competition, and harms the formation of export-competitive industries.

In this regard, studies covering various aspects of the shadow economy, such as its scale, determinants, consequences, and solution policies, are of great relevance for the mentioned countries. Although such studies have been conducted in a limited number for each of these economies separately so far, there is no separate comprehensive study dedicated to the problem of the shadow economy in the Turkic Republics. Therefore, this book, entitled "Shadow Economies in Turkic Republics," can be considered the first comprehensive academic initiative with the important goal of filling the mentioned gap to a certain extent. One of the features that makes the book special is that each of its chapters is written by experienced and advanced specialists in the field of the country under study. This allows the local characteristics of that country to be taken into account as much as possible and thus to reach more reliable academic results.

The book covers all Turkic Republics that are members of the Organization of Turkic States, with the exception of Turkmenistan (which is not yet possible due to insufficient data). Since the chapters of the book cover not only the problems of the shadow economy of these countries but also their economic and institutional profiles, it can also be a useful source for those who want to study the overall economic landscape of the Organization of Turkic States as an emerging regional economic group.

2 Conceptual Clarifications and Theoretical Anchors

In the literature, more than 30 different terms such as "shadow," "informal," "unofficial," "underground," "non-observed," and "unregistered" are used to describe economic activities that are outside the official economy—in other words, those that are not covered by government policy, regulation, and control measures and, as a result, are not reflected in official statistics (Bagirzade, 2012a; Williams, 2023). In fact, it is possible to reveal some general trends in the use of these terms depending on the emphasis on any feature of economic activities outside the official economy, the level of coverage of these activities, their differentiation in international documents, and the language in which the research is published. However, there are also cases where the same author expresses the same economic activities outside the official economy with different terms in different studies, and at the same time, it is often possible to find different uses of terms differentiated in international documents by some researchers. All these cases clearly reveal the lack of a common approach in the use of the numerous existing terms. Therefore, the most common practice in the literature is that the researcher uses any term, clearly stating which part of the economic activities outside the official economy they are studying (Bagirzade, 2012a). This book also adopts the same approach, choosing mainly non-criminal unofficial economic activities as the research subject, and preferring the term "shadow economy" to describe them.

If we approach shadow economic activities as a phenomenon from the perspective of economic actors avoiding obligations arising from existing institutional norms, we can easily say that the emergence of such activities is as old as human history. However, because economics has developed over a long period primarily based on the official sector of the economy, theories regarding the shadow economy emerged later (Bagirzade, 2012b). Today, four different theories can be identified in the literature that attempt to explain the shadow economy. According to the *dualistic/modernization theory*, the main drivers of the shadow economy are unmodern governance systems and economic under-development. *Legalist/neoliberal theory*, on the other hand, argues that excessive state intervention (e.g., high tax rates, burdensome regulations) is a determining factor in the emergence of shadow economies. *Structuralist/political economy theory* argues the opposite, stating that the shadow economy is caused by inadequate state intervention in work and welfare. *Institutionalist theory* approaches the issue from an institutional perspective, demonstrating that formal institutional failures create an asymmetry between formal rules and society's norms, values, and beliefs, thus leading to a more widespread shadow economy (Williams, 2023). It should be noted that each of these theories alone is insufficient to explain the shadow economy problem in the Turkic Republics. Therefore, in the analyses in this book, each of these theories is used to a certain extent, depending on the country and the specifics of the problem.

3 Shared Legacies and Diverging Paths

The long and common past of the Turkic countries, which share the same language, religion, and culture has led to the similarity of their current production and business cultures. However, there are also a number of differences arising from this heritage between those of these countries that have the former Soviet heritage and those that do not, which are more evident in political systems, economic reforms, and state capabilities—in short, in institutions. The peoples of the post-Soviet Turkic Republics have been living with the problem of the shadow economy since the Soviet period. In this situation, which we can explain more with the institutional theory mentioned above, the Soviet Union tried to suppress all free economic initiatives by banning them, and people, in response, often chose the shadow economy as a way out to meet their essential needs. Toward the end of the Soviet Union, when state control was gradually weakening, the shadow economy had already become a kind of normal for the Soviet people, including officials, and was widely studied by social scientists in the United States and Europe under the name of the "second economy" (Grossman, 1977; Shelley, 1990). This "second economy" of the Soviet era, although it included elements such as corruption and theft of state property to a significant extent, consisted mostly of private initiatives with market relations. In other words, since the socialist system prohibited capitalist economic relations, capitalism tried to sustain itself through shadow economic activities. As a result, the people developed habits of engaging in economic activities outside the official economy. After the collapse of the Soviet Union, the institutional legacy we mentioned began to manifest itself more strongly in these countries. Faced with the severe consequences of a collapsing economic and political system, the people began to rely more on shadow economic activities (Eilat & Zinnes, 2000; Johnson et al., 1997; Kaufmann & Kaliberda, 1996; Lacko, 2000). This institutional legacy also largely affected market reforms (which were also led mainly by officials left over from the Soviet era), and these reforms often did not produce the expected results (Dabrowski, 2023). As a result, economies that can be explained more by the concept of crony capitalism and based on low-quality institutions emerged in those countries, which also provided a more favorable environment for shadow economic activities.

The situation is somewhat different in Türkiye and Northern Cyprus, which do not have a socialist heritage. Although the size of the shadow economy in these countries is no less than that of other Turkic countries, they have a long history of market economy, rule of law, and democratic institutions. The high level of the shadow economy in these countries can be explained by various factors. In Türkiye, factors such as heavy taxes and state regulations, low quality of institutions, rapid and unplanned urbanization, economic instability and inequality, and refugee and migrant flows seem to be more influential (Altındağ et al., 2020; Ikiz, 2017). Although the economy of Northern Cyprus is currently closely integrated into the economy of Türkiye, there are also unique factors that give rise to the shadow economy there. Among these are political unrecognition and international isolation, the existence of the gambling and casino sector, legal uncertainties in the land and property sector, illegal migrant flows, the dominance of tourism and other service sectors in the economy, and weak state capacity (Besim et al., 2015a, 2015b; Ekici & Besim, 2016).

There is no single determinant of the shadow economy in any country. However, almost all international studies in this field show that the country's institutional structure and quality are key determinants of the problem (Elgin, 2021). In other words, when institutions such as transparency, rule of law, corruption control, regulatory quality, and effective government are weak, countries provide a favorable environment for economic activities that bypass laws, regulations, and official registration systems. In this regard, although the Turkic Republics have followed different paths of institutional development, today they are at roughly the same level in terms of institutional quality, and all lag far behind developed countries (World Bank, n.d.).

4 Measurement and Data: What We Know and Don't Know

Measuring the shadow economy, though conceptually straightforward, remains technically challenging. Despite improvements in methodology, the shadow economy's size cannot be measured precisely by any approach. Most techniques—including the Multiple Indicators Multiple Causes (MIMIC) model, the Dynamic General Equilibrium (DGE) model, and the currency demand method—yield approximations rather than precise estimates. These methods differ in scope: while MIMIC and DGE aim to estimate activities meant to evade taxes and regulations, they do not account for illegal production, informal household enterprises, or unpaid household production. Currency demand models can capture some of these excluded areas but have become less reliable with the expansion of digital payments and cryptocurrencies.

Because each method captures different components of informality, cross-country comparisons are most meaningful when based on a consistent methodology applied across countries and years. In this book, most of the shadow economy estimates rely on the MIMIC approach, which allows for coherent comparative analysis across the Turkic Republics. Where the World Bank's global informal economy database is unavailable, authors have used national-level MIMIC-based studies or constructed new series using consistent frameworks. In some cases, these are supplemented with alternative indicators such as electricity consumption, expert surveys, or household budget data—but only for country-specific analysis.

The next section builds on this measurement foundation by drawing on the World Bank's global informal economy database, which integrates multiple informality indicators. This enables a systematic overview of the evolution and relative size of shadow economies in the Turkic Republics, grounding the country-specific chapters that follow in a shared empirical baseline.

5 Shadow Economy Trends in the Turkic Republics: A Comparative Overview

The ability to conduct meaningful cross-country comparisons of shadow economies depends critically on the quality, consistency, and breadth of available data. In this regard, the global database of informal economic activity constructed by the World Bank's Prospects Group represents a major contribution. Covering up to 196 economies over the period 1990 to 2020, this database brings together eleven widely used measures of informality. These indicators are grouped under three broad categories: output, employment, and perceptions.

The output-related measures estimate the size of informal production as a share of GDP using two modeling frameworks. The first is based on a dynamic general equilibrium model, while the second uses the Multiple Indicators Multiple Causes, or MIMIC, approach. These model-based estimates rely on structural relationships among observable variables to infer the scale of hidden economic activity.

The employment-related measures reflect labor market informality using direct survey data and administrative sources. Four indicators are included in this group: the share of self-employment in the labor force, the share of informal employment as defined by the International Labour Organization (ILO), the share of employment outside the formal sector, and the share of the labor force not covered by pension insurance. These indicators offer a complementary view of informality by focusing on employment status rather than output.

The perception-based measures rely on subjective assessments obtained through surveys of firms and households. One indicator is derived from the World Economic Forum's Executive Opinion Survey, four are taken from the World Bank's Enterprise Surveys, and one comes from the World Values Survey. These indicators capture how informality is perceived and experienced by economic agents rather than how it is measured directly.

Taken together, the database offers both indirect, model-based estimates and direct, survey-based indicators. This combination strengthens the robustness of cross-country analyses and allows for the triangulation of findings across different types of data. The methodological details and applications of the database are documented in a discussion paper by Elgin et al. (2021) .

Importantly, the internal consistency of the indicators is supported by high pairwise correlations among conceptually related measures.

For instance, the correlation between DGE and MIMIC model-based estimates is 0.99, indicating near-perfect alignment. Similarly, the two informal employment series track each other closely, with a correlation of 0.97. The correlation between self-employment and informal employment is 0.81, while pension coverage and self-employment are negatively correlated at −0.67. Among the perception-based indicators, firms that report facing many informal competitors also tend to feel constrained by them, with a correlation of 0.77. These findings suggest that despite differences in methodology and source, the indicators in the database are largely consistent and mutually reinforcing. A summary of the key correlations is presented in Table 1.

Data Availability and Selection of Comparable Estimates

Of the six countries examined in this volume, four—Azerbaijan, Kazakhstan, Kyrgyzstan, and Türkiye—are included in the World Bank's global informal economy database. Uzbekistan and the Turkish Republic of Northern Cyprus, however, are not covered in this dataset. For Uzbekistan, MIMIC-based estimates spanning the period 2007 to 2018 are available from Donaev (2019). For the Turkish Republic of Northern Cyprus (TRNC), a consistent time series covering 2011 to 2023 has been constructed by Besim (2025), also using the MIMIC approach. Given the high internal consistency among informality indicators, as shown in Table 1, and the availability of comparable estimates for all six countries

Table 1 Correlation between informality indicators

Pair of indicators	*Pearson r*	*Interpretation*
DGE p ↔ MIMIC p	0.99	Two model-based output estimates move almost one-for-one
Infsize p ↔ Infemp p	0.97	The ILO's twin informal employment series track each other closely
SEMP p ↔ Infemp p	0.81	More self-employment is associated with more informal jobs
Pension p ↔ SEMP p	−0.67	Broader pension coverage correlates with less self-employment
WBentp1 ↔ WBentp4	0.77	Firms facing more informal rivals also feel more constrained by them

using the same methodological framework, this volume relies exclusively on MIMIC-based series for cross-country analyses.

Analytical Strategy and Baseline Comparisons

To frame the country-level chapters that follow, we begin with a set of comparative exercises using the MIMIC-based estimates described above. These comparisons serve to establish a regional context and identify broad patterns. First, we compare the average trajectory of the four OTS countries included in the World Bank database to the global average over the period 1993 to 2020. This allows us to assess whether the group has been converging toward or diverging from global norms in informality. Second, we examine how the three post-Soviet OTS members—Azerbaijan, Kazakhstan, and Kyrgyzstan—have performed relative to Russia between 1993 and 2020, in light of their shared institutional legacies. Third, we compare all six countries over the common period from 2011 to 2018 to evaluate relative progress, identify the best and worst performers, and explore convergence or divergence trends within the group. These baseline comparisons provide the necessary empirical background for interpreting the findings presented in subsequent chapters.

Figure 1 compares the average size of the shadow economy in four OTS countries—Azerbaijan, Kazakhstan, Kyrgyzstan, and Türkiye—with the global average over the period 1993 to 2020, based on MIMIC estimates. In 1993, the average shadow economy size in the OTS group stood at 44.4 percent of GDP, compared to the world average of 34.6 percent. By 2020, these figures had declined to 39.9 and 32.7 percent, respectively. Although both series exhibit a downward trend, the gap between them narrowed only slightly, from 9.8 percentage points in 1993 to 7.2 percentage points in 2020. This persistent gap underscores the structural nature of informality in the region. While the world average declined by 1.9 percentage points over the observed period, the four OTS countries achieved a somewhat larger reduction of 4.5 percentage points. Nevertheless, the consistently elevated levels across the OTS group point to region-specific institutional and policy constraints that continue to sustain informality, despite gradual improvements.

Figure 2 illustrates the evolution of the minimum, maximum, and average size of the shadow economy among the four OTS countries—Azerbaijan, Kazakhstan, Kyrgyzstan, and Türkiye—over the period 1993 to 2020, based on MIMIC estimates. The shaded area represents the

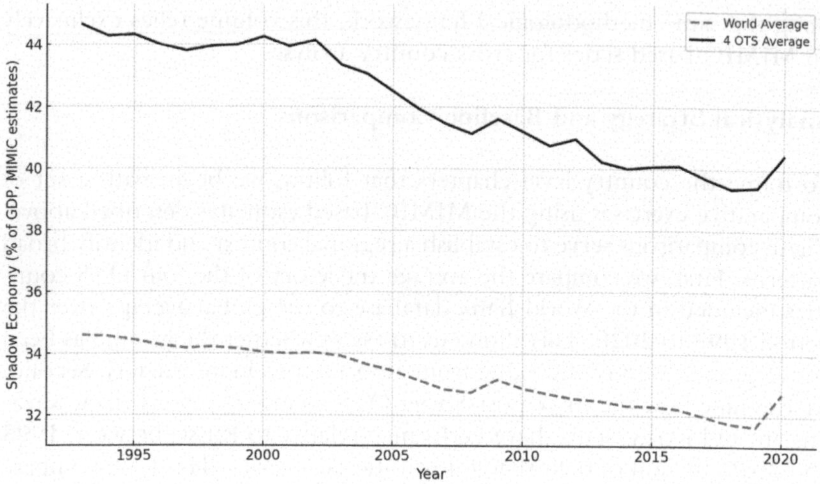

Fig. 1 Shadow economy in 4 OTS countries vs. world average (MIMIC estimates, 1993–2020)

annual range between the country with the lowest and the highest informality level, while the black line indicates the group average.

In the early 1990s, the within-group disparity was substantial. In 1993, Türkiye recorded the lowest shadow economy size at 32.6 percent of GDP, while Azerbaijan reached the highest at 61.2 percent, producing a gap of 28.6 percentage points. Although this gap narrowed intermittently in the following decades, divergence remained a consistent feature. For instance, in 2020, the minimum value was again observed in Türkiye at 31.0 percent, while Azerbaijan still held the maximum at 54.8 percent—maintaining a 23.8-point difference.

Over the full period, Türkiye consistently posted the lowest levels of informality, while Azerbaijan remained the highest throughout. Kazakhstan and Kyrgyzstan fell in between, alternating positions over different years but generally moving in parallel. The average for the group declined moderately, from 44.4 percent in 1993 to 39.9 percent in 2020, suggesting slow but steady formalization.

Despite these improvements, the persistence of a wide min–max range underscores that the four OTS countries have followed divergent paths in tackling informality. The group average masks significant internal

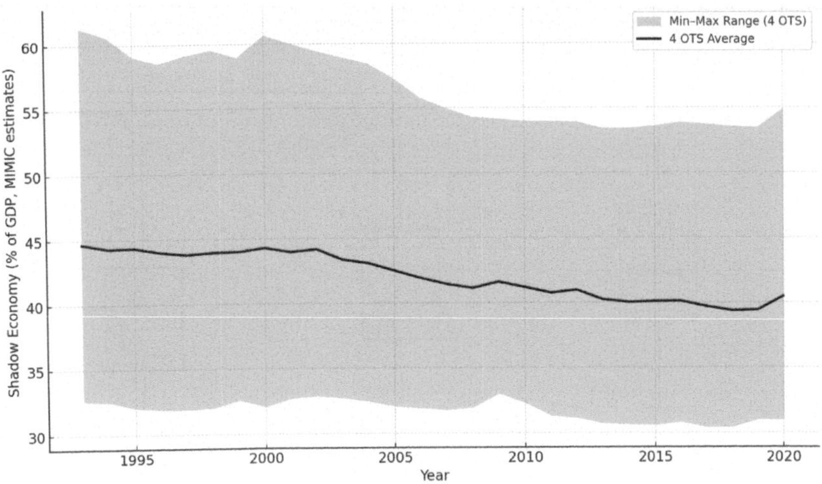

Fig. 2 Range and average of shadow economy in 4 OTS countries (MIMIC estimates, 1993–2020)

variation, making it essential to interpret regional trends alongside country-specific dynamics.

Figure 3 displays the distribution of shadow economy estimates in the four OTS countries—Azerbaijan, Kazakhstan, Kyrgyzstan, and Türkiye—across three decades: the 1990s, 2000s, and 2010s. Each boxplot reflects the spread of annual MIMIC-based estimates for all country-year combinations within the respective decade. The results reveal two consistent patterns: a gradual decline in overall informality and a modest reduction in dispersion over time.

In the 1990s, the median shadow economy size across the group was 42.4 percent of GDP, with values ranging from 32.0 percent (Türkiye, 1996) to 61.2 percent (Azerbaijan, 1993). The interquartile range was wide, indicating substantial variation across countries and years. In the 2000s, the median fell to 40.1 percent, and by the 2010s, it had declined further to 38.3 percent. The narrowing of the interquartile range in the 2010s suggests partial convergence among the four countries, though significant differences persisted.

The boxplots confirm that while formalization has progressed steadily over the decades, the pace and depth of that transition have varied

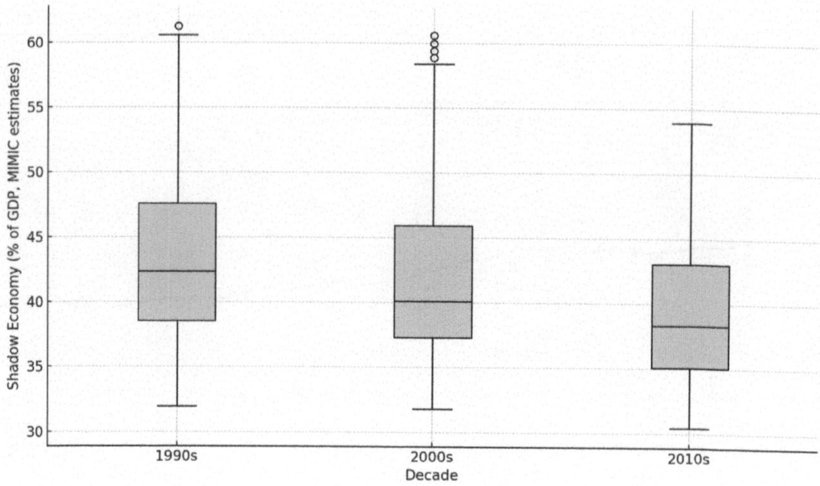

Fig. 3 Shadow economy distributions in 4 OTS countries by decade

considerably within the OTS group. This highlights the importance of examining country-specific institutional trajectories and reform efforts, which are explored in detail in the chapters that follow.

Figure 4 compares the shadow economy size in four OTS countries—Azerbaijan, Kazakhstan, Kyrgyzstan, and Türkiye—between the years 1993 and 2020, based on MIMIC estimates. In 1993, Azerbaijan recorded the highest level of informality at 61.2 percent of GDP, followed by Kazakhstan at 43.4 percent, Kyrgyzstan at 41.3 percent, and Türkiye at 32.6 percent. By 2020, all four countries had reduced their shadow economy shares to varying degrees. Türkiye maintained its position as the least shadow economy, dropping to 31.0 percent. Kazakhstan and Kyrgyzstan converged toward similar levels of 38.4 and 37.6 percent, respectively. Azerbaijan, despite a modest decline, remained the most informal, with an estimate of 54.8 percent.

The absolute reductions between 1993 and 2020 were most pronounced in Azerbaijan (−6.4 percentage points) and Kazakhstan (−5.0 percentage points), while Türkiye achieved a more modest decline of 1.6 percentage points. Kyrgyzstan experienced a small improvement, with only a 3.7 percentage points drop over the entire period. These results highlight the persistence of structural differences in informality

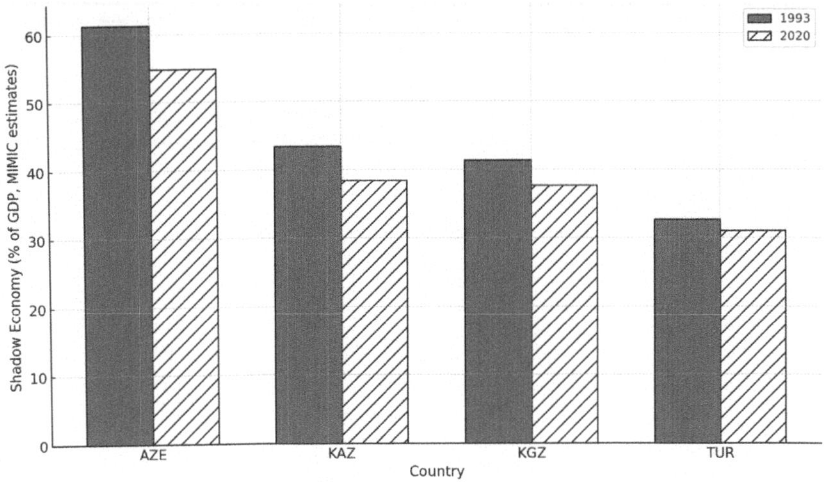

Fig. 4 Shadow economy in 4 OTS countries: 1993 vs. 2020 (MIMIC estimates)

across the region, as well as the uneven progress made by individual countries despite broad similarities in regional context.

Figure 5 traces the evolution of shadow economy estimates for three post-Soviet OTS countries—Azerbaijan, Kazakhstan, and Kyrgyzstan—alongside Russia over the period 1993 to 2020. These countries share a common institutional legacy shaped by their experience under Soviet central planning, which left behind similar state structures, administrative habits, and informal coping mechanisms. Comparing their trajectories since independence provides insight into how different reform paths, political choices, and economic shocks have shaped the evolution of informality in the region.

In 1993, the size of the shadow economy was broadly similar across the four countries, with estimates ranging from 41.3 percent of GDP in Kyrgyzstan to 61.2 percent in Azerbaijan. Russia stood at 45.2 percent, slightly above Kazakhstan and Kyrgyzstan, but considerably below Azerbaijan. Although the percentage of the shadow economy declined in all four countries after 1993, the situation remained almost unchanged. In 2020, with a shadow economy of 43.1 percent of GDP, Russia was slightly above Kazakhstan and Kyrgyzstan, but significantly below Azerbaijan.

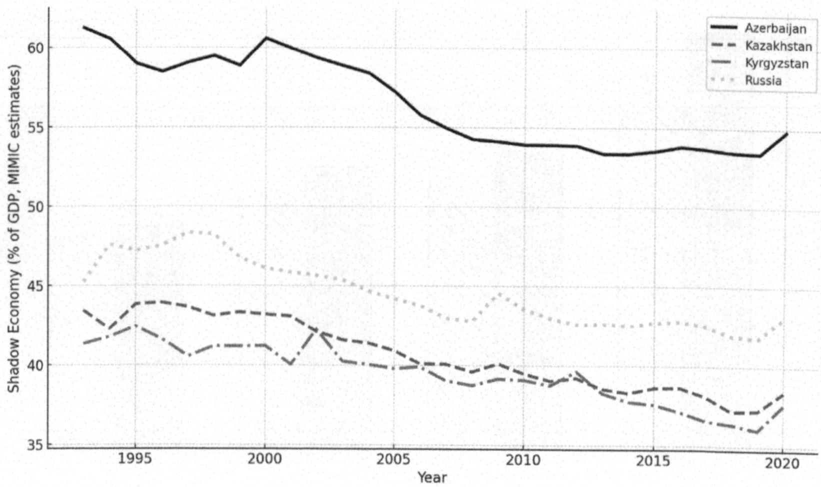

Fig. 5 Shadow economy in post-Soviet OTS countries and Russia (MIMIC estimates, 1993–2020)

Azerbaijan stands out for its persistently high informality levels, ending the period with an estimate of 54.8 percent—well above the others. Russia's trend is remarkably stable, with only a marginal decline over nearly three decades. Overall, the percentage of the shadow economy decreased more in all three OTS countries, particularly Azerbaijan, than in Russia during the period 1993–2020. This result indicates that the dynamics driving the economy towards formalization are stronger in all three OTS countries compared to Russia.

Figure 6 presents the net change in the size of the shadow economy for six countries—Azerbaijan, Kazakhstan, Kyrgyzstan, Türkiye, Uzbekistan, and the Turkish Republic of Northern Cyprus (TRNC)—between 2011 and 2018, based on MIMIC estimates. This period is the only stretch for which comparable data is available for all six countries, allowing for a direct evaluation of relative progress in formalization.

The most significant reduction occurred in Uzbekistan, where the shadow economy share fell from 57.9 percent of GDP in 2011 to 50.0 percent in 2018, marking a drop of 7.9 percentage points. Kyrgyzstan and Kazakhstan also recorded substantial improvements, with declines of

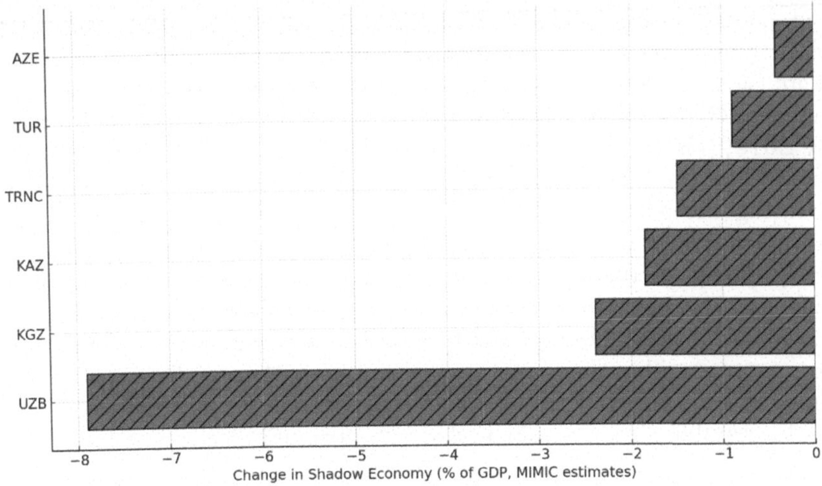

Fig. 6 Change in shadow economy in six countries (MIMIC estimates, 2011–2018)

2.3 and 1.8 percentage points, respectively. TRNC showed a meaningful but smaller reduction of 1.5 points, from 32.5 to 31.0 percent.

Türkiye and Azerbaijan posted only marginal improvements. Türkiye's shadow economy declined by 0.9 percentage points, from 31.3 to 30.4 percent, while Azerbaijan's decreased by just 0.4 points, from 53.9 to 53.5 percent. This limited movement suggests relative stagnation, particularly in Azerbaijan, where informality remained persistently high despite regional progress.

Overall, the results highlight a widening performance gap. While some countries—most notably Uzbekistan—have accelerated formalization efforts during this period, others have made little or no measurable progress. This divergence raises important questions about the effectiveness of institutional reforms, enforcement capacity, and the underlying political will to address informality across the OTS region.

Figure 7 displays the dispersion and average of shadow economy estimates across the six countries in our sample—Azerbaijan, Kazakhstan, Kyrgyzstan, Türkiye, Uzbekistan, and the Turkish Republic of Northern Cyprus—over the period 2011 to 2018, using MIMIC-based data. The shaded area represents the range between the countries with the lowest and highest estimated levels of informality each year, while the solid black line tracks the group average. In 2011, the shadow economy share ranged from a low of 31.3 percent (Türkiye) to a high of 57.9 percent (Uzbekistan), reflecting a substantial 26.6 percentage point gap. By 2018, this range narrowed modestly, with the lowest estimate again for Türkiye (30.4 percent) and the highest for Azerbaijan (53.5 percent), reducing the dispersion to 23.1 percentage points. Despite this slight contraction in the min–max spread, the group average remained relatively stable, fluctuating within a narrow band between 42.2 and 39.7 percent. The persistence of a wide gap, particularly driven by consistently high informality in Azerbaijan and Uzbekistan, indicates that full convergence within the group has not yet materialized. This visualization underscores the heterogeneity of informal economic activity across the Turkic republics, even within a relatively short and recent time frame.

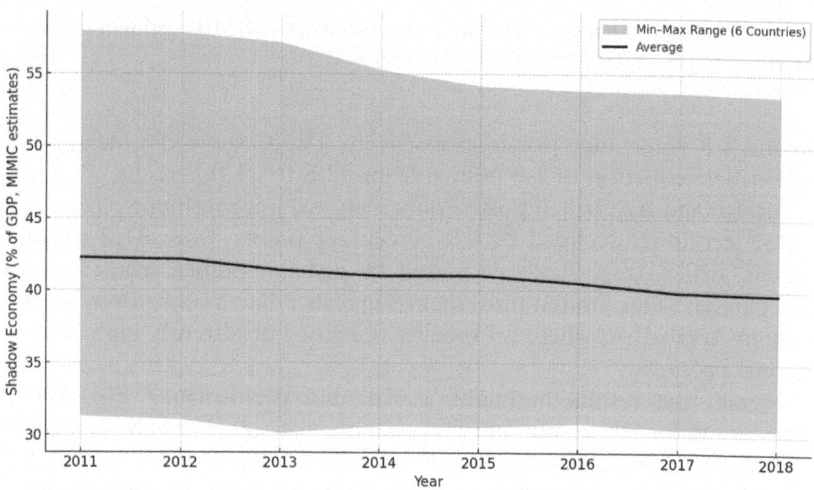

Fig. 7 Shadow economy dispersion among six countries (MIMIC estimates, 2011–2018)

6 Emerging Themes Across Country Analyses

The following seven chapters in this volume—covering Azerbaijan, Kazakhstan, Kyrgyzstan, Türkiye, the Turkish Republic of Northern Cyprus (TRNC), and Uzbekistan—offer a rich comparative picture of how shadow economies evolve across diverse institutional, technological, and social contexts. Despite country-specific differences, several recurring themes stand out.

Institutional trust and accountability emerge as central explanatory factors in both Azerbaijan and TRNC. In Azerbaijan, survey results show that control-based measures since 2018 have produced only limited success because weak institutional trust, and the absence of strong incentives continue to constrain formalization. TRNC extends this perspective by emphasizing the behavioral and psychological underpinnings of informality. The authors show that individuals often justify underreporting of income when there is a lack of trust in policymakers and little perceived risk of being held accountable. This dimension highlights how informality is sustained not only by structural weaknesses but also by social attitudes and norms.

Technological transformation is another major theme, particularly in Kazakhstan and Uzbekistan. One Kazakhstan study demonstrates that greater internet penetration reduces informality by enhancing transparency, while the expansion of mobile cellular subscriptions may encourage informal practices, illustrating the dual nature of digitalization. The Uzbekistan chapter builds on this by applying an enhanced Electricity Consumption Model (ECM) to measure informality, showing how reforms in digital payments and tax procedures are associated with a steady decline in shadow activity. Together these studies suggest that technology can be both a risk and a remedy, requiring complementary policy measures in digital literacy, financial integration, and infrastructure.

Labor market dynamics and human capital also play a decisive role. The second Kazakhstan chapter finds that the earnings gap between formal and informal self-employed workers widened sharply between 2019 and 2022, with university education standing out as the strongest factor limiting informality. The Kyrgyzstan chapter similarly shows that informality is deeply embedded in labor markets, affecting two-thirds of the workforce, and is concentrated in construction, trade, transport, and processing industries. It also highlights declining female participation and gender disparities, underscoring how informality intersects with demographic and social inequalities.

Finally, new policy frontiers emerge that connect informality to broader sustainability concerns. Türkiye's chapter demonstrates that shadow economy activity, public debt, and energy efficiency policies all shape ecological quality. It finds that while energy efficiency measures improve environmental outcomes, financialization and credit expansion can worsen them. Uzbekistan complements this finding by stressing the importance of energy infrastructure and transparency in tracking informality. Kyrgyzstan adds a focus on the fairness of tax and social protection systems, pointing to the need for reforms that balance enforcement with equity.

Taken together, these chapters show that the shadow economy is not merely a fiscal challenge but a multidimensional phenomenon shaped by institutions, technology, human capital, environmental sustainability, and social trust. While punitive enforcement remains part of the policy toolkit, the emerging evidence suggests that developmental and enabling approaches—focused on trust-building, inclusion, and fairness—are gaining ground as more sustainable solutions.

7 Structure of the Book

This volume is organized into seven chapters, each following a uniform structure to ensure cross-country comparability and coherence. Authors provide an introduction, an economic profile, a review of the country's shadow economy, a deeper exploration of country-specific issues, and concluding policy recommendations. This common framework allows the reader to trace thematic, empirical, and policy parallels across the Turkic republics.

Chapter 2 (Azerbaijan) provides a comprehensive assessment of efforts to tackle informality through an expert survey with 87 specialists from academia, the public sector, business, and civil society. It shows that while punitive measures have had some impact, weak institutional trust and insufficient incentives continue to sustain informality. The chapter concludes that a policy shift toward inclusive strategies—emphasizing fiscal transparency, legal predictability, and public–private cooperation—is required for long-term progress.

Chapter 3 (Kazakhstan I) focuses on the digital revolution and its contradictory effects. Using a mixed-method approach, it finds that internet penetration reduces the shadow economy through enhanced monitoring, but mobile cellular subscriptions are associated with an expansion of informal activity. The analysis stresses that digitalization must be supported by policies in financial integration and digital literacy to maximize its benefits while containing risks.

Chapter 4 (Kazakhstan II) turns to the labor market, using Labour Force Survey data from 2019 and 2022 to analyze the determinants of informal self-employment. It documents that the earnings gap between formal and informal self-employed workers has widened nearly fivefold, driven mainly by unexplained factors. The probability of informality increased slightly after the COVID-19 pandemic, while education—particularly university attainment—emerges as the most influential factor reducing informal work.

Chapter 5 (Kyrgyzstan) offers a detailed review of the country's shadow economy, estimated at between 28 and 46 percent of GDP. It shows that informality in the labor market affects two-thirds of workers and is especially prevalent in construction, trade, and transport. Gender disparities are significant, with female participation in the labor force declining over the past decade. The chapter argues that policies since 2007 have focused excessively on tax control while neglecting incentives to formalize. It calls for balanced reforms that include tighter enforcement, targeted labor market interventions, sustainable funding for social protection, and gender-sensitive strategies.

Chapter 6 (Türkiye) links shadow economy dynamics to environmental quality, analyzing data from 1990 to 2020. Using econometric techniques, it finds that shadow economy activity, rising public debt, and energy efficiency measures can improve ecological outcomes, while financialization undermines them. The study supports the Environmental Phillips Curve hypothesis for Türkiye and highlights the importance of sustaining energy efficiency policies and expanding green finance to align economic and ecological goals.

Chapter 7 (Turkish Republic of Northern Cyprus) examines informality in a de-facto state that remains internationally unrecognized. It estimates the shadow economy at about one-third of GDP and finds extremely high levels of income underreporting. Beyond measurement, the chapter's distinctive contribution is its analysis of behavioral and psychological drivers, showing how distrust in policymakers and a lack of accountability normalize informal behavior. These findings underline that combating informality requires not only institutional reform but also strategies that address social attitudes and norms.

Chapter 8 (Uzbekistan) applies an enhanced Electricity Consumption Model (ECM) to measure the size and trajectory of informality using hourly electricity data. It estimates that the shadow economy accounted for more than 60 percent of GDP in the early 2000s but declined steadily to around 35–40 percent by 2023. This decline corresponds with reforms in tax compliance, currency liberalization, and SME formalization. The chapter argues that ECM, when adapted to local contexts, provides a robust tool for measuring informality and stresses the importance of energy infrastructure, digital payments, and data transparency for sustaining progress.

The sequence of chapters moves from institutional trust and governance challenges (Azerbaijan and TRNC), through the technological and labor market dynamics of Kazakhstan and Kyrgyzstan, to broader policy frontiers of environmental sustainability and structural reform in Türkiye and Uzbekistan. This progression highlights both the diversity of contexts and the commonalities that link them, offering readers a coherent comparative framework for understanding the shadow economies of the Turkic republics.

8 Lessons Learned

The country chapters in this volume provide a wealth of empirical findings and conceptual insights. Drawing from them, we as editors identify twelve key lessons that shed light on the dynamics of shadow economies across the Turkic republics. While each case reflects a unique national context, taken together they illustrate recurring institutional, fiscal, and social challenges, as well as emerging areas of policy innovation.

First, the study on Türkiye demonstrates that the environmental consequences of shadow economy activities depend heavily on their sectoral composition. In Türkiye, informal activity is concentrated in labor-intensive rather than heavy industrial sectors. This pattern contrasts with African cases, where shadow activities in pollution-intensive industries degrade ecological quality. The Turkish evidence suggests that the shadow economy's impact on sustainability cannot be generalized but must be understood through sector-specific dynamics.

Second, the chapters on Türkiye and the TRNC reveal that frequent tax amnesties have become a structural feature of fiscal policy. Rather than facilitating compliance, these recurrent amnesties encourage businesses and individuals to remain informal, waiting for the next amnesty to regularize their obligations. This tendency is specific to these two cases and is not observed to the same degree in the other Turkic republics.

Third, a pervasive culture of clientelism appears across nearly all the Turkic republics. Clientelism undermines impartial enforcement and reinforces selective tolerance for informality. As a result, shadow economy practices often become embedded in broader patronage networks, making them more resistant to conventional regulatory interventions.

Fourth, corruption emerges as a central driver of shadow economic activity in every country studied. Corruption not only facilitates underreporting and informal transactions but also shapes the incentives of officials, who may tolerate or even benefit from informality. This reinforces the conclusion that combating informality cannot succeed without addressing corruption at its core.

Fifth, the general weakness of institutional quality is a shared feature across all cases. Low predictability of the legal system, inconsistent enforcement, and administrative inefficiency create an environment where informality thrives. This highlights that institutional reform, rather than narrow tax measures, is fundamental to reducing shadow activity.

Sixth, fiscal dependence on non-tax revenues has long discouraged governments from prioritizing tax collection. In the TRNC, external aid has cushioned fiscal shortfalls, while in Azerbaijan, Kazakhstan, and Uzbekistan natural resource revenues have played the same role. This reliance has weakened incentives to build strong tax administrations, delaying reforms to expand the tax base.

Seventh, in Türkiye, the TRNC, and Kyrgyzstan, indirect taxes form a much larger share of government revenues compared to other cases. This reliance signals the difficulty of collecting direct taxes and indicates low voluntary compliance rates. By contrast, in resource-rich economies revenues from oil, gas, or other rents have offset weak tax collection.

Eighth, in all republics the practice of declaring wages at or near the minimum wage level is widespread. This phenomenon obscures the true scale of informal incomes, reduces contributions to social security systems, and complicates the measurement of labor market informality. It highlights that underreporting of income is as central as unregistered employment in understanding shadow economy dynamics.

Ninth, the Kazakhstan chapter produces a particularly striking finding: internet penetration is associated with reductions in informality by improving monitoring capacity, while the spread of mobile phone subscriptions has the opposite effect, correlating with higher informality. This paradox points to the need to rethink the notion of the "digital shadow economy" and to recognize that technology can simultaneously constrain and enable informal activities.

Tenth, none of the countries examined has developed comprehensive policies that facilitate a transition from informality to formality. Instead, governments have tended to rely on tax-based approaches, particularly tighter inspections and higher penalties. Yet these measures often fail due to weak institutions and limited enforcement capacity. A sector-specific, enabling approach would be more effective in supporting gradual formalization.

Eleventh, a structural feature common to nearly all the republics is the predominance of small, low-capital, labor-intensive enterprises. This composition complicates state oversight, since the costs of monitoring often exceed the taxes that could be collected. Moreover, many businesses deliberately fragment into smaller units to remain less visible to authorities. In such contexts, staying in the shadows becomes a rational survival strategy rather than merely a tax avoidance tactic.

Twelfth, the TRNC chapter adds an original dimension by analyzing the psychological and behavioral underpinnings of informality. It shows that income underreporting is often justified by citizens as normatively acceptable in an environment where policymakers are not trusted and accountability is absent. This behavioral perspective broadens the scope of shadow economy research, suggesting that effective policies must address not only fiscal incentives but also social attitudes and perceptions of legitimacy.

Taken together, these twelve lessons underline that shadow economies in the Turkic republics are sustained by a combination of institutional weaknesses, fiscal structures, social practices, and technological dynamics. They also point toward new research frontiers, from the role of behavioral norms to the environmental and digital dimensions of informality. By placing these lessons at the center of analysis, this volume highlights the need for policies that go beyond punitive enforcement, focusing instead on trust-building, fairness, and inclusive pathways to formalization.

References

ACCA. (2017). Emerging from the shadows: The shadow economy 2025. *ACCA Global*. Retrieved February 12, 2025, from https://www.accaglobal.com/content/dam/ACCA_Global/Technical/Future/pi-shadow-economy-report.pdf

Altındağ, O., Bakış, O., & Rozo, S. V. (2020). *Blessing or burden? Impacts of refugees on businesses and the informal economy. Journal of Development Economics, 146*(C), Article 102490. https://doi.org/10.1016/j.jdeveco.2020.102490

Bagirzade, E. (2012a). Kayıt Dışı Ekonomi Kavramına Ortak Yaklaşım Sorunu: Makroiktisat Kapsamlı Kavramsal Analiz. *Sosyoekonomi*, 18(18). Retrieved April 02, 2025, from https://dergipark.org.tr/en/pub/sosyoekonomi/issue/21078/226941

Bagirzade, E. (2012b). İktisat Biliminde Kayıtdışı Ekonomi Araştırmaları Üzerine. *Yakın Doğu Üniversitesi Sosyal Bilimler Dergisi*, *5*(1), 34–51. Retrieved April 02, 2025, from https://dergi.neu.edu.tr/public/journals/7/yazardizini/bagirzade-e-r-2012-nisan.pdf

Besim, M. (2025). Measuring the size of underground economy in TRNC using MIMIC approach: Updated evidence, *Eastern Mediterranean University Working Paper.*

Besim, M., Ekici, T., & Jenkins, G. P. (2015a). Informality in a micro economy: Measurement, composition and consequences. *International Labour Review*, *154*(3), 353–371. https://doi.org/10.1111/j.1564-913X.2015.00246.x

Besim, M., Mungan, Z., Güpınar, A., & Saydam, G. (2015b). Kuzey Kıbrıs Türk Cumhuriyeti'nde Kayıtdışı Ekonomi: Boyutlaırnın Ölçümü, Çözüm Önerileri ve Eylem Planı. *Kıbrıs Türk Ticaret Odası Yayını*. Retrieved August 7, 2025, from https://ktto.net/wp-content/uploads/2015/04/Kay%C4%B1td%C4%B1%C5%9F%C4%B1-Ekonomi.pdf

Dabrowski, M. (2023). *A limping transition: The former Soviet Union thirty years on*. Essay 01/2023, Bruegel.

Donaev. (2019). *Estimating the shadow economy in Uzbekistan*, M.S. thesis, Central European Univ., Retrieved August 1, 2025, from https://www.etd.ceu.edu/2019/donaev_farkhod.pdf

Eilat, Y., & Zinnes, C. (2000). *The evolution of the shadow economy in transition countries: Consequences for economic growth and donor assistance*. CAER II Discussion Paper No.83, Harvard Institute for International Development.

Ekici, T., & Besim, M. (2016). A measure of the shadow economy in a small economy: Evidence from household-level expenditure patterns. *Review of Income and Wealth*, Series 62, Number 1, March. https://doi.org/10.1111/roiw.12138

Elgin, C. (2021). *The informal economy: Measures, causes, and consequences*. Routledge.

Elgin, C., Kose, M. A., Ohnsorge, F., & Yu, S. (2021). *Understanding informality*. CERP Discussion Paper 16497, Centre for Economic Policy Research. Retrieved February 12, 2025, from https://www.worldbank.org/en/research/brief/informal-economy-database

EY. (2025). *Shadow economy exposed: Estimates for the world and policy paths. Report*. March. Retrieved April, 02, from https://www.ey.com/content/dam/ey-unified-site/ey-com/en-gl/insights/tax/documents/ey-gl-shadow-economy-report-02-2025.pdf

Grossman, G. (1977). The "Second Economy" of the USSR. *Problems of Communism*, 26, September–October (pp. 25–40).

Ikiz, A. S. (2017). Shadow economy and economic growth in Turkey. In M. Bilgin, H. Danis, E. Demir, & U. Can (Eds.), *Regional studies on economic growth, financial economics and management Eurasian studies in business and economics.* (Vol. 7). Springer. https://doi.org/10.1007/978-3-319-54112-9_17

Johnson, S., Kaufmann, D., & Shleifer, A. (1997). The unofficial economy in transition. *Brookings Paper on Economic Activity, 2*, 159–221.

Kaufmann D., & Kaliberda A. (1996). *Integrating the unofficial economy into the dynamics of post-socialist economies: A framework of analysis and evidence.* Policy Research Working Paper 1691, The World Bank Europe and Central Asia Country Department.

Lacko, M. (2000). Hidden economy—An unknown quantity? Comparative analysis of hidden economies in transition countries in 1989–1995. *Economics of Transition, 8*(1), 117–149.

Medina, L., & Schneider, F. (2018). *Shadow economies around the world: What did we learn over the last 20 years?* IMF Working Paper, WP/18/17, January. Retrieved July 16, 2025, from https://www.imf.org/en/Publications/WP/Issues/2018/01/25/Shadow-Economies-Around-the-World-What-Did-We-Learn-Over-the-Last-20-Years-45583

OTS. (2021). *Turkic World Vision 2040*. Retrieved February 12, 2025, from https://www.turkicstates.org/en/news/turkic-world-vision-2040

Shelley, L. I. (1990). The second economy in the Soviet union. In M. Łoś (Ed.), *The second economy in Marxist states.* Palgrave Macmillan. https://doi.org/10.1007/978-1-349-20422-9_2

Williams, C. C. (2023). *A modern guide to the informal economy*. Edward Elgar Publishing. https://doi.org/10.4337/9781788975612

World Bank (n.d). *World governance indicators.* Retrieved August 7, 2025, from https://www.worldbank.org/en/publication/worldwide-governance-indicators/interactive-data-access

World Economics. (2025). Informal economy sizes. *Quarterly Informal Economy Survey (QIES)*. Retrieved July 22, 2025, from https://www.worldeconomics.com/Rankings/Economies-By-Informal-Economy-Size.aspx

CHAPTER 2

Tackling the Shadow Economy in Azerbaijan: Are There Any Results?

Elshan Bagirzadeh and Ibrahim Niftiyev

1 Introduction

Azerbaijan, as a typical post-Soviet developing economy, is one of the countries facing the problem of the shadow economy. Studies show that although this problem grew in the 1990s, it has begun to decrease since 2000 (Medina & Schneider, 2018). Nevertheless, the shadow economy in Azerbaijan remains a persistent and relevant issue. Since 2018, the government has placed the issue on its agenda to an unprecedented degree compared to previous years, incorporating it into official documents and implementing a range of measures to address it. Although the outcomes of this policy against the shadow economy are reflected in the reports by various institutions (EY, 2025), there remains a notable lack of comprehensive scientific studies that systematically examine this policy

E. Bagirzadeh (✉) · I. Niftiyev
Department of Economics, Azerbaijan State University of Economics, Baku, Azerbaijan
e-mail: elshan.bagirzadeh@unec.edu.az

I. Niftiyev
e-mail: ibrahim.niftiyev@unec.edu.az

E. Bagirzadeh and O. Gokcekus (eds.), *Shadow Economies in Turkic Republics*, https://doi.org/10.1007/978-3-032-12872-0_2

and assess its effectiveness. This study seeks to help address the existing gap in the literature.

Thus, in the study, we are analyzing the policy of tackling the shadow economy implemented in Azerbaijan in recent years. For this, we conducted an anonymous survey among experts consisting of prominent scholars familiar with the problem of the shadow economy in Azerbaijan, as well as specialists working in the public and private sectors and non-governmental organizations (NGOs). The expert evaluation method is one of the most widely used approaches for studying the shadow economy and offers the advantage of providing more detailed insights into the issue. At the same time, the expert evaluation method is often preferred in studies that involve complex conceptual and methodological dimensions, such as the analysis of public policy in this domain (Gasparėnienė et al., 2016; Krumplytė, 2010; Remeikiene et al., 2018; Voicu, 2008).

The study seeks to answer the following three questions: (1) What is the current scale of the shadow economy problem in Azerbaijan? (2) How sufficient and effective has been the policy against shadow economy in Azerbaijan in recent years? (3) How to improve the current policy to significantly limit the shadow economy in Azerbaijan?

2 Country's Economic Profile

Azerbaijan, a small South Caucasian country and former Soviet republic, has a population of just over 10 million people in 2023 (World Bank, 2024a) and a gross domestic product (GDP) per capita of 7,133 current US dollars (World Bank, 2024b). The World Bank classifies Azerbaijan as an upper-middle-income country, with an official national unemployment rate of 5.7% in 2022 and relatively low poverty rates of 5.2% (Asian Development Bank, 2025; World Bank, 2024c). Between 1991 and 2023, the country's GDP composition was as follows: industry value added—including construction but excluding manufacturing—amounted to 47.7%, manufacturing value added to 7.5%, agriculture value added to 12.2% and services value added to 33.4% (World Bank, 2024d, 2024e, 2024f, 2024g).

Azerbaijan's strategic location between Europe and Asia positions it as a critical energy corridor, facilitating the transportation of energy resources to international markets. The country's main exports include crude oil and natural gas, along with fruit, vegetables, chemicals and metal products between 2010 and 2022. Azerbaijan's most important trading partners include Italy, Türkiye, Russia, China, Israel, Greece and India (Observatory of Economic Complexity, 2024). In addition, Azerbaijan plays an important role in the European Union's energy security, especially in light of recent geopolitical shifts (Dinçer, 2024). The country primarily imports machinery, transportation equipment, metal products and chemicals from Russia, Türkiye and China. Azerbaijan's trade openness averaged 87% between 2000 and 2023, with the trade balance increasing from—31.8% of GDP in 1998 to 42.3% in 2008 and 33% in 2022 (World Bank, 2024h, 2024i).

The Azerbaijani economy since the collapse of the Soviet Union can be conceptualized through four distinct phases of development: recession (1991–1994), recovery (1995–2004), oil boom (2005–2014) and post-boom (2015 onwards). The recession phase was characterized by the recovery from transitional shocks, the war with Armenia and political instability. The recovery phase brought economic stabilization, the development of infrastructure for international energy projects (e.g., Baku–Tbilisi-Ceyhan) and regulatory measures. The oil boom period was the most significant with record-breaking economic growth of 34.5% in 2006 (World Bank, 2024j), which led to a rapid structural shift toward a commodity-based economy. The post-boom period began after the sharp drop in commodity prices in 2014, which marked the end of the oil boom.

3 Azerbaijan's Shadow Economy

Currently, the global database on the shadow economy created by the World Bank's Prospects Group provides the most comprehensive (between 1990 and 2020) information on the size of the shadow economy in Azerbaijan (Elgin et al., 2021). The results of measuring the size of the Azerbaijan's shadow economy using the Dynamic General Equilibrium (DGE) and Multiple Indicators Multiple Causes (MIMIC) model approaches are presented in Fig. 1. The results of measurements conducted using both methods show that the share of the shadow economy in GDP in Azerbaijan continued to increase over the years in the 1990s and began to decrease since 2000. As a result, it turned out that the share of the shadow economy in GDP for 2020 was 39.1% using the DGE method and 54.8% using the MIMIC method. This means that the size of the shadow economy in Azerbaijan is nominally between $16.7 and 23.4 billion for the mentioned year.

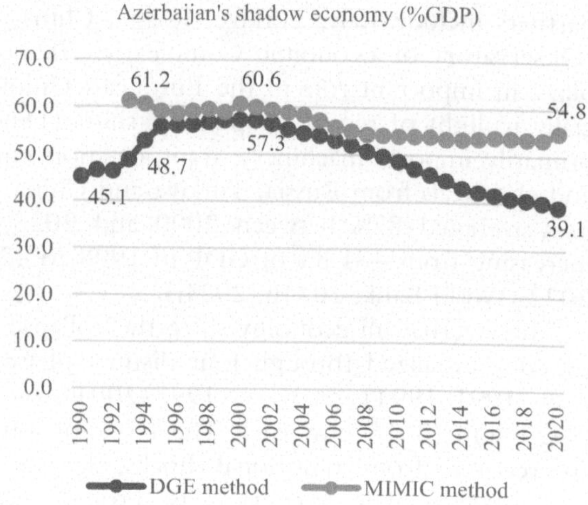

Fig. 1 The size of the Azerbaijan's shadow economy over the years (*Source* Elgin et al. [2021])

The relative decrease in shadow economic activities in Azerbaijan over the years is also supported by some micro-studies. One of the most reliable among these studies is the World Bank Enterprise Surveys (Elgin et al., 2021). As seen in the results presented in Fig. 2 of this survey, the percentage of firms that reported competing with the informal sector and perceived it as a constraint in competition was significantly lower in 2019 compared to 2009.

Although the percentage of firms reporting competition with informal sector firms and perceiving this sector as a constraint decreased by approximately 10 percentage points in 2019 compared to 2009, the problem still appears to persist on a significant scale. Thus, in 2019, the "percent of firms competing against unregistered or informal firms" was 29.9%, and the "percent of firms identifying practices of competitors in the informal sector as a constraint" was 21.7%. As can be seen, approximately 1 in 3 companies surveyed compete with unregistered or informal firms (Fig. 2). This survey was conducted among firms, but it should be noted that there are a large number of economic entities in Azerbaijan that are not firms. For example, the self-employment rate (% of total employment) in Azerbaijan was 65.2% in 2020, and this rate has almost never been lower than 60% in the country (Elgin et al., 2021). As in all other countries, unregistered and shadow economic activities may be significantly more widespread among these types of economic entities.

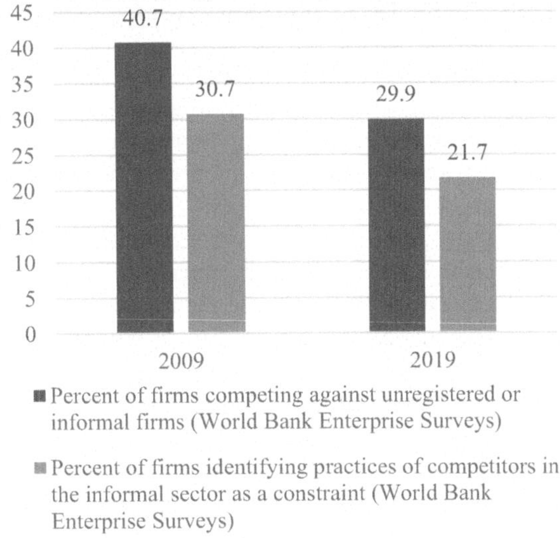

Fig. 2 The size of the shadow economy according to companies in Azerbaijan (*Source* Elgin et al. [2021])

In different years, the government has put forward various measures against shadow economic activities, which are widespread in the economy of Azerbaijan. More intensification of government activities in this direction is observed from 2018. Starting from that period, many official documents of the government began to use the expression "whitening" of shadow economic activities and several policy measures were taken in this direction. These measures, which mainly aim to detect unofficial turnover, encourage economic entities to "whiten" their income, and formalize jobs and wages, have been implemented primarily through numerous changes in tax legislation. Among these measures, in addition to strengthening control, there are also a number of incentive mechanisms aimed at voluntary compliance. Moreover, the tackling the shadow economy has been selected as one of the main priorities in a number of important official documents currently in force, such as "Azerbaijan 2030: National Priorities for Socio-Economic Development," "Socio-Economic Development Strategy of the Republic of Azerbaijan for 2022–2026" and "National Action Plan for Combating the Legalization of Property Obtained by Crime and the Financing of Terrorism for 2023–2025." However, scientific studies that comprehensively evaluate the results of these measures implemented by the government are not at an adequate level.

4 Review of Existing Studies on Azerbaijan's Shadow Economy

According to many studies, the origins of shadow economies in the post-Soviet space, including Azerbaijan, date back to the economic practice that existed during the Soviet Union and was expressed by the concept of "second economy." During the Soviet period, especially in its final decades, misreporting, manipulation of official data and informal relationships between state officials and entrepreneurs were widespread (Sayfutdinova, 2017). These claims are supported by empirical evidence from several post-Soviet countries, where a growing appreciation of the market economy and competition since the 1980s led certain economic actors to enter informal and shadow economic relationships (Heinzen, 2020; Ivanov & Aisin, 2024; Rasanayagam, 2011). Consequently, the persistence of shadow economies in the post-Soviet and post-socialist states is thought to be due to this legacy, which still exists today and to some extent weighs on the economic well-being of these nations. Undoubtedly, the informal institutions and behavioral norms that have developed over many years in post-socialist countries like Azerbaijan are important for understanding their shadow economies (Gërxhani & Cichocki, 2023). However, in our opinion, studying the nature of post-Soviet reforms, new official institutions and economic development in these countries is more important for understanding their current shadow economies.

Comparative studies show that although post-Soviet countries have implemented numerous reforms to form the foundations of a market economy, the policies and institutions preferred in many of these countries have been suboptimal and distortive. As a result, this factor has significantly affected the nature and quality of the economic transition in those countries (Dabrowski, 2023). The literature suggests that institutional quality and economic factors play an important role in shaping the size and impact of the shadow economy in transition countries. For example, institutional quality (mainly measured by the rule of law) and economic growth reduce the shadow economy in transition countries (Luong et al., 2020). Lyulyov et al. (2021) found that economic growth and foreign direct investment (FDI) help reduce shadow economy activities, whereas improvements in energy efficiency and increases in taxes tend to expand them—ultimately exerting a negative effect on life expectancy. Rakhmonov and Elmurodov (2021), focusing on post-Soviet economies, have empirically demonstrated how state-induced distortions, limited business and fiscal freedom and ineffective state interventions contribute to informal economic activities. ACCA (2017) found corruption control, democratic accountability and GDP growth are the top three factors determining the extent of the shadow economy in Azerbaijan and Russia, while in Ukraine, bureaucratic quality, GDP per capita and political stability. Gokcekus et al. (2023) found that there is a complementary relationship between corruption and the shadow economy in post-Soviet countries that are members of the Economic Cooperation Organization (ECO).

Studies focusing exclusively on Azerbaijan's shadow economy were virtually non-existent in the 1990s. However, in the 1990s, some studies on the shadow economies of transition countries also measured the Azerbaijan's shadow economy. These studies, which estimated the size of the shadow economy using various adaptations of the electricity consumption method, revealed that the share of Azerbaijan's shadow economy in GDP rose steadily from 12% in 1989 and surpassed 100% by the late 1990s. (Eilat & Zinnes, 2000; Johnson et al., 1997; Kaufmann & Kaliberda, 1996; Lacko, 2000).

Schneider (2004), who used the Dynamic Multiple Indicators Multiple Causes (DYMIMIC) and Currency Demand Method in his calculations, found that the share of the Azerbaijan's shadow economy in GDP was 61% on average between 2000 and 2003, which was considered a low figure among post-Soviet countries, only compared to Georgia. Schneider et al. (2010) extended these calculations and demonstrated that the relative level of the shadow economy in Azerbaijan continued to decrease in the following years, falling 52% of GDP by 2007. In the last study, which was further developed on the basis of the same measurement method, it was shown that the share of the shadow economy in the GDP in Azerbaijan decreased in the following years and was 43.66% in 2015. Also, according to this study, the shadow economy in Azerbaijan averaged 52.19% of GDP between 1991 and 2015 (Medina & Schneider, 2018). The results of another global study conducted by Elgin and Oztunali (2012) and based on the Dynamic General Equilibrium Model also showed that the share of the shadow economy in GDP in Azerbaijan gradually decreased in the 2000s. Thus, according to the study results, this decrease continued over the years and the shadow economy accounted for 51.21% of GDP in 2008.

There are also international studies that provide forecast indicators of the size of the shadow economy in Azerbaijan. ACCA (2017) shows that the share of the shadow economy in GDP in Azerbaijan will gradually decrease from 66.12% in 2017 to 58.38% in 2025. Elgin (2021: 55) predicts that this indicator, which was 45.05% in 2021, will decrease slightly to 45.02% in 2025.

These studies are important in terms of obtaining certain comparative data on the Azerbaijan's shadow economy. However, it should be noted that none of these studies specifically aimed to study the Azerbaijan's shadow economy. Therefore, it would be unrealistic to expect the aforementioned studies to fully capture the specific dynamics of Azerbaijan's economy. The first set of comprehensive studies on the Azerbaijan's shadow economy were conducted by Bagirzade (2007, 2010, 2013). These studies attempted to estimate the scale of the shadow economy in Azerbaijan using various methods, analyzed its main causes and proposed comprehensive policy measures to formalize this sector. In the aforementioned studies, measurements conducted using the Currency Ratio Method (Gutmann) revealed that the share of the shadow economy in GDP in Azerbaijan decreased by 13.7 percentage points between 2001 and 2011, while measurements conducted using the Currency Demand Method (Tanzi) showed that it decreased by 25.5 percentage points between 2001 and 2007. Bagirzade (2013) also tried to measure the level of informal employment in Azerbaijan using the Employment Method and found that the share of informal employment in total employment decreased by 8.3 percentage points between 2007 and 2011. The above measurement, conducted using the Currency Ratio Method (Gutmann), was later continued by Guliyev (2019) for other years, and it was revealed that the share of the shadow economy in GDP in Azerbaijan also decreased in subsequent years and was 31% in 2018. Calculations based on the Currency Demand Approach, as part of a global report prepared by EY in 2025, show that the share of the shadow economy in GDP in Azerbaijan in 2023 was 17.7%. According to this report, the share of the shadow economy in GDP in Azerbaijan decreased by 15.1 percentage points between 2000 and 2023, by 4.0 percentage points between 2013 and 2023, and by 4.7 percentage points between 2019 and 2023 (EY, 2025).

As can be seen, various studies show that the share of the shadow economy in GDP in Azerbaijan increased rapidly and reached large scales in the 1990s but gradually decreased in the 2000s. The emergence of such a situation in the 1990s can be explained to a significant extent by economic problems and the low quality of institutions. However, the situation in the 2000s can largely be attributed to the relative weakening of these factors compared to earlier years, along with the rapid rise in the share of the oil sector in the GDP, a sector that is more thoroughly recorded (Bagirzade, 2013; Chantzi, 2013; Glinkina & Rosenberg, 2003; Kaser, 2003; Kintsurashvili & Kresic, 2019; Sayfutdinova, 2015, 2017). Yet, in all cases, as can be seen from the above studies, the size of the shadow economy in Azerbaijan is still significant.

Although there are a number of studies in the existing literature assessing the scale of the shadow economy in Azerbaijan, there are very few studies that include a comprehensive analysis and evaluation of policies aimed at restricting this sector. Bagirzade (2013) proposed to analyze and evaluate the policy of tackling the shadow economy in Azerbaijan in four main directions: improving the macroeconomic environment, increasing the advantageousness of the official economy, strengthening administrative measures against the shadow economy and forming public awareness against the shadow economy. In this work, the state of the policy of tackling the shadow economy in Azerbaijan was analyzed, and recommendations were made for improving this policy. A comparable study is the report authored by Williams and Nazarov (2018). The report recommends that policies addressing the shadow economy should rely on a combination of direct and indirect control mechanisms. At the same time, the authors emphasize the need to take into account that the repressive fight against the shadow economy is no longer relevant and propose an action plan for Azerbaijan that supports the transition from the shadow economy to the formal economy.

However, there is also very limited scientific research that allows analyzing and evaluating the policy implemented in Azerbaijan in recent years in the field of tackling the shadow economy. Guliyev (2019) links the significant decrease in the share of the shadow economy in the GDP in Azerbaijan in 2018 compared to 2017 to changes in the tax system, and notes that these are changes that serve the voluntary adaptation of taxpayers. He also shows that the tax burden of the private and non-oil sectors was significantly reduced by the changes made to the tax legislation in 2019, which will have an even more restrictive effect on the shadow economy in the coming years. At the same time, the calculations conducted by EY (2025) are also important in terms of assessing the results of the policy implemented in recent years to tackle the shadow economy in Azerbaijan. So, the calculations in the report show that the share of the shadow economy in Azerbaijan's GDP decreased by 15.1 percentage points between 2000 and 2023, and this decrease is 4.7 percentage points between 2019 and 2023. However, despite this, since the mentioned study was not conducted separately for Azerbaijan, the conclusions that we can draw from it are remain limited.

In recent years, Azerbaijan has been experiencing a slowdown in economic growth, increased efforts to improve institutional quality, and declining share of the oil sector in the economy. Under these conditions, there is a clear need to updated studies on the shadow economy. In particular, evaluating the effectiveness of recent anti-shadow economy measures and formulating relevant policy recommendations have become especially important.

5 Model/Data

As part of the study, the questionnaire shown in Appendix was distributed to pre-selected experts, with responses collected between September 13 and October 20, 2024. The questionnaire was developed based on the model proposed by Bagirzade (2013) for analyzing policies aimed at addressing the shadow economy in Azerbaijan. The questionnaire included 17 multiple-choice questions focused on the size of Azerbaijan's shadow economy and the analysis and assessment of recent policy efforts to combat it, along with three open-ended questions aimed at gathering suggestions for policy improvement. The answers to the multiple-choice questions were analyzed using statistical methods. The answers to the open questions were thematically analyzed using the Quirkos software (version 2.5.3).

As part of the study, 157 experts who are considered specialists in this field in Azerbaijan were selected, and the questionnaire was sent to them anonymously via the Internet. 87 out of 157 experts, in other words, 55.4%, answered the survey. The distribution of experts by field of work and work experience is presented in Fig. 3. As can be seen, a significant part of the experts covering various fields are from universities and scientific research institutions. This can be seen as one of the factors contributing to the increased objectivity of the responses. Moreover, 64 of the 87 experts have more than 10 years of work experience in their field of work, and 50 have more than 15 years. This suggests that the experts are quite experienced.

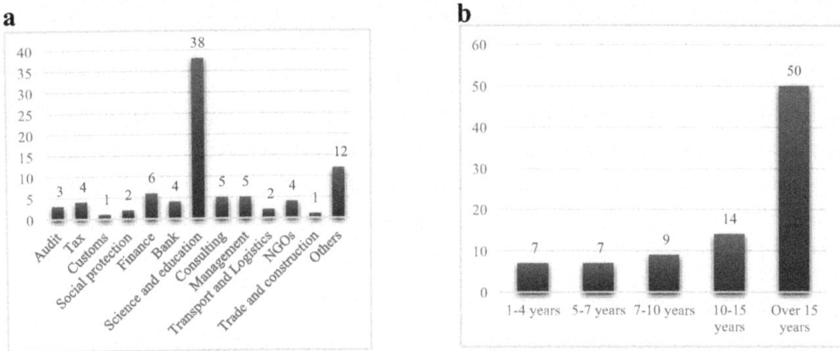

Fig. 3 Distribution of the experts. (a) Distribution of the experts by operation fields, in persons (number) (b) Experts' work experience in current occupation field, in persons (number)

Considering that there are different views in the literature and practice regarding the concept of shadow economy, we also asked the experts the question "*The shadow economy is a set of economic activities that are not declared in order to avoid official obligations, while they must be declared to the relevant official institutions by law. Do you agree with this definition?*" 21.8% of the experts answered "completely agree," 59.8% "mostly agree," 17.2% "partially agree," and 1.1% "disagree." These results show that the approach to the concept of shadow economy is not uniform among the experts, but at the same time, the vast majority agree with the definition presented or are close to it.

In this study, Braun and Clarke's (2012) thematic analysis (TA) was applied to the answers to the last three open questions of the expert survey. TA is increasingly favored for qualitative data analysis due to its simplicity, flexibility and cost-effectiveness (Vaismoradi et al., 2013). A strong foundation in this approach enables researchers to transition to more complex qualitative methods, but accurate identification of themes is always the essential starting point (Shoufan, 2023). Similar to grounded theory approaches or cultural model development, TA requires researchers to engage deeply with the data and interpret it meaningfully (Terry et al., 2017).

TA method allowed us to tailor the qualitative analysis to our research objectives and questions in order to thematize our data set. In particular, TA was used to analyze the brief expert opinions on the shadow economy in Azerbaijan to support a descriptive and exploratory approach to the qualitative data analysis. Therefore, firstly, all 87 expert opinions were read by the authors. Secondly, some approximation of the potential themes was made through initial coding—the second and third phases. After manual review and naming, the final report was written in text form. Of all the phases of TA, qualitative coding needs to be explained in more detail to ensure the validity and robustness of the current study.

In this study, the three open-ended questions were coded qualitatively in order to make them applicable in the context of TA. Qualitative coding is a process that organizes, categorizes and reduces raw data into manageable and meaningful excerpts (Williams & Moser, 2019). Qualitative coding not only helps researchers streamline the research process but also highlights the relationships between key concepts and reflects the researchers' perception of the phenomenon being analyzed (Williams & Moser, 2019).

We adopted Williams and Moser's (2019) non-linear qualitative coding approach, which allowed us to identify key themes, rigorously code the data and interpret the results. During the coding process, we used an inductive approach, meaning that the codes were generated directly from the data without relying on preconceived notions or predefined terms (Armat et al., 2018). Hence, given the limited qualitative analysis of the shadow economy in the context of the Azerbaijani economy, we chose a flexible coding process to ensure both adaptability and depth in the construction of themes. Table 1 provides an overview of the codes used and their corresponding higher-level codes (or themes).

For the sake of simplicity, each theme was constructed based on the corresponding open-ended question. This approach differs slightly from traditional TA; however, it is important to note that TA serves as a complementary research method in this study and not as the primary method.

As a result, three themes were developed:

Theme 1: Implementing Long-Term and Multidimensional Solutions: A Strategic Approach.
Theme 2: Emphasizing the need for public-private partnerships.
Theme 3: Emphasizing the alignment of international partnerships and global standards with local economic realities to tackle the shadow economy.

Table 1 Themes and their qualitative codes used in the thematic analysis, frequency in times (occurrences)

Theme 1: Implementing Long-Term and Multidimensional Solutions: A Strategic Approach	*Frequency*	*Theme 2: Emphasizing the need for public-private partnerships*	*Frequency*
1. Tax	44	Transparency	48
2. Legal system	41	Accountability	22
3. Educational and cultural measures	38	Public-private partnership	13
4. Competition	36	Corruption	9
5. Anticorruption measures	25	Incentives for businesses	9
6. Digitalization and artificial intelligence (AI)	23	Anti-monopoly measures	5
7. Governance and regulation	22	Financial regulations	5
8. Involvement of the state in business	20	Inconclusive statements	5
9. Public trust	19	Civil society	4
10. State support	15	State's image and related matters	4
11. Income transparency	12	Privatization	4
12. Inconclusive statements	5	Legal protection	3

Theme 3: Alignment of international partnerships and global standards with local economic realities to tackle the shadow economy	*Frequency*
1. International standards/experiences	41
2. Inconclusive statements	17
3. Enabling environment	15
4. National interests	14
5 Targeted approach	9
6. Financial aspects	8
7. Domestic matter	8
8. World Trade Organization (WTO)	5

Themes 1 and 2 were each based on twelve qualitative codes, while Theme 3 was derived from eight codes. The most frequently used qualitative code in each theme was as follows: Theme 1: "Tax" (44 occurrences); Theme 2: "Transparency" (48 occurrences); Theme 3: "International standards/experiences" (41 occurrences).

Further details about the context of these qualitative codes and the overarching narrative can be found in the thematic report through content mapping. Specifically, we briefly summarize the short excerpts, which in most cases are not full quotes from the experts, to reinforce the key survey findings. In some appropriate places, we provide direct quotes from the experts from our qualitative data set. The validity of the present study was further enhanced by inter-coder reliability on the part of the authors.

6 Findings

This section presents the responses to the key multiple-choice questions posed to the experts, as illustrated in Figs. 4 and 5. Subsequently, the results of the thematic analysis of the experts' answers to the open-ended questions are presented under Themes 1, 2 and 3. All of these research findings will be discussed in the next section.

Theme 1: Implementing Long-Term and Multidimensional Solutions: A Strategic Approach

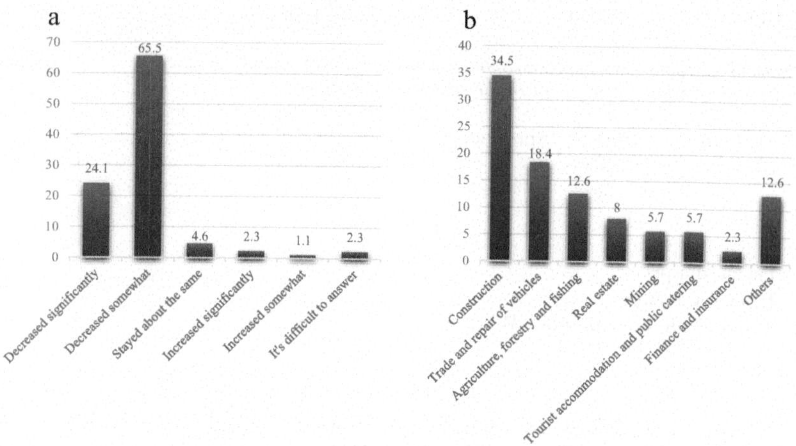

Fig. 4 Dimensions of the shadow economy in Azerbaijan (a) "In your opinion, how has the scale of the shadow economy changed in Azerbaijan in recent years?" (in percentage) (b) "In your opinion, what is the sector in Azerbaijan where the shadow economy is the most widespread?" (in percentage)

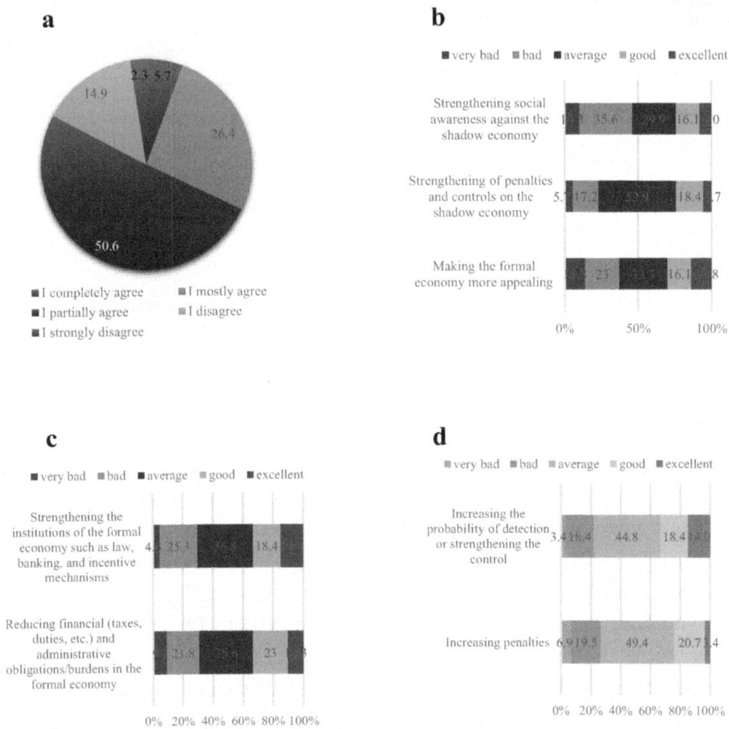

Fig. 5 The current policy of tackling the shadow economy in Azerbaijan (a) "Do you agree with the opinion that the policy implemented by the government in Azerbaijan in recent years in the field of tackling the shadow economy is generally satisfactory?" (in percentage) (b) "Please, evaluate the effectiveness of the following areas in tackling the shadow economy in Azerbaijan" (in percentage) (c) "Please, evaluate the effectiveness of the Azerbaijan government's measures in the following two areas to increase the appeal of the formal economy" (in percentage) (d) "Please, evaluate the effectiveness of the Azerbaijan government's measures in the following two administrative areas to tackle the shadow economy" (in percentage) (e) "Please, evaluate the effectiveness of the Azerbaijan government's measures to strengthen social awareness against the shadow economy in the following areas" (in percentage) (f) "Please, choose the causes for the shadow economy that you believe are most pertinent to the Azerbaijan economy" (in percentage)

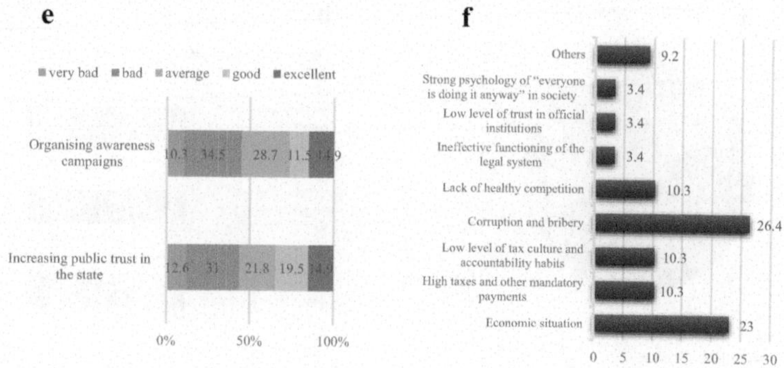

Fig. 5 (continued)

Based on the expert opinions gathered in the open-ended questions of the survey, it is clear that tackling the shadow economy cannot be achieved just in a few years. This realization gave rise to the first major theme entitled "Implementing Long-Term, Multidimensional Solutions: A Strategic Approach," which sums up the complexity of the topic.

The shadow economy in Azerbaijan is driven by high tax burdens, complex regulations, and a lack of trust between businesses and the government, according to expert opinions captured in the largest qualitative code "Tax" (44 codes). To address these issues, it is important to lower tax rates and reduce the financial burden on small and micro businesses. Simplifying tax systems and ensuring transparency are also essential to encourage voluntary compliance and reduce informal practices. In addition, promoting a tax culture through awareness campaigns that emphasize the societal benefits of tax compliance can increase public confidence in the system. Fair taxation, where all companies are treated fairly and benefit proportionately from public spending, is necessary to eliminate the sense of injustice that often leads to tax evasion.

> The threats posed by public finances as one of the potential catalysts of the shadow economy should be assessed in terms of possible scenarios. (Source 33, science and education, upper management with 10–15 years of experience)
>
> The greatest negative impact of the shadow economy on long-term economic development is that these economic actors choose a strategy of non-growth in order to avoid taxes and other official obligations. If there are many economic entities that do not grow and develop, long-term

> economic development is jeopardized. (Source 65, science and education, lecturer with 1–4 years of experience)

Experts emphasized that building trust between the government and businesses is essential for curbing the shadow economy. Entrepreneurs need to see that their tax contributions lead to tangible benefits, while strategic investment in high-value industries can promote tax compliance and reduce informal practices.

The analysis of the code "Legal system" (41 entries) underlines the need to strengthen Azerbaijan's legal and judicial framework in order to tackle the shadow economy. Key issues include ensuring transparency and independence of the judiciary to promote trust and fair practices, as well as reforms to combat institutional mistrust and bias. Respondents emphasize improving enforcement mechanisms, such as stricter penalties, risk-based audits, and automated monitoring systems such as Automated Risk Analysis System (ARAS), to prevent illegal activities.

The third largest qualitative code used to construct the current theme is "Educational and cultural measures" (38 codes), which emphasize the crucial role of awareness raising and education in tackling the shadow economy in Azerbaijan. A prevalent theme is public awareness and tax culture, emphasizing the need for systematic campaigns to promote understanding of the risks of the shadow economy and the benefits of formal economic participation. This includes targeted efforts to increase tax literacy, explain the contributions of taxes to public services and instill a sense of civic responsibility.

> People need to be educated; measures need to be taken. I do not believe that anyone steals for fun and gets stressed in the process. Penalties should be a deterrent, but there should also be training, and fees should encourage people. (Source 74, consultant with 1–4 years of experience)

Education at all levels is emphasized as a fundamental element of possible strategies to tackle shadow economy in the long term. According to the responses, programs from early childhood education to vocational training should instill values such as honesty, compliance and business ethics.

The fourth largest qualitative code concerned competition-related aspects of long-term measures against the large share of the shadow economy in Azerbaijan. It is clear from the experts' responses on "Competition" (36 codes) that ensuring fair and healthy competition is key to tackling the shadow economy in Azerbaijan. A recurring idea is the creation of a healthy competitive environment through a sound legal framework, including the effective implementation of the Competition Law and measures to combat monopoly practices. If competitive environment is not ensured, the motivation and recognition for companies that contribute to economic value creation will remain low. This could further exacerbate the spread of the shadow economy in the country. Encouraging compliance with laws through rewards and incentives, such as recognizing high taxpayers or innovators, is seen as complementary to deterrent measures such as penalties, which would reinvigorate competitive forces in the markets.

> A fair and healthy competitive environment and transparent public administration can increase the responsibility of the private sector. (Source 46, science and education, lecturer with 1–4 years of experience)

The fifth largest qualitative code in the current theme was "Anticorruption measures" (25 codes). The central idea of this code is the elimination of corruption and bribery, which respondents see as crucial to creating a transparent and fair business environment. This includes minimizing the risk of evading penalties, reducing nepotism and curbing illegal interference by state institutions that often force companies to relocate or operate informally. There is also a focus on aligning the fight against corruption to broader socio-economic reforms. Respondents argue for a reduction in inequality, an increase in income and an improvement in overall living standards in order to reduce society's dependence on corrupt systems.

There were other qualitative codes that collected additional ideas from respondents in relation to the current theme. "Income transparency" (12 codes) was mainly about a more detailed analysis of income distribution, which can be distorted for various reasons (e.g., corruption, lack of experience in income reporting). Respondents pointed to certain reforms that need to be pushed forward in order to disclose the income and expenditure of all individuals regardless of their profession, which would ensure transparency and accountability.

The qualitative code "State support" (15 codes) listed all the ideas that defended the need for more incentives by the state to enlarge the private business, liberalize the economy and decrease the tax pressure over the employment. Healthy business environment, provision of equal opportunities for the private agents of the markets, better working conditions and better policymaking were also among the suggestions.

The qualitative codes such as "Governance and regulation" (22 codes), "Involvement of the state in the business" (20 codes) and "Public trust" (19 codes) were about improving the quality of governance in the state apparatus in order to overcome coordination problems, corruption and inefficiency and to clear the way for SMEs. In other words, the basic idea is that the state's current regulatory capacity is hampered by various bureaucratic malpractices that need to be corrected.

Finally, one of the most interesting lines of qualitative coding within the first theme was "Digitalization and artificial intelligence (AI)" (23 codes) where numerous respondents spoke out in favor of increasing digitalization and the use of AI. At the heart of this narrative is the transition to a cashless economy, facilitated by reforms to promote digital payment systems and reduce reliance on cash transactions. According to the experts, this transition not only increases transparency but also minimizes tax evasion and unregistered activity.

> Electronic invoicing and digital tax systems. The digitalization of tax returns and payment systems will reduce tax evasion. (Source 78, science and education, research fellow with 7–10 years of experience)

Another central dimension of "Digitalization and AI" was the advocacy for the introduction of e-governance and digital services. This includes the development of mechanisms for online income declarations, the simplification of company registrations and the introduction of risk-based verification systems such as the ARAS. In addition, blockchain technology and big data analytics are highlighted for their ability to monitor commercial transactions and more accurately identify fraudulent activity.

Theme 2: Emphasizing the need for public-private partnerships

Several qualitative codes within Theme 2 collectively addressed the multilayered nature of the shadow economy in Azerbaijan in the context of public-private partnerships. Transparency emerges as a cornerstone supported by accountability mechanisms and public-private cooperation. International standards provide a framework for reform, while cultural change ensures long-term sustainability. Taken together, these efforts aim to create a transparent, equitable and competitive business environment to minimize the shadow economy, but without a strong commitment, it could persist for some time.

The largest qualitative code in this theme was "Transparency" (48 codes). Transparency serves as a basis for accountability and trust between stakeholders, which are essential for effectively tackling the shadow economy. For this reason, several aspects of transparency appeared particularly frequently in the theme, which primarily called for strengthening the transparency of government institutions and processes such as procurement, privatization and financial reporting. Measures include the introduction of digital governance tools, open and competitive tendering systems and independent audits. In addition, encouraging companies to adopt transparent financial practices, publishing financial data and complying with international accounting standards were mentioned several times.

> Transparency should not be a major financial burden on the private sector. The government should support this with mechanisms that encourage transparent activity. (Source 68, tax specialist, head of department with the experience more than 15 years)
> The most important thing is that transparency is increased. There should be strict control over the preparation of financial statements. In particular, the persons who prepare the financial statements must have extensive knowledge of the process of preparing international financial reporting and the financial statements. (Source 76, science and education, lecturer with 15 years of experience)

The second largest qualitative code was "Accountability" (22 codes). Many expert responses emphasize the need for robust systems to ensure accountability in governance and business operations. In addition, the integration of international financial reporting standards and rigorous monitoring of financial statements is emphasized as critical to accountability. It is suggested that financial reporting should be accurate and accessible to stakeholders, with significant penalties for non-compliance, to promote a culture of accountability.

> Real statistical indicators of the economy and sectors should be made available to scientists and the public. (Source 25, finance sector, manager with 10–15 years of experience)

The third largest qualitative code was "Public-private partnership" (13 codes). The excerpts in this qualitative code emphasize the need to strengthen public-private partnerships in Azerbaijan through increased dialog, clear regulatory standards and principles of mutual trust. Respondents emphasize the promotion of an improved business environment by supporting SMEs, ensuring transparency in the legal and judicial system and promoting compliance with international standards.

Other qualitative codes in this theme included the main ideas about greater public participation on the part of entrepreneurs to ensure more legal protection. Civil societies were recommended to expand the necessary institutional framework to improve the quality of legal protection. In line with these ideas, it was also suggested to include privatization in a public-private partnership.

Theme 3: Alignment of international partnerships and global standards with local economic realities to tackle the shadow economy

Using eight qualitative codes, the third theme was constructed to see how international partnerships and global standards can be useful in addressing the challenges related to shadow economy in Azerbaijan. Therefore, the largest qualitative code "International standards/experiences" was used 41 times and mainly describes the application of international standards and successful practices that were emphasized as cornerstones for tackling the shadow economy. Examples from countries such as Estonia and Singapore illustrate the need to adopt global standards in the areas of financial transparency, anticorruption and regulatory frameworks.

The experts pointed out that cooperation with international organizations (e.g., International Monetary Fund–IMF, OECD–Organization for Economic Co-operation and Development, WTO–World Trade Organization) and peer countries is crucial for learning and implementing effective strategies. Partnerships can facilitate the exchange of expertise, monitoring practices and the adaptation of regulatory models.

> The experience of countries that have successfully tackled the shadow economy in the recent past should be used, taking into account local particularities. This work, in particular the development of strategies to tackle this problem, should be based on advice from international experts and pilot projects should be carried out. (Source 12, science and education, manager with more than 15 years of experience)

While the second largest qualitative code "Inconclusive statements" was the highest among the other themes (17 codes), the third and fourth codes, namely "Enabling environment" (15 codes) and "National interests" (4 codes), described the expert opinions on the exact measures that should be applied in Azerbaijan regarding the shadow economy. These two codes mainly included the idea that the local economic and regulatory realities of the Azerbaijani economy should be based on international experience, taking into account the unique Azerbaijani context.

"Targeted approach" (9 codes) included the ideas that international standards and experiences should be adapted and applied in the specific sectors or subsectors that are in line with the country's strategic economic model. This is probably the reason why the qualitative code "Domestic matter" (8 codes) picks up on the recurring ideas that the tackling the shadow economy is primarily a domestic issue and that each country should develop its own policy practice to tackle it effectively. In addition, encouraging FDI and granting financial amnesties can boost investor confidence and support long-term development (covered by "Financial aspects," 8 codes).

> It will be useful to examine and test country models that could serve as pilot projects in the individual sectors/areas. (Source 84, audit sector, head of department with 5–7 years of experience)

Finally, membership of the WTO (5 codes) is seen as an important step toward addressing existing economic challenges and promoting transparency in trade. By adopting and implementing advanced international trade rules, Azerbaijan can promote a more competitive and efficient trading environment.

> Commercial transactions can be more transparent and registered under WTO membership and free trade agreements. (Source 78, science and education, research fellow with 7–10 years of experience)

7 Discussion

As already mentioned, the first question that this research should answer is how the scale of the shadow economy in Azerbaijan has changed in recent years and at what level it is now. Because the answer to this question is very important in terms of assessing the results of the policy of tackling the shadow economy, which the government has actively announced to put on its agenda since 2018. As shown in Fig. 4a, 24.1% of experts answered "decreased significantly" and 65.5% "decreased somewhat" to the question of how the scale of the shadow economy in the country has changed over the past period, in other words, the absolute majority of experts, approximately 90%, believe that this decrease has occurred. In addition to confirming the results of the study conducted by EY (2025), this can be considered as a good result in light of the decrease in the share of the oil sector, which is considered more transparent, and the gradual increase of the share of the non-oil sector in the economy of Azerbaijan in recent years. However, the experts' responses to questions eight and nine of the survey (See: Appendix) show that they believe that the shadow economy in the country accounts for about 1/3 of GDP and informal employment accounts for about 1/3 of the labor force. This reveals that the problem of the shadow economy in the country is slightly lower than the level indicated by the current international studies (See: Elgin et al., 2021), but still significant.

In a situation where the share of the relatively transparent and registered oil sector in the country's GDP is gradually decreasing, while the share of the non-oil sector is increasing, the decrease in the share of the shadow economy in GDP also gives reason to think that this is the result of government measures aimed at "whitening" economic activities and significantly reducing the tax burden of the non-oil sector in recent years. However, although the absolute majority of experts participating in our survey stated that the scale of the shadow economy in the country has been limited in recent years, they demonstrated a different position regarding the idea that the government's policy in this direction is sufficient. As can be seen from Fig. 5a, 5.7% of experts answered "I completely agree" to this idea, and 26.4% answered "I mostly agree." 50.6% of experts, in other words, more than half, stated that they partially agree with this idea, 14.9% disagreed, and 2.3% strongly disagreed. This result gives us a strong basis to focus on improving the policy implemented in Azerbaijan to tackle the shadow economy.

The effectiveness of the policy to tackle the shadow economy in Azerbaijan was assessed by experts on the three main elements of the policy model developed by Bagirzade (2013), and the results are presented in Fig. 5b. As can be seen, the percentage of experts who assessed the effectiveness of the applied policy as "bad" and "very bad" in the following areas was as follows: "making the formal economy more appealing"—36.8%, "strengthening of penalties and controls on the shadow economy"—22.9% and "strengthening of social awareness against the shadow economy"—45.9%. Overall, it can be seen from Fig. 5b that although experts report that the government's punitive and control measures in tackling the shadow economy are relatively successful, they believe that it should do more to increase the attractiveness of the formal economy and to form public awareness against the shadow economy. In this regard, experts assess the effectiveness of existing measures to increase the attractiveness of the formal economy on "strengthening the institutions of the formal economy" and "reducing financial and administrative obligations/burdens in the formal economy" at approximately the same level (See: Fig. 5c). This view is also approximately similar in the approach to the formation of social awareness against the shadow economy. Thus, experts believe that in this direction, the current level of effectiveness of both "organizing awareness campaigns" and "increasing public trust in the state" measures is close to each other (See: Fig. 5e). However, among the existing punitive and control measures, experts consider "increasing the probability of detection or strengthening the control" measures to be relatively more successful than "increasing penalties" measures (See: Fig. 5d). The general conclusion from these assessments is that experts believe that the policy to tackle the shadow economy in Azerbaijan focuses more on strengthening direct or administrative measures, while indirect aspects such as increasing the attractiveness of the formal economy and strengthening public awareness against the shadow economy should be further developed. This coincides with approaches (Bagirzade, 2013; Williams & Nazarov, 2018) that emphasize the importance of governments supporting the transition from the shadow economy to the formal economy.

The fact that experts emphasize the need to further develop non-administrative or indirect ways to tackle the shadow economy in Azerbaijan is also reflected in their answers to the question asked about the main reasons for the shadow economy in the country (question 17 in the survey) and to the open-ended questions presented regarding the improvement of this policy (questions 18, 19 and 20 in the survey). As presented in Fig. 5f, they see "corruption and bribery," "economic situation," "high taxes and other mandatory payments," "low level of tax culture and accountability habits" and "lack of healthy competition" as the main reasons for the shadow economy in the country. At the same time, the results of the TA show that experts consistently highlight the following topics to improve the tackling the shadow economy in the country: "transparency," "tax," "legal system," "international standards/experiences," "educational and cultural measures," "competition," "anticorruption measures," "digitalization and AI," "governance and regulation," "accountability" (See: Table 1, Theme 1, 2, 3). These problems, which are mainly related to the quality of economic institutions, are also consistent with the research results presented by ACCA (2017), Luong et al. (2020), Rakhmonov and Elmurodov (2021), Gërxhani and Cichocki (2023), Dabrowski (2023), and Gokcekus et al. (2023). Undoubtedly, this institutional situation is largely related to the Soviet legacy, as emphasized by Sayfutdinova (2015, 2017). Thus, in the Soviet era, when poverty was distributed approximately equally and any private initiative was severely punished by the state, people often had no other options than to turn to the shadow economy and corruption to meet their needs. At the same time, in the Soviet economy, where all resources and enterprises were state-owned, institutions such as competition, taxation and business-friendly regulation were out of the question. Unfortunately, this legacy, combined with the economic difficulties of the transition period, had its impact on economic transformation reforms in post-Soviet countries such as Azerbaijan and became one of the main factors determining the quality of institutions formed during this period.

However, certain positive results of the policy implemented by Azerbaijan against the shadow economy in recent years, which were also revealed in this study, provide grounds for optimism for the future and may encourage economic decision-makers to take more effective steps in this direction. This will require a greater focus on policy measures that promote the transition from the shadow economy to the formal economy, the basics of which we will try to present in the next section. However, it is important to note that our research findings and policy recommendations largely related to the macro level. Future research could benefit from further analyzing this issue across sectors and with regard to specific policy measures.

8 Policy Recommendations

1. First of all, it should be noted that the tackling the shadow economy requires a comprehensive approach. The results of this study also show that the tackling the shadow economy is not only a problem that tax authorities should deal with. It is a complex problem with many reasons, such as economic, institutional, social and technological and requires a long-term struggle. In this regard, there is a need to implement separate government programs developed on the basis of a comprehensive approach to tackle the shadow economy in Azerbaijan.

2. It is useful for economic decision-makers to take into account the existence of economic and business environment factors that push economic entities into shadow economic activities in Azerbaijan. The analysis of the answers to questions 11, 12 and 17 of the questionnaire we presented to experts within the framework of this study (See Appendix) also significantly strengthens this conclusion. Thus, to the question "Do you agree that the participation of economic entities in the shadow economy can be justified, in other words, that it is dictated by the current economic and business environment?" (Question 11), 4.6% of experts answered "I completely agree," 17.2% "I mostly agree" and 47.1% "I partially agree." Only 1/3 of the experts stated that they did not agree with this opinion. The answers to the question "Do you agree that the macroeconomic environment in Azerbaijan in recent years encourages the shadow economy?" (Question 12) also supports this opinion. Thus, 58.6% of experts answered this question with "I completely agree," "I mostly agree" and "I partially agree." Again, in response to question 17, respondents indicated "economic situation: low incomes, inequality, unemployment and poverty" as the second reason among the main reasons for the shadow economy in the country. As GDP per capita increases, income distribution improves, good jobs increase, and a profitable, fair and stable business environment develops, the tendency of economic entities to turn to shadow economic activities will also decrease. This can be largely justified in terms of small and medium-sized businesses, where shadow economic activities are usually widespread. Because when looking at the business structure in Azerbaijan, the number of micro, small and medium-sized business entities and self-employed people is significantly higher. Therefore, the government's focus on providing a more favorable business environment for these business entities can make significant positive contributions to economic growth, employment, improved income distribution and limiting the shadow economy in the country. In addition, policy measures that will increase productivity in the economy as a whole, including strengthening the economy's innovation capacity, can be effective in weakening the economic foundations of the shadow economy.

3. *In order to ensure a fair business environment, it is important to achieve the application of competition legislation without any exceptions.* As can be seen from the results of the TA, one of the most emphasized issues by experts in the tackling the shadow economy in Azerbaijan is the importance of a healthy competitive business environment and anti-monopoly measures. The participation of businesses with high market shares, as well as smaller businesses that are trying to compete with them and stay in the market, in shadow economic activities is a widespread practice in many developing countries. In this practice, large businesses do not shy away from shadow economic activities, mainly relying on their strengths. As for smaller businesses, they often turn to the shadow economy to reduce their costs. As a result, increased shadow economic activities push those economies further away from the goal of a fair business environment.

4. *The existence of a developed and favorable business infrastructure of the formal economy can significantly weaken the incentive for economic entities to participate in the shadow economy.* From this point of view, the existence of a legal system that protects the rights of entrepreneurs and a banking system that ensures their access to favorable financial resources is extremely important. If economic entities see that their opportunities to use an effective legal system and favorable financial resources are limited by participating in the shadow economy, their incentives to participate in shadow economic activities will decrease. Policy measures applied in this direction can yield better results, especially in terms of small and medium-sized businesses. Another effective measure that can be taken in this direction, especially in terms of large businesses, may be the development of capital markets in the country. The development of capital markets will require economic entities that want to go to market capitalization to adapt to high transparency standards. On the other hand, developing capital markets will also expand the opportunities for the population to invest their savings in the formal economy.

5. *It is important to note that the high transparency and efficiency of the public sector, especially public finances, have a significant positive*

impact on the transition of economic entities to the formal economy. This issue has been raised several times from different aspects in the experts' responses presented in Themes 1 and 2. When economic entities do not have sufficient information about what and how the taxes and other mandatory payments they pay to the state are spent on, when they do not have any influence on these expenditures, when they do not see that a significant part of these mandatory payments are returned to them in the form of public services or when they see that they are returned insufficiently, their tendency to engage in shadow economic activities also increases significantly. In other words, their incentives for the transition to the formal economy also decrease significantly. In such a situation, economic entities think that they can manage these financial resources they pay to the state more efficiently than the state.

6. In the tackling the shadow economy, it may be more useful to correctly select the sectors where this problem is widespread and take specific measures aimed at those sectors. It is true that shadow economic activities can appear in one way or another in almost all sectors of the economy. However, identifying sectors where unregistration, tax evasion, informal and non-transparent relations are more widespread and taking adequate measures for them may have a greater impact on limiting the share of the shadow economy in the economy as a whole. It should be borne in mind that shadow economic activities also have a "contagion" feature. Thus, in many cases, even transparent businesses that are in contact with shadow businesses can turn to shadow economic activities in order to both maintain their relations with these businesses and reduce their own costs. Therefore, effective measures by the government in sectors where shadow economic relations are widespread may lead to better results in the tackling the shadow economy. The answers to the 6th question (See: Appendix) that we presented to the respondents in the study (See: Fig. 4b) show that experts believe that the top three sectors where the shadow economy is most widespread in Azerbaijan are "construction," "trade and repair of vehicles" and "agriculture, forestry and fishing." Considering that these sectors are interconnected with many other sectors of the economy and have wide opportunities to influence them, then the government's activities aimed at limiting shadow economic relations in these sectors may also lead to better results overall.

7. Effective continuation of anti-corruption measures can significantly limit the shadow economy. The fact that the experts we asked for their opinion listed corruption and bribery as the first causes of the shadow economy in the country and, at the same time, included topics such as corruption, bribery, transparency and income declaration of officials in their answers to open questions supports this idea to a large extent. International studies also show that in high-income countries there is a mainly substitutive relationship between corruption and the shadow economy, and in middle- and low-income countries there is a mainly complementary relationship. As a study conducted for ECO countries revealed, this relationship is mainly complementary in post-Soviet countries, including Azerbaijan (Gokcekus et al., 2023). In the fight against corruption, it is necessary to focus not only on simple corruption mechanisms but also on complex corruption mechanisms that are widely observed in modern times. In particular, advanced digital technologies open up wide opportunities for officials to use more complex corruption mechanisms. The situation has even reached the point where the concept of digital corruption has already entered the literature. Thus, it is widely observed that bribe payments are made using blockchain, card to card, etc. mechanisms and are presented as fees for various fictitious services (consulting, e-education, etc.). In most of these cases, corruption income can be "laundered" directly by paying taxes. It seems that one of the areas where the government should focus in the fight against corruption is the tender system in the public sector. A transparent and competitive tender system will both weaken corruption in this area and encourage market entities wishing to participate in this system to be more transparent. In this direction, it is especially useful to close all the ways for fictitious companies to enter tenders.

8. There is a need to develop a policy to tackle the increasingly widespread digital shadow economy. Although a significant part of the experts we asked for their opinion noted the need to use digital technologies, AI, big data analytics, etc. in the tackling the shadow economy, it should also be taken into account that the development of digital technologies has also created conditions for the emergence of a new phenomenon—the digital shadow economy. The development of the digital shadow economy is also observed in Azerbaijan. In particular, it is observed that shadow e-commerce conducted through social networks and various digital services are increasingly widespread. It seems that the most widespread payment mechanisms of the digital shadow economy include currencies such as card to card and bitcoin. The use of such cashless payment mechanisms in shadow economic activities also increasingly reduces the reliability of methods that try to measure the volume of the shadow economy using cash demand methods. In this regard, it may be useful for the government to strengthen the tackling the digital shadow economy by using the most modern digital technologies.

9. It is important to adopt business practices and the economy as a whole in the country into line with progressive international standards. As the experts we consulted in this area noted, compliance with international transparency and financial reporting standards, cooperation with international organizations such as the WTO, IMF, OECD and the adoption of their transparency standards, especially corporate governance principles, are of great importance. In order for such good practices to spread rapidly in the economy, it is necessary to focus especially on public-private partnerships and attracting FDI to the economy.

10. There is a need to strengthen social awareness against the shadow economy, especially in the rural regions of the country. Most of the experts surveyed in this study emphasized the need to develop measures to strengthen social awareness in the tackling the shadow economy in Azerbaijan. In particular, observations show that this awareness is very weak in areas outside the country's major cities and that unregistered economic activities are widespread in these areas. In addition to developing control mechanisms in this direction, it is important to provide the necessary knowledge at all stages of the education system and conduct targeted awareness campaigns. At the same time, these measures should be sustainable.

9 Conclusion

The results of the study show that in parallel with the policy of tackling the shadow economy, which has intensified in recent years in Azerbaijan, the relative share of the shadow economy has also decreased. However, despite this, the share of the shadow economy in the economy still remains at a significant level—approximately 1/3 of the official economy—and this currently makes the question of how effective the policy of tackling it is relevant. There is almost no research in the existing literature that attempts to answer this question. In this regard, this study sought a detailed answer to the question and, based on the answers of experts, a comprehensive assessment of the policy of tackling the shadow economy in Azerbaijan was made. The assessment results show that the policy of tackling the shadow economy in Azerbaijan is more direct or administrative in nature than indirect or environment-creating, ensuring the transition from the shadow economy to the formal economy. Therefore, experts are of the opinion that punitive and control measures are more effectively applied in Azerbaijan than measures to increase the attractiveness of the formal economy and strengthen social awareness against the shadow economy. Against the background of all this, it turns out that the economic and institutional causes of the shadow economy in the country are more decisive, which increases the need for government policies aimed at eliminating or weakening the mentioned factors. It is not enough for this policy to be a policy of a punitive and control nature carried out by tax authorities. For this, there is a need to implement separate comprehensive state programs that combine the economic, institutional, social, and technological aspects of the shadow economy and, in addition to punishing such economic activities, also encourage the transition to the formal economy.

Appendix: Expert Survey

Dear Expert,

Thank you for agreeing to respond to this peer review survey.

We, Dr. Elshan Bagirzadeh and Dr. Ibrahim Niftiyev from Azerbaijan State University of Economics (UNEC) conduct this survey within the framework of a research that will be published in the prestigious "Palgrave Macmillian" Publishing House. The purpose of conducting the research is to assess the results of the policy announced and implemented by the government in the field of tackling the shadow economy in Azerbaijan in recent years. By answering the questions in this survey, you will greatly help us scientifically assess the main results of the mentioned policy and the effectiveness of this policy as a whole. We would like to note in advance that the confidentiality of your answers will be protected by us.

We consider your participation in this survey to be very important and would be pleased to share the published final results of the study with you, if you wish.

Please follow this link for the expert survey: https://forms.gle/kX5CVE1g4NCh4Xvd6.

Part I. General Information About the Expert

1. **Your field of work:**
    - Audit
    - Tax
    - Customs
    - Social protection
    - Finance
    - Bank
    - Statistics
    - Science and education
    - Consulting
    - Management
    - Other (please specify)
2. **Your position in the field you work in:**
    - Upper management
    - Specialist
    - Other (please specify)
3. **Your experience in your field of work:**
    - 1–4 years
    - 5–7 years
    - 7–10 years
    - 10–15 years
    - More than 15 years

Part II: About the Size of the Shadow Economy in Azerbaijan

4. **"The shadow economy is a set of economic activities that are not declared in order to avoid official obligations, while they must be declared to the relevant official institutions by law." Do you agree with this definition?**
    - I completely agree
    - I mostly agree
    - I partially agree
    - I disagree
    - I strongly disagree

- It is difficult to answer

5. **As you know, for more than 5 years now, the Azerbaijani government has been mentioning the existence of the problem of the shadow economy in many official documents and has listed tackling it as one of its main priorities. How do you think the size of the shadow economy in the country has changed over the past period?**

    - Decreased significantly
    - Decreased somewhat
    - Stayed about the same
    - Increased somewhat
    - Increased significantly
    - It is difficult to answer

6. **Please choose the top three industries from the list below where you believe the shadow economy is widespread in Azerbaijan:**

    - Agriculture, forestry and fishing
    - Mining
    - Manufacturing
    - Energy production, distribution and supply
    - Water supply, waste treatment and recycling
    - Trade and repair of vehicles
    - Construction
    - Transport and warehousing
    - Tourist accommodation and public catering
    - Information and communication
    - Finance and insurance
    - Real estate
    - Education
    - Health
    - Culture
    - Other service areas

7. **Please rank the following three shadow economy forms according to how common they are in Azerbaijan:**

- Illegal (without TIN) business activity No.______
- Tax evasion No.______
- Informal employment No.______

8. **As you know, until now, various studies on the size of the shadow economy of Azerbaijan have revealed different results. In your opinion, what is the approximate share of the shadow economy in GDP in Azerbaijan?**

   - 5–10%
   - 10–20%
   - 20–30%
   - 30–40%
   - 40–50%
   - More than 50%
   - It is difficult to answer

9. **What do you think is the approximate share of informal employment in the labor force in Azerbaijan?**

   - 5–10%
   - 10–20%
   - 20–30%
   - 30–40%
   - 40–50%
   - More than 50%
   - It is difficult to answer

Part III: On the Tackling Shadow Economy in Azerbaijan

10. **Do you agree with the opinion that the policy implemented by the government in Azerbaijan in recent years in the field of tackling the shadow economy is generally satisfactory?**

    - I completely agree
    - I mostly agree
    - I partially agree
    - I disagree

- I strongly disagree
- It is difficult to answer

11. **Do you agree with the idea that it is possible to "justify" the participation of market subjects in the shadow economy in Azerbaijan (in other words, the current economic and business environment dictates it)?**

    - I completely agree
    - I mostly agree
    - I partially agree
    - I disagree
    - I strongly disagree
    - It is difficult to answer

12. **Do you agree with the opinion that the macroeconomic condition (the general economic situation shaped by parameters such as economic growth, interest rates, exchange rates, unemployment, balance of payments, GDP per capita and income distribution) in Azerbaijan in recent years is encouraging for shadow economy?**

    - I completely agree
    - I mostly agree
    - I partially agree
    - I disagree
    - I strongly disagree
    - It is difficult to answer

13. **Please evaluate the effectiveness of the following areas in tackling the shadow economy in Azerbaijan on a 5-point scale** ***(1 = very bad, 2 = bad, 3 = average, 4 = good, 5 = excellent)*****:**

- Making the formal economy more appealing Point _____
- Strengthening of penalties and controls on shadow economy Point _____
- Strengthening social awareness against the shadow economy Point _____

14. **Please evaluate the effectiveness of the Azerbaijan government's measures in the following two areas to increase the appeal of the formal economy on a 5-point scale** ***(1 = very bad, 2 = bad, 3 = average, 4 = good, 5 = excellent)*****:**

- Reducing financial (taxes, duties, etc.) and administrative obligations/burdens in the formal economy Point _____
- Strengthening the institutions of the formal economy such as law, banking and incentive mechanisms Point _____

15. **Please evaluate the effectiveness of the Azerbaijan government's measures in the following two administrative areas to tackle the shadow economy on a 5-point scale *(1 = very bad, 2 = bad, 3 = average, 4 = good, 5 = excellent)*:**

- Increasing penalties Point _____
- Increasing the probability of detection or strengthening the control Point _____

16. **Please evaluate the effectiveness of the Azerbaijan government's measures to strengthen social awareness against the shadow economy in the following areas on a 5-point scale *(1 = very bad, 2 = bad, 3 = average, 4 = good, 5 = excellent)*:**

- Increasing public trust in the state Point _____
- Organizing awareness campaigns Point _____

17. **Please choose the top three causes for the shadow economy that you believe are most pertinent to the Azerbaijan economy from the list below *(Please enter the numbers in the boxes next to the available options)*:**

- Economic situation: low incomes, inequality, unemployment and poverty
- High taxes and other mandatory payments
- Low level of tax culture and accountability habits
- Corruption and bribery
- Lack of healthy competition
- Ineffective functioning of the legal system
- Low level of trust in official institutions
- Low probability of detection of shadow economic activities
- Inadequate cashless payment infrastructure
- Heavy bureaucratic burden of the state
- Heavy regulatory burden of the state
- Society's tolerant view of shadow economic activities

- Strong psychology of "everyone is doing it anyway" in society

18. **In your opinion, in the long term, what policy measures should be prioritized to significantly reduce the share of the shadow economy in Azerbaijan economy?** ***(Please comment below)***

    ____
    ____
    ____

19. **How should the government and the private sector regulate the issues of transparency and accountability so that the shadow economy does not threaten the long-term economic development of Azerbaijan?** ***(Please comment below)***

    ____
    ____
    ____

20. **In your opinion, what role should international collaboration and alignment to global standards play in Azerbaijan's initiatives to tackle the shadow economy, and how may these initiatives be successfully integrated into national strategies?** ***(Please comment below)***

    ____
    ____
    ____

We Appreciate Your Cooperation!

References

ACCA—The Association of Chartered Certified Accountants. (2017). *Emerging from the shadows: The shadow economy 2025*. ACCA Global. https://www.accaglobal.com/content/dam/ACCA_Global/Technical/Future/pi-shadow-economy-report.pdf. Accessed 12 February 2025.

Armat, M. R., Assarroudi, A., & Rad, M. (2018). Inductive and deductive: Ambiguous labels in qualitative content analysis. *The Qualitative Report, 23*(1), 219–221.

Asian Development Bank. (2025). *Poverty data: Azerbaijan*. https://www.adb.org/where-we-work/azerbaijan/poverty. Accessed 1 March 2025.

Bagirzade, E. (2007). *Gizli iqtisadiyyatin Kemiyyet qiymetlendirmesinin Gutmann Metodu ve Azerbaycan üzre Tetbiqi İmkanlari* (AMEA İqtisadiyyat İnstitutu Milli İqtisadiyyatin Problemləri: Meqaleler Toplusu, No. 2, 43–55).

https://avesis.unec.edu.az/publication/details/ac9ee554-e238-4115-bc6a-bfe87a1e9991/gizli-iqtisadiyyatin-kmiyyt-qiymtlndirmsinin-gutmann-metodu-v-azrbaycan-uzr-ttbiqi-imkanlari. Accessed 12 February 2025.

Bagirzade, E. (2010, May 30–June 6). *Nakit Para Talebi veya Tanzi Yöntemiyle Azerbaycan Kayıtdışı Ekonomisinin Tahmini Üzerine bir Deneme.* 2. Uluslararası Balkanlarda Sosyal Bilimler Kongresi, Prizren, Kosovo (pp. 925–936). https://avesis.unec.edu.az/publication/details/ab7efb1b-e2d4-4f8c-96cc-86d6031c5ab5/nakit-para-talebi-veya-tanzi-yontemiyle-azerbaycan-kayitdisi-ekonomisinin-tahmini-uzerine-bir-deneme. Accessed 12 February 2025.

Bagirzade, E. (2013). *Qeyri-resmi iqtisadiyyatin leqallasdirilmasinin esas istiqametleri* (Felsefe Doktorlugu Dissertasiyasi). Azerbaycan Devlet İqtisad Universiteti, Bakı. https://avesis.unec.edu.az/file?id=da2e6b4a-374d-468a-8a20-e10093d5da37. Accessed 12 February 2025.

Braun, V., & Clarke, V. (2012). Thematic analysis. In *APA handbook of research methods in psychology, Vol 2: Research designs: Quantitative, qualitative, neuropsychological, and biological* (pp. 57–71). American Psychological Association. https://doi.org/10.1037/13620-004

Chantzi, G. (2013). *The emergence of Azerbaijan as regional leader* (ICBSS Policy Briefs, 28).

Dabrowski, M. (2023). *A limping transition: The former Soviet Union thirty years on.* Essay 01/2023, Bruegel.

Dinçer, M. (2024). The role of Azerbaijan as the EU's energy supplier: A secondary alternative partner in natural gas. *European Politics and Society, 25*(4), 624–642.

Eilat, Y., & Zinnes, C. (2000). *The evolution of the shadow economy in transition countries: Consequences for economic growth and donor assistance* (CAER II Discussion Paper No. 83). Harvard Institute for International Development.

Elgin, C. (2021). *The informal economy: Measures, causes, and consequences.* Routledge.

Elgin, C., Kose, M. A., Ohnsorge, F., & Yu, S. (2021). *Understanding informality (CERP Discussion Paper 16497).* Centre for Economic Policy Research.

Elgin, C., & Oztunali, O. (2012). *Shadow economies around the world: Model based estimates* (Working Paper No. 2012/05). Bogazici University, Department of Economics, Istanbul.

EY. (2025, March). *Shadow economy exposed: Estimates for the world and policy paths.* Report. https://www.ey.com/content/dam/ey-unified-site/ey-com/en-gl/insights/tax/documents/ey-gl-shadow-economy-report-02-2025.pdf. Accessed 2 April 2025.

Gasparėnienė, L., Remeikienė, R., Sadeckas, A., & Ginevičius, R. (2016). Level and sectors of digital shadow economy: The case of Lithuania. *Entrepreneurship and Sustainability Issues, 4*(2), 183–197. https://doi.org/10.9770/jesi.2016.4.2(6)

Gërxhani, K., & Cichocki, S. (2023). Formal and informal institutions: Understanding the shadow economy in transition countries. *Journal of Institutional Economics, 19*(5), 656–672. https://doi.org/10.1017/S1744137422000522

Glinkina, S. P., & Rosenberg, D. J. (2003). The socioeconomic roots of conflict in the Caucasus. *Journal of International Development: The Journal of the Development Studies Association, 15*(4), 513–524. https://doi.org/10.1002/jid.1000

Gokcekus, O., Bagirzadeh, E., & Scribner, D. (2023). The shadow economy and corruption in ECO countries. *Sosyoekonomi, 31*(58), 179–180. https://doi.org/10.17233/sosyoekonomi.2023.04.09

Guliyev, H. (2019). Estimating the size of the shadow economy in Azerbaijan. *Voprosy Upravleniya i Ekonomiki: Sovremennoye Sostoyaniye Aktualnykh Problem, Sbornik Statey Po Materialam XXVIII Mezhdunarodnoy Nauchno-Prakticheskoy Konferentsii, 10*(26), 43–46.

Heinzen, J. (2020). Soviet entrepreneurs in the late socialist shadow economy: The case of the Kyrgyz affair. *Slavic Review, 79*(3), 544–565. https://doi.org/10.1017/slr.2020.157

Ivanov, D., & Aisin, A. (2024). Market under the radar: Soviet shadow economy and post-Soviet preferences in Georgia. *Communist and Post-Communist Studies, 57*(1), 74–100.

Johnson, S., Kaufmann, D., & Shleifer, A. (1997). The unofficial economy in transition. *Brookings Paper on Economic Activity, 2*, 159–221.

Kaser, M. (2003). V. The economic and social impact of systemic transition in central Asia and Azerbaijan. *Perspectives on Global Development and Technology, 2*(3), 459–473. https://doi.org/10.1163/156915003322986352

Kaufmann, D., & Kaliberda, A. (1996). *Integrating the unofficial economy into the dynamics of post-socialist economies: A framework of analysis and evidence* (Policy Research Working Paper 1691). The World Bank Europe and Central Asia Country Department.

Kintsurashvili, K., & Kresic, A. (2019). *Azerbaijan diagnostic.* European Bank of Reconstruction and Development. https://www.ebrd.com/content/dam/ebrd_dxp/assets/pdfs/country-strategies/azerbaijan/archive/azerbaijan-diagnostic.pdf. Accessed 7 January 2026.

Krumplytė, J. (2010). The shadow economy factors and causes analysis by expert evaluation method: Case of Lithuania. *Business, Management and Economics Engineering, 8*(1), 122–138. https://doi.org/10.3846/bme.2010.09

Lacko, M. (2000). Hidden economy—An unknown quantity? Comparative analysis of hidden economies in transition countries in 1989–1995. *Economics of Transition, 8*(1), 117–149.

Luong, T. T. H., Nguyen, T. M., & Nguyen, T. A. N. (2020). Rule of law, economic growth and shadow economy in transition countries. *The Journal of Asian Finance, Economics and Business, 7*(4), 145–154. https://doi.org/10.13106/jafeb.2020.vol7.no4.145

Lyulyov, O., Paliienko, M., Prasol, L., Vasylieva, T., Kubatko, O., & Kubatko, V. (2021). Determinants of shadow economy in transition countries: Economic and environmental aspects. *International Journal of Global Energy Issues, 43*(2–3), 166–182. https://doi.org/10.1504/IJGEI.2021.115142

Medina, L., & Schneider, F. (2018, January). *Shadow economies around the world: What did we learn over the last 20 years?* (IMF Working Paper, WP/18/17). https://www.imf.org/en/Publications/WP/Issues/2018/01/25/Shadow-Economies-Around-the-World-What-Did-We-Learn-Over-the-Last-20-Years-45583. Accessed 16 July 2025.

Observatory of Economic Complexity. (2024). *Azerbaijan*. https://oec.world/en/profile/country/aze?yearSelector1=2016. Accessed 16 January 2025.

Rakhmonov, A., & Elmurodov, S. (2021). Institutional Determinants of shadow economy in the former Soviet Union countries. *European Proceedings of Social and Behavioural Sciences* (pp. 1048–1060). https://doi.org/10.15405/epsbs.2021.09.02.116

Rasanayagam, J. (2011). Informal economy, informal state: The case of Uzbekistan. *International Journal of Sociology and Social Policy, 31*(11/12), 681–696.

Remeikiene, R., Gaspareniene, L., & Schneider, F. G. (2018). The definition of digital shadow economy. *Technological and Economic Development of Economy, 24*(2), 696–717. https://doi.org/10.3846/20294913.2016.1266530

Sayfutdinova, L. (2015). Negotiating welfare with the informalizing state: Formal and informal practices among engineers in post-Soviet Azerbaijan. *Journal of Eurasian Studies, 6*(1), 24–33. https://doi.org/10.1016/j.euras.2014.08.002

Sayfutdinova, L. (2017). Post-Soviet small businesses in Azerbaijan: The legacies of the Soviet second economy. *Caucasus Survey, 5*(1), 11–26. https://doi.org/10.1080/23761199.2017.1280927

Schneider, F. (2004). *The size of the shadow economies of 145 countries all over the world: First Results over the Period 1999 to 2003* (IZA Discussion Papers, No.1431). Institute for the Study of Labor (IZA), Bonn.

Schneider, F., Buehn, A., & Montenegro, C. E. (2010). New estimates for the shadow economies all over the world. *International Economic Journal, 24*(4), 443–461. https://doi.org/10.1080/10168737.2010.525974

Shoufan, A. (2023). Exploring students' perceptions of ChatGPT: Thematic analysis and follow-up survey. *IEEE Access, 11*, 38805–38818.

Terry, G., Hayfield, N., Clarke, V., & Braun, V. (2017). Thematic analysis. *The SAGE Handbook of Qualitative Research in Psychology, 2*(17–37), 25.

Vaismoradi, M., Turunen, H., & Bondas, T. (2013). Content analysis and thematic analysis: Implications for conducting a qualitative descriptive study. *Nursing & Health Sciences, 15*(3), 398–405.

Voicu, C. C. (2008). The perception of specialists on Romanian underground economy. *Synergy, 4*(2), 254–267.

Williams, C., & Nazarov, I. (2018, July 14). *Supporting the transition from the informal to formal economy in Azerbaijan*. https://ssrn.com/abstract=4136684 or https://doi.org/10.2139/ssrn.4136684

Williams, M., & Moser, T. (2019). The art of coding and thematic exploration in qualitative research. *International Management Review, 15*(1), 45–55.

World Bank. (2024a). *Population, total—Azerbaijan*. https://data.worldbank.org/indicator/SP.POP.TOTL?locations=AZ. Accessed 16 January 2025.

World Bank. (2024b). *GDP per capita (current US$)—Azerbaijan*. https://data.worldbank.org/indicator/NY.GDP.PCAP.CD?end=2023&locations=AZ&start=1991. Accessed 16 January 2025.

World Bank. (2024c). *Unemployment, total (% of total labor force) (national estimate)—Azerbaijan*. https://data.worldbank.org/indicator/SL.UEM.TOTL.NE.ZS?end=2022&locations=AZ&start=1991&view=chart. Accessed 16 January 2025.

World Bank. (2024d). *Industry (including construction), value added (% of GDP)—Azerbaijan*. https://data.worldbank.org/indicator/NV.IND.TOTL.ZS?locations=AZ. Accessed 16 January 2025.

World Bank. (2024e). *Manufacturing, value added (% of GDP)—Azerbaijan*. https://data.worldbank.org/indicator/NV.IND.MANF.ZS?end=2023&locations=AZ&start=2000&view=chart. Accessed 16 January 2025.

World Bank. (2024f). *Agriculture, forestry, and fishing, value added (% of GDP)—Azerbaijan*. https://data.worldbank.org/indicator/NV.AGR.TOTL.ZS?end=2023&locations=AZ&start=2010&view=chart. Accessed 16 January 2025.

World Bank. (2024g). *Services, value added (% of GDP)—Azerbaijan*. https://data.worldbank.org/indicator/NV.SRV.TOTL.ZS?end=2023&locations=AZ&start=1990&view=chart. Accessed 16 January 2025.

World Bank. (2024h). *Trade (% of GDP)—Azerbaijan*. https://data.worldbank.org/indicator/NE.TRD.GNFS.ZS?end=2023&locations=AZ&start=1990&view=chart. Accessed 16 January 2025.

World Bank. (2024i). *External balance on goods and services (% of GDP)—Azerbaijan*. https://data.worldbank.org/indicator/NE.RSB.GNFS.ZS?end=2023&locations=AZ&start=1991&view=chart. Accessed 16 January 2025.

World Bank. (2024j). *GDP growth (annual %)—Azerbaijan*. https://data.worldbank.org/indicator/NY.GDP.MKTP.KD.ZG?locations=AZ. Accessed 16 January 2025.

CHAPTER 3

Digital Revolution and the Shadow Economy: Opportunities and Challenges for Kazakhstan

Saltanat Kondybayeva and Zhansaya Temerbulatova

1 Introduction

The digital revolution has become one of the key driving forces behind the current economic transformation, significantly changing the way we do business, interact between economic agents, and regulate economic activity. The introduction of digital technologies, such as the Internet and mobile devices, not only increases the efficiency of economic processes, but also creates new opportunities for controlling and monitoring economic activity. However, along with the positive effects, digitalization can also contribute to the development of the

S. Kondybayeva
Al-Farabi Kazakh National University, Almaty, Kazakhstan
e-mail: Saltanat.Kondybaeva@kaznu.edu.kz

Z. Temerbulatova (✉)
Almaty Management University, Almaty, Kazakhstan
e-mail: t.zhansaya.s@mail.ru; Zh.Temerbulatova@almau.edu.kz

E. Bagirzadeh and O. Gokcekus (eds.), *Shadow Economies in Turkic Republics*, https://doi.org/10.1007/978-3-032-12872-0_3

shadow economy, providing more flexible and difficult-to-trace channels for informal economic activity.

In this study, we define digitalization as the process of integrating digital technologies into economic and administrative activities to enhance efficiency, transparency, and service delivery. Following OECD (2023) and ITU (2024) frameworks, we operationalize digitalization through two key measurable dimensions: (1) internet penetration, which captures population-wide access to online infrastructure and reflects the level of digital connectivity; and (2) mobile cellular subscriptions, which indicate the scale and accessibility of mobile communication technologies. These indicators serve as proxies for digital inclusion and infrastructure, enabling us to analyze their differentiated effects on the shadow economy. While e-government development, digital public services, and fintech expansion are important aspects of digitalization, they are not directly included in our quantitative model due to data limitations but are discussed qualitatively in the policy section.

The main purpose of this study is to examine the impact of digital technologies on the shadow economy in Kazakhstan. In particular, it analyzes how Internet penetration and the spread of mobile technologies affect informal economic activity, as well as what macroeconomic factors can strengthen or weaken this effect.

The shadow economy remains an important problem for many countries, including Kazakhstan, as it undermines the stability of the state budget, reduces tax revenues, creates unfavorable conditions for business, and distorts the statistical picture of economic development (World Bank, 2024). In the context of digitalization, when financial flows become more transparent and controllable, new opportunities for reducing informal economic activity appear. However, digital technologies can also create new opportunities for tax evasion if they are not accompanied by adequate control measures. This study focuses on the analysis of the impact of key digitalization factors, such as the level of internet penetration and the spread of mobile technologies, as well as macroeconomic factors, such as GDP per capita, unemployment, inflation, and tax revenues, on the size of the shadow economy. This allows for a deeper understanding of the factors determining the dynamics of the informal sector and the formulation of practical recommendations for the development of economic policies aimed at reducing the share of the shadow economy.

2 Country's Economic Profile

Kazakhstan, the largest country in Central Asia in terms of territory and economic potential, has demonstrated sustainable macroeconomic development in recent years. This is happening against the backdrop of ongoing reforms, institutional changes, and active integration into the global economy. The country's economic profile, presented in the World Bank's open sources, allows us to assess the current situation and growth prospects based on quantitative data and international comparisons.

Macroeconomic characteristics. According to the World Bank (2024), Kazakhstan's nominal GDP in 2023 was $259.7 billion, which corresponds to the status of a country with an upper-middle income. Per capita, it was $13,088, an indicator that is ahead of neighboring countries in the region and confirms the relative stability of the economy.

Economic growth in 2023 was positive, but the pace began to slow down slightly: real GDP grew by 5.1%. This was largely possible due to an increase in oil production, the restoration of external demand, and the growth of domestic consumption. Despite the consequences of the pandemic, Kazakhstan's economy has shown the ability to adapt, including through active government support measures and the use of the National Fund's resources (World Bank, 2024).

Inflation, however, remains high. In 2023, the annual inflation rate reached 21.3%. This is due to both internal problems—structural imbalances and price unevenness—and external factors: exchange rate fluctuations, rising prices of imported products, and rising logistics costs (World Bank, 2024).

In the first half of 2024, Kazakhstan's GDP growth rate slowed to 3.2%. The main reasons were a decrease in investment and a reduction in government spending. Thus, real investment fell by 3.5% compared to growth of 13.3% a year earlier, and government spending decreased by 4.5% (after + 17% in the first half of 2023). The slowdown also affected consumer demand: retail sales growth slowed to 3.9% against 10.4% last year (World Bank, 2024).

On the supply side, industrial production grew by 2.7%, which is slightly below the level of last year (3.8%). This is partly due to a decrease in oil production by 1.6%. At the same time, the construction sector showed an acceleration to 8.6% (against 7.7% previously), and the service sector slowed to 3.3%. Despite these fluctuations, the official unemployment rate in the second quarter remained stable at 4.7%. To improve living standards, the government continues to digitalize the social sphere and management. It was also decided to increase the minimum wage by 21.4% in nominal terms. Since 2021, it has actually doubled—an increase of 70% in real terms (World Bank, 2024).

An analysis of the GDP structure shows that the economy still largely depends on extractive industries: agriculture provided about 3.9% of GDP, industry—32.3%, services—56.3% (World Bank, 2024). The high share of the services sector indicates a gradual transition to a post-industrial model, but the dominance of raw material exports emphasizes the need to continue the policy of economic diversification laid down in the Strategy for Industrial and Innovative Development of Kazakhstan.

Foreign economic positions and investment attractiveness. Kazakhstan occupies a favorable geographical position between Europe and Asia, which creates potential for the development of logistics and transit. However, the structure of foreign trade remains raw materials: the main share is oil, gas, metals, uranium, and grain. Key trading partners are China, Italy, Russia, the Netherlands, and Türkiye. Foreign direct investment continues to play an important role in the country's economy, especially in terms of attracting capital and technology. Kazakhstan remains one of the leaders in FDI in the region, but most of it is still concentrated in the oil and gas sector. According to the OECD (2024), in sectors such as telecommunications and transport, there is still a high level of regulatory restrictions, which hinders the inflow of investment into the non-resource sector.

Human capital and socio-economic indicators. According to the World Bank's Human Capital Index (2020), Kazakhstan's score is 0.63. This means that a child born today realizes, on average, 63% of his or her potential, given access to quality education and healthcare. This is higher than the Central Asian average, but still below the OECD average. The poverty rate by national threshold in 2022 was 5.2%. At the same time, significant socio-economic differences remain between regions. Average life expectancy has reached 71.4 years—a positive result against the backdrop of the modernization of the healthcare system (World Bank, 2024).

The Shadow Economy. The shadow economy continues to play a significant role in Kazakhstan's economic development. Its scale affects not only tax policy, but also how government regulation works, how the labor market is structured, and how great social inequality is. the World Bank published an interesting database that collected estimates of shadow production volumes for almost 30 years, from 1990 to 2020 (Elgin et al., 2021). The study presents data for 196 countries, including Kazakhstan, and uses two approaches: the MIMIC model and the DGE model. This allows us to get a fairly comprehensive picture of how the shadow economy has developed in different regions.

According to the data, in the early 1990s, the share of the shadow economy in Kazakhstan reached 43–45% of GDP, according to the MIMIC model (Fig. 1). This is not surprising, given the post-Soviet institutional vacuum, problems with tax administration, and the widespread use of barter transactions in those years.

The DGE model gave slightly lower estimates—about 37–39%, which, nevertheless, confirmed the scale of the problem, albeit with less pronounced fluctuations.

After 2003, both models recorded a steady decline in the share of the informal sector. This is most likely due to the digitalization of the tax system, tightening of customs controls, and simplification of business conditions.

Nevertheless, as of 2020, the shadow economy still occupies a significant place: according to the MIMIC model—about 37% of GDP, according to the DGE—about 35%. That is, despite positive shifts in the institutional environment, the problem remains relevant.

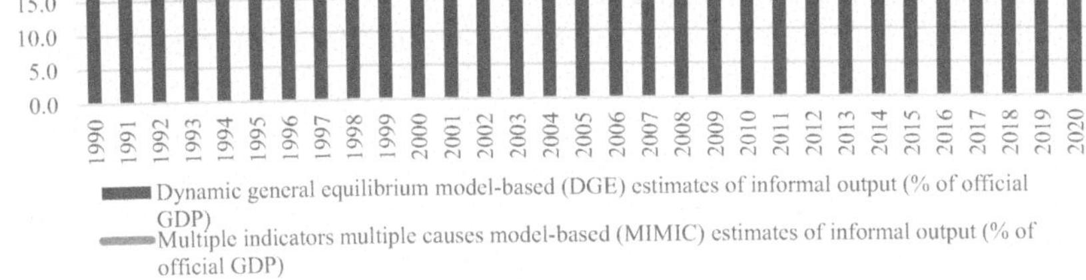

Fig. 1 Shadow economy in Kazakhstan: dynamics and scale based on DGE and MIMIC model estimates. *Source* Authors' compilation based on Elgin et al. (2021)

Environmental sustainability and digitalization of the economy. In the context of the global transition to a carbon–neutral development model, Kazakhstan has set itself the goal of achieving climate neutrality by 2060. To this end, steps are being taken to develop renewable energy sources, modernize industry, and digitally transform public administration.

Digitalization is becoming one of the key areas of sustainable growth. The introduction of smart management technologies (GovTech) helps increase labor productivity, improve the business climate, and reduce transaction costs. The slowdown in economic growth requires strategic decisions, and one of them is the Digital Kazakhstan program. It is aimed at developing digital infrastructure, introducing AI, automating production, and digitalizing public services, which should contribute to the growth of productivity and GDP in the long term (World Bank, 2021).

Digitalization is especially important against the backdrop of declining traditional investments and slowing global economic activity. Thus, the banking sector continues to demonstrate resilience: lending volumes grew by 13.8% in the first half of 2024 (World Bank, 2024). The development of fintech and digital financial services increases the population's access to financial resources, including through non-banking channels. In addition, the active growth of e-commerce helps maintain domestic demand, compensating for the decline in traditional consumption.

According to forecasts (IMF, 2025; World Bank, 2025), Kazakhstan's real GDP growth is expected to temporarily accelerate to around 4.7% in 2025—driven by higher oil output, investment stimulus, and infrastructure spending—and then moderate toward its medium-term potential growth of 3–3.5%. However, further digitalization is necessary for sustainable growth, especially in services exports and innovation. Internet of Things technologies, automation, and big data can become important factors in increasing competitiveness.

Inflation is expected to continue to decline in 2025, although the risk of pressure on prices remains in the services sector. At the same time, digitalization of public administration and the financial sector can improve monetary policy management and reduce inflation expectations.

The budget deficit is expected to shrink from approximately 2.7% of GDP in 2024 to around 2.5% in 2026, and further decline to about 1.8% in 2027 and 1.4% by 2028, supported by tax reform and more precise fiscal planning (Government of Kazakhstan, 2025). Digitalization of tax administration will play a significant role here, increasing tax collection and reducing the shadow economy. Despite the challenges, Kazakhstan continues to actively integrate into the digital economy, focusing on the development of innovative technologies and the expansion of digital capabilities in various industries. All this makes digital transformation not just an element of economic strategy, but a key condition for the country's sustainable development in the future.

3 Literature Review

The relationship between digitalization and the shadow economy has become a critical area of research in recent years. Digital technologies, such as the internet and mobile phones, have significantly transformed economic systems by increasing transparency, reducing transaction costs, and improving the traceability of financial operations. However, digitalization also presents new challenges, as it can simultaneously facilitate informal economic activities, creating a complex dynamic between technological progress and economic formality.

Digitalization is generally associated with a reduction in the size of the shadow economy, primarily through enhanced transparency and improved government oversight. For example, Haruna and Alhassan (2022) found that in African countries, digitalization, particularly through improved telecommunications infrastructure and expanded government online services, contributes to a significant decrease in informal economic activities. Similarly, Amanova (2022) reported that in Uzbekistan, higher R&D expenditure and increased availability of personal computers are negatively correlated with the size of the shadow economy and informal employment. However, Konovalov and Konovalova (2023) emphasized that digitalization can also create new risks, such as illegal labor markets, hidden information resources, and cryptocurrencies, complicating efforts to control the informal sector.

Mobile technologies have a particularly complex relationship with the shadow economy. While mobile phones can reduce transaction costs and increase market access, they may also expand the scope of informal activities. Larsson and Svensson (2018) observed that mobile phones in Kampala enabled market women to conduct transactions outside of traditional street markets, increasing their financial autonomy but potentially expanding the informal economy. Similarly, Hyde-Clarke (2013) found that mobile phones are vital for the economic welfare of small market enterprises in Johannesburg but do not necessarily facilitate a transition to the formal sector. In contrast, Hassan (2024) and Ghislain (2022) argued that mobile financial services and ICT diffusion can reduce the size of the shadow economy by enhancing transparency and accessibility, particularly in Sub-Saharan Africa. However, the effectiveness of these technologies depends heavily on regulatory quality and broader economic conditions.

Macroeconomic factors also play a crucial role in shaping the size and dynamics of the shadow economy. Achim and Mare (2024) highlighted that income inequality and unemployment are positively correlated with the shadow economy, while good governance and effective institutions are associated with its reduction. Bitzenis et al. (2016) further noted that the important determinants of the shadow economy are factors related to macroeconomic conditions, such as unemployment and GDP growth, and institutional factors, such as tax morale and the rule of law.

In the context of Kazakhstan, digitalization presents both opportunities and challenges for reducing the shadow economy. Tulemetova et al. (2024) noted that while Kazakhstan has made significant progress in digital transformation, including advancements in e-commerce, digital literacy, and e-government, substantial challenges remain. These include regional disparities in ICT adoption, insufficient investment in digital skills training, and persistent structural barriers to formal economic participation. Muminov et al. (2020) suggested that digitalization could be a powerful tool for formalizing shadow economic activities, particularly in sectors like electronic commerce and retail trade. However, as Kydyrova et al. (2020) pointed out, issues such as insecure property rights, monopolies, and repressive taxation continue to drive informal economic activities in Kazakhstan.

Overall, the literature suggests that while digitalization has the potential to reduce the shadow economy by improving transparency and reducing transaction costs, it also introduces new risks and challenges. Effective policy interventions, including stronger regulatory frameworks, targeted investments in digital infrastructure, and enhanced digital literacy, are essential for leveraging the benefits of digitalization while minimizing its potential drawbacks.

Despite the significant progress in understanding the relationship between digitalization and the shadow economy, several research gaps remain. First, most studies focus on either the positive or negative impacts of digitalization, without fully accounting for its dual nature. While some researchers emphasize the transparency and formalizing potential of digital technologies (Amanova, 2022; Haruna & Alhassan, 2022), others highlight the risks of increased informality through digital platforms (Konovalov & Konovalova, 2023). This creates a need for a more nuanced analysis that captures the complex, often contradictory effects of digitalization on the shadow economy.

Second, much of the existing literature is region-specific, often focusing on African or Asian contexts, with limited attention to Central Asian economies like Kazakhstan. Given the unique economic, institutional, and regulatory conditions in Kazakhstan, it is essential to conduct more context-specific studies that address the specific challenges and opportunities associated with digital transformation in this region (Muminov et al., 2020; Tulemetova et al., 2024).

Finally, there is a lack of comprehensive empirical studies that simultaneously consider the effects of both digitalization and traditional macroeconomic factors, such as GDP per capita, unemployment, inflation, and tax revenue, on the size of the shadow economy. Most existing models either focus solely on digital factors or emphasize broader macroeconomic trends, without integrating these two perspectives.

Addressing these gaps will provide a more complete understanding of the factors driving the shadow economy in digitally transforming economies like Kazakhstan and will offer more precise policy recommendations for reducing informality.

4 Data and Methodology

The data used in this analysis were collected from multiple reliable sources, including the World Bank and the International Monetary Fund (IMF). The dataset covers the period from 2006 to 2020 and includes annual observations for Kazakhstan. The primary focus is on examining the impact of digitalization on the size of the shadow economy in Kazakhstan. This specific period was selected because estimates of informal output are available for these years in the Informal Economy Database of the World Bank (Elgin et al., 2021), providing a consistent basis for analysis. The key variables used in this study are given in Table 1.

The following hypotheses were put forward:

H1 An increase in the percentage of the population using the internet leads to a significant reduction in the size of the shadow economy, reflecting the positive effects of digital transparency and enhanced economic monitoring.

Table 1 Key variables used in the study

Variable	*Designation in the model*	*Description*	*Source*
Dependent variable			
Dynamic general equilibrium model-based (DGE) estimates of informal output (% of official GDP)	*Shadow*	Estimated share of the shadow economy as a percentage of GDP, capturing the size of unregistered economic activities	Informal economy database of World Bank (Elgin et al., 2021)
Main independent variables			
Individuals using the Internet (% of population):	*Internet*	A measure of digital penetration and internet accessibility among the population	World Bank
Mobile cellular subscriptions (per 100 people)	*Mobile*	Reflects the extent of mobile technology adoption and connectivity	World Bank
Control variables			
GDP per capita (thousand USD)	*GDPpc*	Represents the overall economic development and income level in the country	International Monetary Fund
Unemployment rate (%)	*Unempl*	An economic indicator reflecting the share of the labor force that is without work but actively seeking employment	International Monetary Fund
Inflation rate (%)	*Infl*	The annual percentage change in the consumer price index (CPI), capturing the rate of price level changes	International Monetary Fund
Tax revenue (% of GDP)	*Tax*	The share of tax collections in the total GDP, reflecting the fiscal capacity of the government	World Bank

Note Compiled by the authors

H2 An increase in mobile cellular subscriptions is positively associated with the size of the shadow economy, potentially reflecting the role of mobile technologies in informal economic activities.

H3 Control variables (GDP per capita, unemployment rate, inflation rate, and tax revenue) have varying impacts on the size of the shadow economy and are included to control for broader economic conditions.

To assess the relationship between variables, multiple linear regression models were developed using the Ordinary Least Squares (OLS) method.

The general specification of the model is as follows:

$$\begin{aligned} Shadow_t =& \beta_0 + \beta_1 \cdot Internet_t + \beta_2 \cdot Mobile_t + \beta_3 \cdot GDPpc_t \\ &+ \beta_4 \cdot Unempl_t + \beta_5 \cdot Infl_t + \beta_6 \cdot Tax_t + \varepsilon_t \end{aligned}$$

However, to avoid possible errors in the specification, an analysis for multicollinearity was performed. Variables with excessively high correlation coefficients were used separately to improve model stability.

Then, various combinations of independent variables were tested, allowing up to one statistically insignificant variable in each model to improve flexibility while maintaining overall robustness. The models were ranked based on Akaike Information Criterion (AIC) to identify the most efficient specifications with significant coefficients.

Following this, additional tests, including the Durbin-Watson statistic for autocorrelation and residual normality, were conducted to validate the models.

The final selection of models prioritized those with high explanatory power (R-squared), low AIC values, and acceptable levels of multicollinearity. These models serve as the basis for interpreting the impact of digitalization on the shadow economy in Kazakhstan.

While the dataset spans the period from 2006 to 2020, the primary objective of our empirical analysis is to explore structural associations rather than dynamic forecasting. Therefore, we rely on cross-sectional OLS-type specifications applied to annual data, controlling for key macroeconomic variables. Although time series techniques (e.g., stationarity tests, cointegration analysis) may offer additional insights, their application is limited by the short sample size. Furthermore, preliminary diagnostics suggest that the inclusion of lag structures or transformations does not substantially alter the direction of key coefficients. As such, our approach prioritizes interpretability and policy relevance within the constraints of available data.

5 Findings

This section presents the main results of the regression analysis conducted to test the above hypotheses. First, descriptive statistics were conducted.

Table 2 presents the descriptive statistics for the variables used in the analysis, including the dependent variable (*Shadow*) and the main independent and control variables. The shadow economy (*Shadow*) has a mean value of 37.191 with a standard deviation of 1.004, ranging from a minimum of 35.473 to a maximum of 38.624. This indicates relatively low variability in the size of the shadow economy over the study period. The primary independent variables, Internet usage (*Internet*) and mobile cellular subscriptions (*Mobile*), exhibit greater variation, with mean values of 51.893 and 129.546, and standard deviations of 29.96 and 36.005, respectively. Internet usage varies significantly, from a minimum of 3.27 to a maximum of 85.9, reflecting the rapid digital transformation in Kazakhstan. Mobile subscriptions also show a wide range, from 49.143 to 176.786, capturing the rapid growth in mobile connectivity over the years.

Among the control variables, GDP per capita (*GDPpc*) has a mean of 9.583 (thousand USD) with a moderate spread, ranging from 5.29 to 13.89. The unemployment rate (*Unempl*) averages 5.64%, with relatively low variability (standard deviation 0.958) over the period. Inflation (*Infl*) has a higher degree of fluctuation, with a mean of 8.213% and a

Table 2 Descriptive statistics of key variables (2006–2020)

Variable	*Obs*	*Mean*	*Std. dev.*	*Min*	*Max*
Shadow	15	37.191	1.004	35.473	38.624
Internet	15	51.893	29.96	3.27	85.9
Mobile	15	129.546	36.005	49.143	176.786
GDPpc	15	9.583	2.382	5.29	13.89
Unempl	15	5.64	0.958	4.8	7.8
Infl	15	8.213	3.601	4.6	18.6
Tax	15	12.544	2.767	8.319	18.258

Note Compiled by the authors based on calculations in STATA 17

standard deviation of 3.601%, indicating periods of significant price instability. Finally, the tax revenue (*Tax*) as a percentage of GDP has a mean of 12.544 with a standard deviation of 2.767, reflecting the varying fiscal capacity of the government over time.

The next step of the analysis was to check all independent variables for multicollinearity.

Table 3 presents the correlation matrix for the main independent and control variables used in this study. High correlations between certain pairs of variables indicate potential multicollinearity, which can lead to unstable coefficient estimates and reduced reliability of statistical inferences. Specifically, the matrix reveals several critical relationships:

- *Internet* and *Unempl* (−0.960). These two variables exhibit a very strong negative correlation, indicating that as internet penetration increases, unemployment tends to decrease significantly. Including both in the same model is likely to introduce severe multicollinearity, as changes in one variable strongly predict changes in the other.
- *Mobile* and *GDPpc* (0.893). There is a strong positive correlation between mobile subscriptions and GDP per capita, suggesting that more economically developed regions tend to have higher mobile penetration rates. Including both in the same model would likely cause inflated standard errors and unreliable coefficient estimates.
- *Mobile* and *Unempl* (−0.868). This pair also shows a very strong negative correlation, reflecting the possible relationship between economic development (represented by mobile adoption) and

Table 3 Correlation matrix of digital and macroeconomic indicators in Kazakhstan

	Internet	Mobile	GDPpc	Unempl	Infl	Tax
Internet	1					
Mobile	0.594	1				
GDPpc	0.564	0.893	1			
Unempl	-0.96	-0.868	-0.656	1		
Infl	-0.441	-0.459	-0.399	0.456	1	
Tax	-0.226	0.286	0.51	0.026	-0.238	1

Note Compiled by the authors based on calculations in STATA 17

employment levels. Combining these variables in the same model is not recommended due to the risk of multicollinearity.

Inclusion of these highly correlated pairs can undermine the reliability of the regression results, making it difficult to accurately interpret the effects of individual predictors on the dependent variable.

Following this, regression models were built with different combinations of variables, taking into account multicollinearity and the Akaike Information Criterion (AIC) to identify the most efficient specifications with significant coefficients. Table 4 presents the results of the most successful specifications.

The results of the regression analysis presented in Table 4 demonstrate stable and significant relationships between the main independent

Table 4 Results of the regression analysis, dependent variable—Shadow Economy (estimates of informal output, % of official GDP)

Independent variable	*Equation*				
	I	*II*	*III*	*IV*	*V*
Internet	−0.045*** (0.004)	−0.049*** (0.006)	−0.037*** (0.004)		−0.048*** (0.007)
Mobile	0.016*** (0.003)	0.018*** (0.005)			0.018** (0.006)
GDPpc			0.164*** (0.044)	0.223*** (0.065)	
Unempl				1.217*** (0.166)	
Infl			0.008 (0.27)	0.013 (0.037)	0.005 (0.027)
Tax		−0.029 (0.045)			−0.025 (0.051)
Constant	37.511*** (0.302)	37.679*** (0.406)	37.49*** (0.509)	28.082*** (1.396)	37.598*** (0.631)
R^2	0.938	0.94	0.92	0.854	0.94
Fisher test	F(2, 12) = 89.93 [0,0000]	F(3, 11) = 57.15 [0,0000]	F(3, 11) = 42.26 [0,0000]	F(3, 11) = 21.49 [0,0001]	F(4, 10) = 39.09 [0,0000]
AIC	6.086	7.536	11.747	20.779	9.491

Notes (1) In parentheses are the standard errors of the regression coefficient
(2) **, ***—significance of coefficients at 5% and 1% levels, respectively
(3) Compiled by the authors based on calculations in STATA 17

variables and the level of the shadow economy in Kazakhstan. In all specifications, the coefficient of the *Internet* variable is negative and significant at the 1% level (e.g., −0.045 in Model I and −0.048 in Model V). This indicates that an increase in the share of the population using the Internet is associated with a decrease in the level of the shadow economy. This effect can be explained by increased transparency and accessibility of digital payments, which reduces the possibility of tax evasion and other informal transactions. Widespread use of the Internet simplifies control over financial transactions, increases business responsibility, and reduces incentives for participation in the informal economy. The *Mobile* indicator (mobile subscriptions) has a positive and significant effect in specifications I, II (at the 1% level) and V (at the 5% level). This may be due to the fact that high mobile activity may facilitate informal transactions, allowing shadow economy participants to exchange information more quickly and conduct financial transactions outside the formal banking system. However, this effect may also reflect the level of overall economic development, which requires additional control for other variables.

The *GDPpc* variable (GDP per capita) has a positive and statistically significant effect at the 1% level on the size of the shadow economy in Models III and IV (e.g., 0.164 in Model III and 0.223 in Model IV), which may indicate that higher per capita income stimulates consumption, including informal goods and services.

The *Unempl* variable (unemployment rate) in Model IV has a significant positive coefficient at the 1% level (1.217), which is expected, since high unemployment often leads to an increase in informal employment and, consequently, to an increase in the share of the shadow economy. The variables *Infl* (inflation) and *Tax* (tax revenue) turned out to be statistically insignificant in all specifications, which may be due to their relatively low variability or weak direct connection with the level of informal economic activity.

The coefficients of determination (R^2) in all models are high, ranging from 0.854 (model IV) to 0.94 (models II and V), indicating a high explanatory power of the models and a strong dependence of the level of the shadow economy on the selected factors. This means that the selected independent variables explain a significant part of the variation in the dependent variable, which confirms the quality of the constructed models.

It is also important to note that the constants in all models are significant at the 1% level, indicating a stable baseline value of the level of the shadow economy even without taking into account changes in the independent variables.

Table 4 also presents the AIC values. AIC is used to compare different models and assess their quality in terms of accuracy and complexity. Lower AIC values indicate a better model, as this criterion penalizes the excessive number of parameters to avoid overfitting. Model I has the lowest AIC value (6.086), which makes it the most preferable among all specifications. This indicates that the combination of Internet and Mobile explains the change in the share of the shadow economy with minimal loss of information, and these two variables are the main independent variables describing the level of digitalization. Therefore, it was Model I that was chosen for further analysis, in particular to check the normality of the residuals, the absence of heteroscedasticity, and autocorrelation.

To check the normality of the residuals distribution, a Quantile–Quantile Plot was constructed (Fig. 2). The plot shows how much the residuals distribution deviates from normal. Since the points lie close to a straight line, this means that the residuals distribution is close to normal, which confirms the correctness of the selected model.

The absence of heteroscedasticity and autocorrelation in Model I was checked using the Breusch-Pagan and Breusch-Godfrey tests, respectively (Table 5). In the Breusch-Pagan test, p-values above 0.05 indicate the absence of significant heteroscedasticity in the model, that is, the variance of the residuals is approximately constant, which corresponds to one of the main assumptions of classical linear regression. Also, in the Breusch-Godfrey test, high p values (significantly above 0.05) indicate the absence of significant autocorrelation of the residuals, which also confirms the correctness of the model. Thus, both tests confirm the stability and reliability of the model.

Based on the regression analysis, the following conclusions can be drawn on the formulated hypotheses:

H1 In all specifications (I, II, III, V), the coefficients of the *Internet* variable are statistically significant at the 1% level and have a negative sign. This confirms that the growth of Internet penetration does indeed contribute to a decrease in the share of the shadow economy. This effect can be explained by increased digital control over financial transactions, increased transparency, and reduced opportunities for tax evasion through informal channels. Thus, hypothesis H1 is fully confirmed.

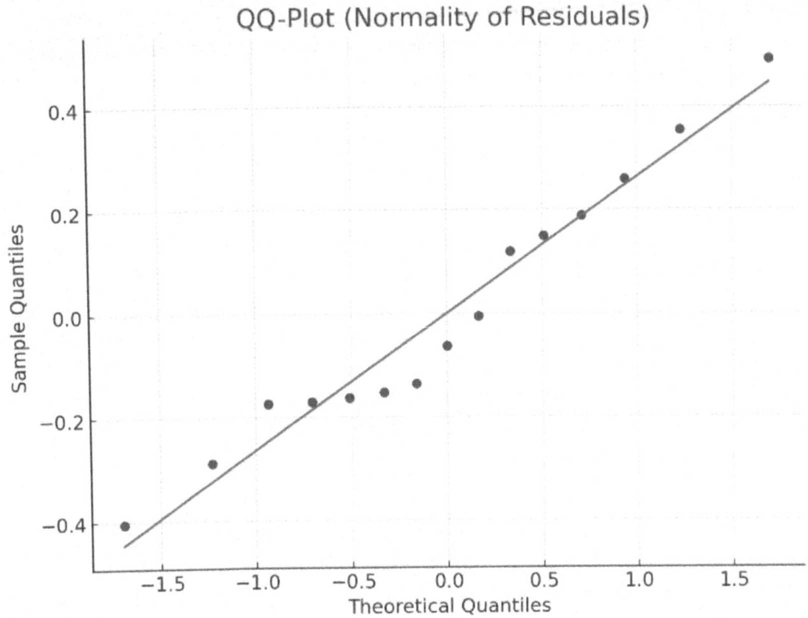

Fig. 2 Quantile–Quantile plot

Table 5 Heteroscedasticity and autocorrelation tests

Result	*Breusch-Pagan test (heteroscedasticity)*	*Breusch-Godfrey test (autocorrelation)*
Test Statistic	3.82	0.26
p value	0.148	0.88
F-Statistic	2.05	0.09
F p value	0.171	0.92

H2 The coefficients of the *Mobile* variable are also statistically significant in all models where it is included. The positive value of the coefficients confirms that increased mobile usage is indeed associated with increased shadow activity, which may be due to the growth of informal transactions through mobile payments and applications. This confirms hypothesis H2.

H3 GDP per capita: Positive and significant coefficients confirm that higher income levels may be associated with increased consumption of informal goods and services, which increases the size of the shadow economy.

> *Unemployment*: The positive and significant coefficient in Model IV confirms that increased unemployment contributes to increased informal employment, which also expands the shadow sector.
> *Inflation*: The coefficients for the *Infl* variable are statistically insignificant, which may indicate a weak impact of inflation on the shadow sector.
> *Tax revenue*: The *Tax* variable is also insignificant in all specifications, which may indicate a weak relationship between tax revenues and the size of the shadow economy.

Hypothesis H3 is partially confirmed, since the influence of control variables is not unambiguous and depends on the specific model.

Thus, all the main hypotheses formulated at the beginning of the study received empirical confirmation. The main independent variables (*Internet and Mobile*) demonstrated stable and statistically significant relationships with the size of the shadow economy, which confirms their key influence on the scale of informal economic activity.

6 Discussion

The results of this study highlight the complex nature of the relationship between digitalization and the shadow economy in Kazakhstan. In contrast to the simpler and more straightforward findings of previous studies, our analysis reveals both positive and negative effects of digital technologies on informal economic activity.

First, the negative and statistically significant effect of internet penetration in all model specifications confirms the critical role of digital transparency in reducing the shadow economy. This effect can be explained by improved traceability of financial transactions, increased use of electronic payments, and increased monitoring of economic activity, which reduces opportunities for tax evasion and registration of informal transactions. However, these results also indicate that internet access alone cannot fully address the shadow economy problem, as it is influenced by broader economic and institutional factors.

On the other hand, the positive and statistically significant coefficients for the mobile subscriptions variable in all models indicate that mobile technologies can contribute to the growth of the shadow economy. This is due to the dual nature of mobile technologies, which, on the one hand, facilitate access to information and economic participation, and, on the other hand, facilitate informal transactions outside the formal financial system. This effect highlights the need for stricter regulation of mobile financial services and digital payment systems to reduce the potential for tax evasion.

Furthermore, mixed results for control variables such as GDP per capita, unemployment, inflation, and tax revenue highlight the complex economic mechanisms that influence the shadow economy. For example, the positive relationship between GDP per capita and the shadow economy suggests that higher income levels may stimulate demand for informal goods and services, while the significant positive effect of unemployment confirms the expectation that economic hardship forces people to seek income outside the formal economy.

Thus, our results highlight the importance of a balanced approach to digitalization policies. While increasing internet access can help reduce the shadow economy, regulatory challenges for mobile financial technologies also need to be addressed. Future research could focus on a more detailed analysis of the role of digital platforms in the processes of formalization and informalization of economic activity.

7 Policy Recommendations

The findings of this study suggest several policy recommendations to effectively address the challenges and opportunities presented by digitalization in reducing the size of the shadow economy in Kazakhstan. To enhance digital infrastructure and accessibility, it is essential to invest in expanding broadband and mobile internet coverage, particularly in rural areas, to reduce the digital divide and ensure equal access to digital technologies across the country. Additionally, improving the quality and speed of internet connections can support digital businesses and reduce the reliance on informal economic activities, while the development of 5G networks and next-generation digital infrastructure can further support high-speed data exchange and advanced digital services.

To strengthen digital financial systems, it is necessary to promote the use of digital payments and electronic financial transactions, which can reduce cash-based, informal transactions that contribute to the shadow economy. Stricter regulations for mobile financial services should be implemented to reduce the risk of tax evasion and money laundering, while fintech solutions should be integrated into the formal economy to enhance transparency and traceability of financial flows.

Improving digital literacy and skills is another critical area, requiring national programs to improve digital skills among the population, particularly in regions with low internet penetration and high levels of informal employment. Collaboration with educational institutions and private sector companies can provide training in digital skills, cybersecurity, and data management, while encouraging digital entrepreneurship can help formalize small and medium-sized enterprises (SMEs) and reduce their reliance on informal economic activities.

Strengthening regulatory frameworks and institutional capacity is also vital. This includes developing a comprehensive legal framework to regulate digital platforms, mobile financial services, and e-commerce, ensuring transparency and accountability. It is equally important to enhance the capacity of tax authorities to monitor digital transactions and enforce compliance with tax regulations, as well as to introduce digital identification systems and blockchain technologies to improve transaction traceability and reduce fraud.

Supporting the formalization of informal sectors can be achieved by providing targeted support to sectors with high levels of informality, such as retail, agriculture, and transportation. This may include reducing administrative burdens for small businesses, offering tax incentives and financial support for enterprises that adopt digital technologies, and creating platforms for knowledge sharing and best practice exchange to strengthen the digital economy.

Promoting public–private partnerships in digital transformation is essential for leveraging innovative digital solutions for economic transparency and financial inclusion. Collaboration between the public and private sectors can drive research and development in digital technologies, including AI, blockchain, and IoT, enhancing economic efficiency and reducing the scope for informal transactions.

Effective monitoring and evaluation are critical to assessing the impact of digitalization on the shadow economy. This includes establishing a comprehensive monitoring framework, using data analytics and AI tools to track informal economic activities, and regularly reviewing and updating digital policies to reflect changing technological and economic conditions.

Finally, international cooperation is crucial for sharing best practices in digital transformation and shadow economy reduction. Kazakhstan should actively engage with international organizations and regional partners, participating in global digital economy forums to ensure its competitiveness in the rapidly evolving digital landscape.

By implementing these policy recommendations, Kazakhstan can more effectively leverage digital technologies to reduce the size of its shadow economy, improve economic transparency, and promote sustainable long-term growth.

8 Conclusion

In conclusion, this study has explored the multifaceted relationship between digitalization and the shadow economy in Kazakhstan. The findings demonstrate that while digital technologies offer significant potential for reducing informal economic activities by enhancing transparency, efficiency, and financial oversight, they also present new challenges. The rapid spread of mobile technologies and the increasing use of digital platforms can, in some cases, expand the scope for informal transactions if not properly regulated.

The analysis confirmed that increased internet penetration is strongly associated with a reduction in the size of the shadow economy, largely due to improved transparency and reduced transaction costs. However, mobile technologies exhibit a more complex relationship with informality, potentially increasing the size of the shadow economy by facilitating untraceable, decentralized transactions. This highlights the need for balanced policies that support digital inclusion while ensuring robust regulatory oversight.

Furthermore, the study underscored the importance of macroeconomic factors such as GDP per capita, unemployment, and tax revenue in shaping the size of the shadow economy. High levels of unemployment, in particular, were found to drive individuals into informal employment as a means of survival, emphasizing the need for comprehensive employment and social protection policies.

To address these challenges, the study proposes several policy recommendations, including expanding digital infrastructure, promoting digital literacy, enhancing financial transparency, and strengthening regulatory frameworks. Effective implementation of these measures can help Kazakhstan fully leverage the potential of digitalization to reduce the size of its shadow economy, promote economic stability, and achieve sustainable long-term growth.

Overall, the findings of this research provide a valuable foundation for policymakers, offering insights into the complex dynamics of digitalization and informality in Kazakhstan. However, further research is needed to fully understand the long-term impacts of digital technologies on the shadow economy, particularly as emerging technologies like blockchain, artificial intelligence, and fintech continue to evolve. Additionally, cross-country comparisons and sector-specific studies could offer further insights into best practices for managing the challenges and opportunities presented by digital transformation.

References

Achim, M.-A., & Mare, C. (2024). Unveiling the factors behind the shadow economy: A global investigation survey utilizing panel data analysis. *Journal of Financial Studies, 9*, 9–23. https://doi.org/10.55654/jfs.2024.9.17.01

Amanova, M. (2022). Do R&D and digitalization affect shadow economy in Uzbekistan? In *ICFNDS '22: The 6th International Conference on Future Networks & Distributed Systems*. December 2022. https://doi.org/10.1145/3584202.3584240

Bitzenis, A., Vlachos, V., & Schneider, F. (2016). An exploration of the Greek shadow economy: Can its transfer into the official economy provide economic relief amid the crisis? *Journal of Economic Issues, 50*(1), 165–196. https://doi.org/10.1080/00213624.2016.1147918

Elgin, C., Kose, M. A., Ohnsorge, F., & Yu, S. (2021). *Understanding informality*. CERP Discussion Paper 16497, Centre for Economic Policy Research. Retrieved July 25, 2025, from https://www.worldbank.org/en/research/brief/informal-economy-database

Ghislain, M. B. (2022). Does the diffusion of information and communication technologies affect the shadow economy in Africa? *African Development Review, 34*(4), 513–526. https://doi.org/10.1111/1467-8268.12676

Government of Kazakhstan. (2025). Kazakhstan set to cut budget deficit to 1.4 % by 2028, PM. In *Government of Kazakhstan Official Statement at Joint Parliamentary Session*. Kazinform News Agency. Retrieved July 25,

2025, from https://qazinform.com/news/kazakhstan-set-to-cut-budget-deficit-to-14-by-2028-pm-daeafe

Haruna, E. U., & Alhassan, U. (2022). Does digitalization limit the proliferation of the shadow economy in African countries? An in-depth panel analysis. *African Development Review, 34*, S34–S62. https://doi.org/10.1111/1467-8268.12653

Hassan, A. (2024). Mobile financial services and the shadow economy in Southern African countries: Does regulatory quality matter? *International Journal of Financial Studies, 12*(4), 115. https://doi.org/10.3390/ijfs12040115

Hyde-Clarke, N. (2013). The impact of mobile technology on economic growth amongst 'Survivalists' in the informal sector in the Johannesburg CBD, South Africa. *International Journal of Business and Social Science, 4*(16), 149–156. Retrieved July 25, 2025, from http://ijbssnet.com/journals/Vol_4_No_16_December_2013/13.pdf

IMF. (2025). *Republic of Kazakhstan: 2024 Article IV Consultation—Press Release*. IMF. Retrieved July 25, 2025, from https://www.imf.org/en/Publications/CR/Issues/2025/01/31/Republic-of-Kazakhstan-2024-Article-IV-Consultation-Press-Release-and-Staff-Report-561424

ITU. (2024). *Measuring digital development: Facts and Figures 2024*. International Telecommunication Union. Retrieved July 25, 2025, from https://datahub.itu.int/data/?Connectivity=Traffic&Markets=Revenues&Sustainability=Emergency+telecommunications&Trust=Applications+and+Services&utm=&e=KAZ

Konovalov, E. L., & Konovalova, D. A. (2023). The impact of digitalization on the spread of the shadow economy. *Economy and Entrepreneurship, 4*(153), 32–37. https://doi.org/10.34925/EIP.2023.153.4.003

Kydyrova, Z., Onlasynov, E., Shadieva, A., Abdrakhmanova, A., Umbitaliev, A., & Seidakhmetov, M. (2020). Contemporary scales of the shadow economy in Kazakhstan. *Journal of Advanced Research in Law and Economics, 11*(2), 475–482. https://doi.org/10.14505/jarle.v11.2(48).20

Larsson, C. W., & Svensson, J. (2018). Mobile phones in the transformation of the informal economy: Stories from market women in Kampala, Uganda. *Journal of Eastern African Studies, 12*(3), 533–551. https://doi.org/10.1080/17531055.2018.1436247

Muminov, N., Olimjanova, S., Salimov, A., & Kim, T. (2020). Digitalization as an important factor of legalization of the shadow economy. *International Journal on Economics, Finance and Sustainable Development, 2*(2), 16–19. Retrieved July 25, 2025, from https://journals.researchparks.org/index.php/IJEFSD/article/view/371

OECD. (2023). *Improving framework conditions for the digital transformation of businesses in Kazakhstan*. OECD Publishing. Retrieved July 25, 2025, from https://www.oecd.org/en/publications/2023/05/improving-framework-conditions-for-the-digital-transformation-of-businesses-in-kazakhstan_c62df12f.html

OECD. (2024). *OECD FDI regulatory restrictiveness index: Key findings and trends*. OECD Business and Finance Policy Papers, No. 72. Retrieved July 25, 2025, from https://www.oecd.org/content/dam/oecd/en/publications/reports/2024/12/oecd-fdi-regulatory-restrictiveness-index_3b446fc8/c56f8a14-en.pdf

Tulemetova, A., Zhanakova, N., Shevchenko, I., & Bekmanova, G. (2024). The digital economy development in Kazakhstan. *Bulletin of the Kazakh University of Economics, Finance and International Trade, 2*(55), 173–180. Retrieved July 25, 2025, from http://vestnik.kuef.kz/web/uploads/file-vestnik/fdb0d5f8171b70e2e859f8a0461d8f3d.pdf

World Bank. (2021). *Program information document: Resilient digital Kazakhstan program*. World Bank Group. Retrieved July 25, 2025, from https://documents1.worldbank.org/curated/en/400941617469177523/pdf/Concept-Stage-Program-Information-Document-PID-Resilient-Digital-Kazakhstan-Program-P176295.pdf

World Bank. (2024). *World development indicators and macro poverty outlook: Kazakhstan data for 2023*. World Bank Group. WDI database and Macro Poverty Outlook table. Retrieved July 25, 2025, from https://documents1.worldbank.org/curated/en/099817104042416085/pdf/IDU159dc271912750142871b2fc11d3c160ca3d2.pdf

World Bank. (2025). *Kazakhstan economic update—funding the future: Boosting revenues for lasting investments*. World Bank Group. Retrieved July 25, 2025, from https://www.worldbank.org/en/country/kazakhstan/publication/economic-update-january-2025

CHAPTER 4

Earnings and Informality Choice Among the Self-Employed in Kazakhstan

Arlan Musayir, G. Reza Arabsheibani, Altay Mussurov, Alma Kudebayeva, Irina Kovaleva, and Dena Sholk

1 Introduction

Recent evidence shows that informal employment remains a defining feature of labour markets in many parts of the world. Across the globe, more than 2 billion people were engaged in informal employment in 2023, representing 58% of the global workforce (UN, 2024a). Although informal employment declined 5 percentage points between 2004 and 2019, informal employment as a share of total employment increased between 2019 and 2022 (ILO, 2023).

This persistence of informality can carry significant consequences for workers, since it is often claimed that informal workers typically

The views expressed in this chapter are solely those of the authors and do not necessarily reflect the positions of their respective institutions or employers.

A. Musayir
London, UK
e-mail: a.musayir@gmail.com

E. Bagirzadeh and O. Gokcekus (eds.), *Shadow Economies in Turkic Republics*, https://doi.org/10.1007/978-3-032-12872-0_4

earn low and unstable incomes, work in unsafe environments, and are often excluded from legal protections and social insurance systems (UN, 2024b). These challenges are exacerbated by the lack of access to skills training, making it difficult to achieve economic security. The COVID-19 pandemic underscored these vulnerabilities, since many joined the informal economy to cushion the impact of lockdowns and the economic downturn (UN, 2024b).

Another important observation is that although informality should fall with economic growth, as argued by Kanbur (2017), it appears that informality nevertheless can remain persistent and widespread. In Kazakhstan, according to estimates based on a dynamic general equilibrium model, the informal economy accounted for 36% of GDP in the 1990s, 38% in the 2000s and 37% in the 2010s (Elgin et al., 2021). Over that same period, Kazakhstan's GDP per capita (constant 2015 US$) more than doubled, rising from approximately $5,600 in 1990 to $11,450 in 2023 (WDI, 2025), suggesting that in certain contexts, there is a weak link between economic growth and formalisation. Recent data also shows that despite economic growth, informal employment stubbornly persists, particularly among the self-employed (National Bureau of Statistics, 2023). This observation suggests that growth alone is not sufficient to stop workers operating in the shadows.

G. R. Arabsheibani
London School of Economics, London, UK
e-mail: g.arabsheibani@lse.ac.uk

A. Mussurov
Enigma Seven, Derby, UK
e-mail: a.mussurov@gmail.com

A. Kudebayeva · I. Kovaleva (✉)
Department of Economics, KIMEP University, Almaty, Kazakhstan
e-mail: irina.kovaleva@kimep.kz

A. Kudebayeva
e-mail: almak@kimep.kz

D. Sholk
Washington, DC, USA
e-mail: dsholk@gmail.com

Next, empirical evidence unveils several characteristics of informal employment in Kazakhstan. Formal workers earn more than informal workers, with around 25% of the wage gap unexplained by observable characteristics, and more self-employed workers work informally than wage workers (Mussurov et al., 2019 and Table 1). Self-employment itself may be a subsistence strategy adopted due to the lack of more secure or lucrative job options or serve as a means to bypass regulatory constraints, taxation, or exploitative practices (Kanbur, 2017). Self-employment is commonly used as a proxy for informal employment, particularly in emerging market and developing economies, since they represent the majority of informal employment, operating without formal registration, contracts, or social security contributions (Ohnsorge & Yu, 2022).

Using data from the 2019 and 2022 Kazakhstan Labour Force surveys, we wish to estimate the extent to which earnings differ between formal and informal self-employed workers and examine the determinants of informality among the self-employed. We also wish to examine the potential impact of the pandemic on informality choice and earnings. By comparing pre- and post-pandemic periods, our aim is to assess whether the crisis influenced the decision to engage in informal work and if it had any effect on the formal–informal earnings gap. In doing so, this chapter contributes to the broader literature on informality in the Turkic states and offers additional empirical evidence to inform labour market policy.

Our empirical findings show that the earnings gap rose almost fivefold between 2019 and 2022, driven primarily by an increase in the unexplained component of the gap. Detailed decomposition estimates show that university education accounted for a larger share of the explained earnings gap after the pandemic. We also find a small rise in the predicted probability of informal self-employment between 2019 and 2022, which was not driven by a deterioration in observable worker characteristics.

2 Kazakhstan's Economic Profile

Kazakhstan's economy grew at an average annual rate of 4.7% since the turn of the millennium up until 2023, averaging 9.7% per year from 2000 to 2007, which was well above the global average (World Bank, 2025). In the same period, Kazakhstan moved from a lower-middle-income to an upper-middle-income country, with higher living standards and lower poverty rates (World Bank, 2025). Between 2006 and 2022, the population expanded by 28%, and total employment also increased (World

Table 1 The economy and labour market, 2013–2024 (%)

	2013	*2014*	*2015*	*2016*	*2017*	*2018*	*2019*	*2020*	*2021*	*2022*	*2023*	*2024*
GDP[a]	6.0	4.2	1.2	1.1	4.1	4.1	4.5	−2.5	4.3	3.2	5.1	4.8
Inflation[b]	5.9	6.8	6.7	14.4	7.4	6.2	5.3	6.7	8.0	15.0	14.7	8.8
Unemployment[c]	5.2	5.1	4.9	5.0	4.9	4.8	4.8	4.9	5.5	4.9	4.8	4.8
Self-employment[d]	29.0	26.8	24.1	24.6	23.3	22.8	22.8	22.3	22.7	22.5	23.0	22.8

Notes [a] Annual percentage growth rate of GDP at market prices based on constant local currency (based on constant 2015 prices, expressed in U.S. dollars). [b] Inflation rate as measured by the consumer price index. [c] Unemployment, total (% of total labour force). [d] Self-employment, % of total employment

Sources [a, b, c] World Development Indicators (2025) [d] National Bureau of Statistics (2025)

Bank, 2025). Most of the new jobs were in services, including education, trade, healthcare, and other service activities. From 2010 to 2022, about 857,000 jobs were added in these sectors, while agriculture lost around 1.2 million jobs. Yet employment in mining, construction, and industry has shown little change.

Employment growth has been concentrated in urban areas, which accounted for 85 percent of net job creation since 2006. Since the end of 2015, real wages have generally been rising, despite a substantial decline during the pandemic, from which they have now largely recovered (World Bank, 2025).

Table 1 shows that the economy shrunk by 2.5% during the pandemic, while the official unemployment rate rose from 4.8% in 2019 to 5.5% in 2021 but then returned to pre-pandemic levels in the following years. Although the share of self-employed workers fell in the 2010s, nearly 23% of workers are self-employed. While not all self-employment occupations are of low quality, the majority are, and most such jobs are classified as vulnerable employment (World Bank, 2024).

3 Literature Review

3.1 Cross-country Studies

Definitions of informality in the literature vary and hence empirical findings may differ depending on the definition adopted (Henley et al., 2009). This heterogeneity complicates the comparison of empirical studies and also makes it even more important to consider the diverse forms and underlying drivers of informality when it comes to policy formulation (Kanbur, 2011). Nevertheless, one of the most consistent empirical findings in the literature is that informal workers are typically paid less than formal workers, on average 19% less (Ohnsorge & Yu, 2022). Evidence from a number of studies supports the above conclusions. For example, Gasparini and Tornarolli (2009), using micro household survey data, look at 14 Latin American and Caribbean countries. Even though the definition of informality is different, in general they find that the informal sector pays lower wages and offers less protection.

Human capital factors such as education and experience play a significant role in explaining these differences in earnings. Kahyalar et al. (2018) estimate wage differentials between formal and informal sectors in Turkey using 2004 and 2009 Household Budget Surveys data. Their results show the formal–informal wage gap was around 0.88–0.90 log points for workers without social security, contracts, and employed in small firms. Their decomposition results show that a substantial portion of the wage gap is explained by differences in observable characteristics such as education and experience.

Evidence from Serbia, reported in Blunch (2015), shows that education is a major contributor to the earnings gap. Using data from the Labour Force Survey for 2008 and 2009 and formal registration of the enterprise as the informality measure, the author finds that while raw wage differentials narrowed after the crisis (from 60 to 47%), the gap adjusted for observable worker characteristics remained stable (between 26 and 27%). For workers with no labour contract and no pension benefits, they find that the unexplained part of the gap decreased substantially, likely reflecting a fall in importance of unobservable factors such as bargaining power and access to networks. Their analysis also reveals that formal workers benefit not only from their endowments, like higher education and employment in better-paying sectors, but also from higher returns to these characteristics. On the determinants of informality, the study finds that informal workers were more likely to be less educated, part-time workers, employed in small firms, and working in agriculture or construction. Informality was slightly more prevalent in rural areas. The author argues that following the crisis, better-educated individuals entered informal employment due to formal sector job losses, while more vulnerable workers exited into unemployment.

Using data from the 2007 Living Standards Measurement Survey, Staneva and Arabsheibani (2014) analyse the formal–informal wage gap in Tajikistan and find evidence to the contrary. They report that informal workers, on average, earned higher net hourly wages than formal workers and that the wage disadvantage for formal workers ranges between "42% of the relevant gap at the bottom of the earnings distribution to around 33% at the top of the distribution" (Staneva & Arabsheibani, 2014: 17). The authors attribute 60–70% of the wage gap to observable characteristics such as education and experience. Even after matching workers with similar characteristics, informal workers in Tajikistan earn, on average, 32% more than formal sector workers. They also report that informal workers are generally less qualified and tend to work in trade and sales-related jobs.

Another interesting result is shown by Gimpelson and Kapeliushnikov (2015). They argue that, in Russia, wage workers rather than self-employed individuals represent most informal employment. Their estimates indicate that informal workers are more educated than those in other countries and that informal workers face a relatively small wage penalty. Evidence reported in Kim et al. (2019) shows that the wage gap in the Russian labour market has widened beginning from the mid-2000s and towards the 2010s and that informal workers (particularly salaried informal workers) were earning lower wages compared to formal workers. This gap widened further during the 2008–2009 global financial crisis and persisted well into the mid-2010s.

Empirical evidence from neighbouring Kyrgyzstan underscores the central role of informality within the broader concept of employment vulnerability. Using longitudinal data from the "Life in Kyrgyzstan" household survey for 2010–2013 and 2016, Karymshakov et al. (2023) adopt a multidimensional framework of employment vulnerability, in which informality is treated as a key dimension of vulnerability. Informality is defined for wage workers as the absence of written contracts or workbooks and for the self-employed as unregistered business activity. They show that approximately 30% of the employed sample fell into these informal categories. The authors conceptualise informality not only as a legal status but also as a marker of employment vulnerability which is characterised by low wages, lack of benefits, and limited upward mobility.

Dell'Anno (2021) and Slonimczyk (2022), both discuss the challenges that emerging and transition economies face in tackling informality. Dell'Anno (2021) argues that inequality in emerging and transition economies pushes low-skilled workers into the informal sector and, for certain individuals, it provides a needed safety net, especially when there is a gap left by inadequate government support. Slonimczyk (2022) argues that improving access to quality education can create incentives to work formally. The author also reports that, for self-employed individuals and entrepreneurs in many transition economies, the choice to work informally is based on a cost-benefit analysis. Finally, Ohnsorge and Yu (2022) report that the COVID-19 pandemic has disproportionately affected informal firms and informal workers, partly due to challenges in adapting to digital operations and accessing government support programmes.

3.2 Empirical Evidence from Kazakhstan

Earlier studies show that informal employment is disproportionately concentrated among rural residents, the self-employed, and those with lower levels of education. Using the 2009 Kazakhstan Labour Force Survey (KLFS), Rutkowski (2011) finds that informality accounts for roughly one-third of total employment, with 70% of informal workers living outside urban centres and 60% employed in agriculture. Informal workers are more likely to be younger, have lower levels of education (elementary education or secondary general education), and are usually self-employed. Strokova et al. (2016), using the 2013 KLFS, also find that informal workers tend to have lower education levels (only 13.5% of informal wage workers have completed tertiary education, compared to 52.5% in the public sector). Their results show that workers in the commerce sector and in South Kazakhstan have a higher probability of informality.

Mussurov and Arabsheibani (2015) explore how informal self-employment responds in times of economic downturn, more specifically the 2008–2009 financial crisis. Using 2006, 2009, and 2011 KLFS data, the authors define informality as self-employment without official registration. They find that the share of informal self-employment declined from 53 to 46% for men and 51% to 43% for women in this period. Only 25% of this decline is explained by improvements in observable characteristics (education, tenure, and working hours). The probability of being informally self-employed is significantly higher among individuals with lower educational attainment, shorter tenure, and fewer weekly working hours. Women who work in Astana or Almaty are less likely to be informal during the crisis period. For men, the negative and significant effects of working in Astana and Almaty on the probability of informality had also been observed prior to the crisis but were no longer present in 2009.

Mussurov et al. (2019) examine the formal–informal wage gap in Kazakhstan, using data from the 2013 KLFS. The authors adopt a "legalistic" definition of informality, classifying employees with labour contracts but without access to mandatory social security benefits as informal. In addition, those employed under civil law contracts or verbal agreements are categorised as informal, since such arrangements typically exclude social protections. According to the authors, the average hourly wage is $2.24 for formal workers and $1.63 for informal workers (a 38% wage premium for formal sector employment). They report that informality is more prevalent among women, younger workers, those with lower educational attainment, rural residents, and agricultural workers. Their empirical results show that at similar education levels, except for university graduates, returns to education are higher in the informal sector when compared to those with only basic or primary education. In the formal sector, university graduates enjoy a slightly higher earnings premium, while it is those with lower levels of education (and university dropouts) who have higher returns to education in the informal sector. Workers who have one year or less of experience earn less in both formal and informal sectors. Managers earn more in the informal sector (almost twice as much as in the formal sector). Firm size negatively affects earnings in both sectors, as wage workers in micro firms (with 10 or fewer employees) earn between 9%–11% less. After matching on observable characteristics (education, experience, firm size, gender, marital status, occupation, and location), they find that approximately half of the raw wage gap is explained by these individual characteristics.

4 Kazakhstan's Informal Economy

4.1 Size and Trend Over Time

As shown in Table 2, informal output, measured as a share of official GDP, shows little signs of decreasing, accounting for nearly 36% of the economy. In Panel B of Table 2, we can also observe that between 2013 and 2024, informal employment shrunk by half but still accounts for 12% of total employment. Furthermore, informality among the self-employed is consistently higher than among the wage workers (e.g. 26.9% vs 9.6% in 2019).

Table 2 Size of the informal sector and informal employment, 2013–2024 (%)

	2013	*2014*	*2015*	*2016*	*2017*	*2018*	*2019*	*2020*	*2021*	*2022*	*2023*	*2024*
Panel A. Size												
Informal output[a]	37.6	36.9	37.0	36.6	36.0	36.1	35.8	35.5	–	–	–	–
Panel B. Informal employment												
Total[b]	24.3	25.0	22.9	18.6	16.2	14.9	13.7	14.1	13.6	12.9	12.8	12.0
Employees[c]	14.6	17.0	15.8	14.2	12.3	11.2	9.6	10.3	9.7	9.7	10.0	9.6
Self-employed[d]	46.2	45.4	42.6	31.3	28.0	26.7	26.9	26.3	26.3	23.0	21.6	19.7

Notes [a] Dynamic general equilibrium model-based estimates of informal output (% of official GDP). [b, c, d] Measured as the ratio of the number of employed/employees/self-employed in the informal sector of the economy aged 15 and over to the total number of employed population/employees/self-employed

Sources [a] Elgin et al. (2021); [b, c, d] Government of Kazakhstan (2025) and National Bureau of Statistics (2023, 2025)

4.2 *Laws, Regulations, and Enforcement*

The law of Kazakhstan effectively recognises three categories of employment contracts: a "traditional" labour contract; a civil law contract; and an oral contract. The labour contract is the standard arrangement for formal salaried workers. Under the 2015 Labour Code, a labour contract is defined as a written agreement between a worker and employer, in accordance with which the worker is required to carry out his/her respective responsibilities. Such agreements apply to wage workers who are formally employed, as they receive the full array of legal protections and social benefits associated with being wage employees. Under this contract, the formally employed individual receives a regular salary, accumulates pension entitlements, and has access to other social benefits such as sick leave and access to public health insurance. Meanwhile, both civil law and oral contracts may be associated with informal employment. The former is not actually defined in the Labour Code but is detailed in the Civil Code. These contracts do not require the employer to provide benefits such as paid vacation, pension contributions, mandatory health insurance, or maternity leave coverage (in addition to the default state-provided coverage).

Self-employed individuals ("own-account workers") working in the informal sector can formalise by registering as an individual entrepreneur ("*individual'nyy predprinimatel'*," or "IP"). An IP-holder is required to make regular tax and social contributions. In 2025, the overall tax burden for an IP-holder amounted to 10% of earnings for mandatory pension contributions, 5% for mandatory health insurance, and 5% for social contributions.[1]

In 2019, in an effort to encourage legalisation of entrepreneurial activities of self-employed workers, the government launched an experimental tax system known as the Single Aggregate Payment ("*Edinyy sovokupnyy platezh*," or "SAP") regime. The SAP regime, which was in effect between 1 January 2019 and 1 January 2024, offered a simplified alternative for calculating and paying taxes for own-account workers operating without an IP registration (KPMG, 2019). Under SAP, instead of paying taxes under the standard regime governing IP-holders, a self-employed individual could make a monthly tax payment specifically calculated to cover contributions for four tax categories: individual income tax, social security contributions, pension contributions, and mandatory health insurance (KPMG, 2019).

Under SAP, the total monthly payment amounted to less than $10 US dollars. To be eligible for the SAP scheme, self-employed workers must have no employees and their annual turnover be below 2,966,875 tenge ($7,500) in 2019 (KPMG, 2019). Activities were restricted to providing services directly to individuals or selling self-produced agricultural goods, excluding excisable goods such as alcohol and tobacco. Occupations that generally qualified for SAP included tailoring; beauty and salon services; small-scale sales of fruits, vegetables, meat, and dairy products (thereby capturing informal workers in rural areas); and residential apartment rentals. Professionals involved in accounting, legal, or consulting professions were prohibited from participating (KPMG, 2019). SAP payers gained pension entitlements and health insurance after three consecutive months of contributions, and eligibility for social benefits such as sick leave, unemployment support, and maternity payments. The government did not extend SAP beyond 1 January 2024. Therefore, following SAP's expiration, workers wishing to retain the benefits of formality had to register as an IP and comply with the standard statutory stipulations.

Informality in Kazakhstan has been a persistent and structural feature of the labour market, shaped by regulatory barriers, uneven enforcement, and lack of stable employment opportunities. To combat this,

[1] https://uchet.kz/news/kak-izmenyatsya-platezhi-ip-V-2025-godu/.

the government has pursued a variety of policy responses to reduce informality. Following the 2008–2009 financial crisis, the government aimed to reduce the regulatory burden placed on businesses by reducing the number of licensed activities and simplifying registration procedures (Mussurov & Arabsheibani, 2015). Further reforms introduced in 2010 reduced the number of procedures required to start a business and mandated one-day registration for small and medium-sized enterprises (SMEs). The government also committed to eliminating a third of the business permits, signalling its intention to lower the bureaucratic burden for entrepreneurs (Rutkowski, 2011). Digital public services and the expansion of the eGov.kz platform to streamline tax registration and payments were also introduced (Government of Kazakhstan, 2023a). On the supply side, these reforms were accompanied with policies that aimed to encourage SME development through targeted loans, training, loan guarantee schemes, leasing finance, and interest subsidies (Mussurov & Arabsheibani, 2015). This was all part of the "Kazakhstan-2050" long-term development strategy introduced in 2012.

Reforms also targeted the structure of employment itself. For example, the Labour Codes of 2007 and 2015 introduced legal recognition of part-time and multiple-job contracts, while the 2016 Law on Employment introduced reforms designed to expand vocational training, improved job placement services, and introduced new measures to support employment in rural areas.

In November 2023, the government approved the Labour Market Development Concept for 2024–2029, marking the next phase of the country's formalisation agenda (Government of Kazakhstan, 2023b). The concept also prioritised the creation of 3.8 million high-quality jobs by 2030—that is jobs with salaries above the region's median, stable tenure, and with a safe workplace environment—with the goal of increasing the share of quality jobs to 45% of total employment. Other priorities include reduction of informal employment, particularly in rural areas where a significant share of the workforce remains outside formal structures, expansion of vocational education, and supporting the transition from household-based and subsistence work to formal employment.

To conclude, formalisation requires a combination of levelling the regulatory playing field, ensuring effective implementation of existing laws, and offering well-designed incentives (World Bank, 2025). Kazakhstan's recent efforts reflect a broader shift towards formalisation through targeted, system-wide reform, and sustained policy commitment.

5 Methodology

We first estimate a Mincer-type earnings equation separately for formal and informal self-employed workers:

$$lnW_F = X_F\beta_F + \varepsilon_F \tag{1}$$

$$lnW_I = X_I\beta_I + \varepsilon_I \tag{2}$$

where, lnW_I is the log hourly earnings for group $j \in \{F, I\}$, F refers to formal and I to informal self-employed individuals. X_j is a vector of observed characteristics and β_j is the vector of estimated returns.

We apply the Oaxaca and Ransom (1994) technique to decompose the gap in log earnings between formal and informal self-employed workers:

$$\overline{lnW}_F - \overline{lnW}_I = \left(\overline{X}_F - \overline{X}_I\right)'\beta^* + (\beta_F - \beta_I)'\overline{X}^* \tag{3}$$

where $\overline{X}_j$ denotes the mean characteristics of group j, β^* is the reference coefficient vector derived from a pooled regression over the combined sample of formal and informal workers.

The decomposition then splits the total mean wage gap into:

i. Endowment effect (explained component): $\left(\overline{X}_F - \overline{X}_I\right)'\beta^*$, the part due to differences in average characteristics;
ii. Coefficient effect (unexplained component): $(\beta_F - \beta_I)'\overline{X}^*$, the part due to differences in the returns to characteristics.

We also carry out a detailed Oaxaca–Ransom decomposition, in which each component of the gap is attributed to individual covariates. To account for the choice of reference group in the decomposition, we follow Oaxaca and Ransom (1994) and apply the Omega-weighting scheme. Specifically, the reference coefficients β^* are calculated as a weighted average of the group-specific coefficients, where $\beta^* = \Omega\beta_F + (1 - \Omega)\beta_I$, to reflect the relative importance assigned to each group in constructing the counterfactual returns.

Next, we decompose changes in the predicted probability of informal self-employment between 2019 and 2022. For this purpose, we employ the non-linear decomposition method proposed by Yun (2000). Yun's technique uses variable-specific weights derived from partial derivatives of the model's prediction function. Specifically, let Y be a binary outcome indicating informal self-employment (or formal otherwise). In a probit model, the expected outcome is given by:

$$E[Y_t] = E[\Phi(X_t \beta_t)] \tag{4}$$

where $\Phi(\cdot)$ is the standard normal cumulative distribution function, X_t is a vector of observable characteristics, and β_t is the corresponding vector of estimated coefficients for year $t \in \{2019, 2022\}$

The difference in average predicted probabilities of informal self-employment between the two periods is expressed as:

$$\Delta = E[\Phi(X_{2022}\beta_{2022})] - E[\Phi(X_{2019}\beta_{2019})] \tag{5}$$

Yun (2000) shows that this difference can be decomposed into two components: an endowment effect, which reflects changes in the distribution of observable characteristics, and a coefficient effect, which captures changes in the association (or return) to those characteristics.

In order to estimate the contribution of each covariate in a non-linear model, Yun proposes variable-specific weights based on the marginal effects of the model:

$$\Delta = \sum_k \left[\left(\overline{X}_{2022,k} - \overline{X}_{2019,k} \right) \cdot W_k^X + \overline{X}_{2019,k} \cdot \left(\beta_{2022,k} - \beta_{2019,k} \right) \cdot w_k^\beta \right] \tag{6}$$

where $\overline{X}_{t,k}$ is the mean of covariate k in year t and W_k^X and W_k^β are weights that capture the relative contribution of each covariate to the predicted probability, adjusted for non-linearity. These weights are derived from the partial derivatives of the probit function and ensure that the decomposition is path-independent, internally consistent, and interpretable.

In our empirical section, we estimate separate probit models for 2019 and 2022, then apply the 'mvdcmp' command in Stata, which implements Yun's decomposition for non-linear models (see: Powers et al., 2011). The command computes both the aggregate decomposition by splitting the total change into explained and unexplained components and the detailed decomposition, attributing changes to individual covariates such as education, occupation, gender, and region. This methodology enables us to evaluate not only whether the probability of informal self-employment has changed between the two periods but also whether those changes are due to compositional shifts in the workforce or to evolving structural relationships between characteristics and informality.

6 Data

This study uses data from the Kazakhstan Labour Force Survey (KLFS), a nationally representative household survey conducted quarterly by the National Bureau of Statistics of the Republic of Kazakhstan. The KLFS is the largest household study in Kazakhstan and represents the most comprehensive labour market dataset available. It is representative of the whole population. The sample design currently consists of around 21,000 responding households. The survey has a panel element, since households stay in the sample for 4 consecutive quarters (or waves), with a fifth of the sample replaced each quarter (first quarter of the year). The data are weighted to ensure representativeness of the working-age population (15 years and older). We focus on the August rounds (third quarter) of 2019 and 2022, which serve as representative snapshots of the pre-pandemic and post-pandemic labour market, respectively.

In line with Mussurov and Arabsheibani (2015), our analysis focuses on informal self-employment, which is defined as non-agricultural own-account work that is not registered or licensed with the state. These individuals may work alone or with occasional help but operate outside formal legal and regulatory frameworks. Respondents who report that their activity is unregistered, unlicensed, or are unsure about their registration status are classified as informally self-employed. By contrast, formal self-employment is defined as registered or licensed entrepreneurial activity. This legalistic definition aligns with Kazakhstan's official criteria and allows us to distinguish between regulated and unregulated self-employment. The restriction to non-agricultural workers excludes subsistence farming and aligns with prior studies of the informal economy.

Table 9 in the Appendix presents descriptive statistics for key variables used in the analysis. In 2019, formal workers earned an average of approximately 5.232 log points per hour, compared to 5.150 log points for informal workers. By 2022, average hourly earnings were 5.690 log points for formal workers and 5.266 log points for informal workers. On average, formal workers were slightly older than informal workers in 2019, but the difference nearly disappeared in 2022, with both groups having similar mean ages. Education differences are also notable: in 2019, the share of workers with a university education is higher among formal workers (21%) than informal workers (14%), and this gap is even larger in 2022 (33% vs. 16%). In contrast, college-level education is more prevalent among informal workers. The share of workers with vocational education was higher in the formal sector before the pandemic (53% vs. 38%). However, this difference disappeared by 2022, with both formal and informal workers showing similar rates (55% and 56%, respectively).

Female workers and those who are married are more likely to be working in the formal sector. Informal workers were more likely to work in agricultural, craft and trade, and plant operation roles, while formal workers dominated service and sales jobs. Informality was slightly more common in rural areas. Formal workers were also slightly more concentrated in Astana and Shymkent than informal workers. In Almaty, the share is very similar in both periods. More informal workers have been in their current job for less than a year than formal workers across both years. Finally, our sample consists of 4,759 self-employed workers in 2019 and 4,329 self-employed workers in 2022, of whom 345 (7.2%) and 357 (8.3%), respectively, are informal.

7 Empirical Results

7.1 Earnings Equations

Table 3 reports the OLS estimates of the earnings Eqs. 1 and 2. We find a positive effect of higher and further education on earnings relative to those with a secondary education or less. For those employed formally, having a college degree is associated with earnings being 34% higher (over secondary education or below) in 2022 and 58% higher in 2022. Having a university education has a weaker effect for the formal sector after the pandemic, while being insignificant in the informal sector before and after the pandemic. Vocational education also has a positive yet somewhat more modest effect on earnings in formal employment in 2019 compared to 2022. For those employed informally, only college education was associated with a statistically significant earnings premium in both waves.

Occupational effects are measured relative to the reference group, which is the managerial and professional workers. In the formal sector, all occupational coefficients are negative and statistically significant in both 2019 and 2022. In contrast, in informal self-employment in 2019, skilled agricultural workers, craft and trades workers, as well as unskilled workers,

Table 3 Earnings equations

	Formal 2019 (coefficients)	*Informal 2019 (coefficients)*	*Formal 2022 (coefficients)*	*Informal 2022 (coefficients)*
Age	0.002	−0.019	0.012	0.030
	(0.007)	(0.028)	(0.010)	(0.036)
Age^2	0.00002	0.0003	−0.0002	−0.0005
	(0.00009)	(0.0003)	(0.0001)	(0.0004)
College	0.344***	0.424***	0.579***	0.622***
	(0.048)	(0.142)	(0.080)	(0.204)
Vocational	0.118***	−0.005	0.277***	0.072
	(0.031)	(0.105)	(0.062)	(0.156)
University	0.280***	0.182	0.197***	0.260
	(0.039)	(0.152)	(0.063)	(0.196)
Female	0.010	−0.054	−0.121***	−0.096
	(0.025)	(0.088)	(0.033)	(0.137)
Married	−0.014	−0.080	−0.037	−0.110
	(0.026)	(0.095)	(0.033)	(0.118)
Unskilled	−0.453***	0.740**	−0.500***	0.278
	(0.045)	(0.324)	(0.054)	(0.401)
Technicians	−0.648***	0.147	−0.203**	0.728
	(0.074)	(0.507)	(0.085)	(0.521)
Clerical	−0.970***	0.595	−0.707***	1.081***
	(0.107)	(0.443)	(0.205)	(0.415)
Service/Sales	−0.573***	0.681**	−0.447***	0.780*
	(0.044)	(0.343)	(0.058)	(0.401)
Agricultural	−0.696***	0.995***	−0.425***	0.204
	(0.068)	(0.331)	(0.085)	(0.467)
Craft/Trades	−0.505***	0.736**	−0.433***	0.640
	(0.056)	(0.343)	(0.075)	(0.406)
Plant/Machine	−0.413***	0.530	−0.409***	0.155
	(0.051)	(0.341)	(0.059)	(0.391)
Rural	−0.107***	−0.214**	−0.301***	−0.141
	(0.028)	(0.098)	(0.036)	(0.134)
Shymkent	−0.044	−0.012	0.474***	−0.142
	(0.041)	(0.216)	(0.048)	(0.293)
Almaty	0.445***	0.856***	0.798***	1.657***
	(0.085)	(0.182)	(0.102)	(0.199)
Astana	0.237**	−0.189	−0.066	0.954
	(0.106)	(0.123)	(0.124)	(0.591)
Tenure < 1	0.058	0.183*	0.187***	−0.109
	(0.041)	(0.109)	(0.062)	(0.151)
Primary	0.066	0.037	−0.084	−0.215
	(0.069)	(0.225)	(0.094)	(0.294)

(continued)

Table 3 (continued)

	Formal 2019 (coefficients)	*Informal 2019 (coefficients)*	*Formal 2022 (coefficients)*	*Informal 2022 (coefficients)*
Tertiary	−0.004	−0.096	0.042	−0.232
	(0.044)	(0.130)	(0.062)	(0.183)
Constant	5.486***	4.861***	5.831***	4.833***
	(0.151)	(0.681)	(0.219)	(0.799)
N	4414	345	3972	357
adj. R^2	0.123	0.162	0.123	0.203

Note Robust standard errors in parentheses. ***$p < 0.001$, **$p < 0.01$, *$p < 0.05$

exhibited earnings premiums. In 2022, however, these effects were no longer statistically significant among informally self-employed workers except for service/sales workers who showed positive and significant returns. Another interesting result that we can observe is that workers in clerical occupations who work informally earn a premium when compared to the reference group of informal workers.

Regional disparities were more pronounced in the informal sector, with informal workers in Almaty consistently showing higher earnings premiums compared to the formal sector workers (85.6% vs. 44.5% in 2019 and 165.7% vs. 79.8% in 2022). Being formal had a statistically significant effect on earnings for workers in Astana in 2019 and Shymkent in 2022. In 2019, having less than one year of tenure was associated with a significant earnings premium in informal self-employment, but no effect in formal self-employment. In 2022, we observe a positive and significant effect in formal self-employment, while in the informal sector the coefficient turned negative and became statistically insignificant.

Overall, formal self-employment increasingly rewards higher qualifications, with university and vocational education associated with significant earnings premiums. College graduates enjoy a higher premium in the informal sector. Returns to occupations are more volatile in the informal sector, with diminishing premiums and weaker rewards for the less experienced. Regional disparities are more pronounced in the informal sector, with Almaty showing consistently higher earnings premiums in both years.

7.2 *Decomposition Estimates*

We apply the Oaxaca and Ransom (1994) method to decompose the differences in log hourly earnings between formal and informal self-employed workers. Table 4 presents a summary of the results. We find a large and significant increase in the earnings gap between formal and informal workers between 2019 and 2022 (from 0.082 log points to 0.424 log points), with formal workers earning approximately 8.54% more per hour on average in 2019, rising to 52.8% in 2022. In 2019, approximately 89% of the gap can be attributed to differences in observable characteristics. However, in 2022, only around 22% of this gap is explained by differences in observable characteristics, while the remaining 78% remains unexplained. This substantial rise in the unexplained component observed in 2022 may reflect increasing institutional or discriminatory barriers faced by informal self-employed workers.

In Table 5, we present the detailed decomposition results. While the explained component of the formal–informal earnings gap changed slightly in size (from 0.073 log points in 2019 to 0.093 log points in 2022), its composition changed. In 2019, occupational differences explained most of the gap: craft and trades, plant and machine, and skilled agricultural work were key positive contributors. University and vocational education added 0.016 log points and 0.014 log points (or 22% and 19%, respectively) to the explained component, while service and sales occupations narrowed the gap.

Table 4 Summary of Oaxaca–Ransom decomposition of mean log hourly earnings

Year	*Mean Log of Earnings*		*Total Gap*	*Explained*	*Unexplained*
	Formal	Informal			
2019	5.232	5.150	0.082*	0.073***	0.008
	(0.012)	(0.041)	(0.042)	(0.014)	(0.042)
			100%	89%	11%
2022	5.690	5.266	0.424***	0.093***	0.331***
	(0.016)	(0.056)	(0.058)	(0.022)	(0.054)
			100%	22%	78%

Notes Robust standard errors in parentheses. Percentages represent each component's share of the raw gap. ***$p < 0.01$, **$p < 0.05$, *$p < 0.1$

Table 5 Detailed Oaxaca–Ransom decomposition of log hourly earnings gaps

	2019 (explained)	*2022 (explained)*	*2019 (unexplained)*	*2022 (unexplained)*
Age	0.001 (0.008)	−0.002 (0.008)	0.853 (1.118)	−0.743 (1.480)
Age^2	0.003 (0.008)	0.003 (0.010)	−0.489 (0.583)	0.656 (0.794)
College	−0.005 (0.005)	−0.006 (0.009)	−0.006 (0.010)	−0.003 (0.015)
Vocational	0.014*** (0.005)	−0.004 (0.008)	0.050 (0.042)	0.115 (0.091)
University	0.016*** (0.006)	0.038*** (0.011)	0.015 (0.022)	−0.015 (0.036)
Female	0.000 (0.003)	−0.014*** (0.005)	0.023 (0.031)	−0.008 (0.043)
Married	−0.002 (0.002)	−0.002 (0.002)	0.043 (0.062)	0.051 (0.082)
Unskilled	−0.002 (0.010)	−0.023** (0.011)	−0.270*** (0.076)	−0.150* (0.078)
Technicians	−0.006 (0.006)	−0.000 (0.002)	−0.023 (0.016)	−0.031 (0.019)
Clerical	0.003 (0.008)	−0.004 (0.002)	−0.036** (0.016)	−0.005 (0.005)
Service/Sales	−0.077*** (0.012)	−0.027*** (0.009)	−0.152*** (0.046)	−0.153*** (0.053)
Agricultural	0.036*** (0.013)	0.012 (0.009)	−0.261*** (0.060)	−0.093 (0.068)
Craft/Trades	0.068*** (0.014)	0.039*** (0.011)	−0.290*** (0.083)	−0.220*** (0.084)
Plant/Machine	0.026*** (0.010)	0.057*** (0.013)	−0.182*** (0.067)	−0.158 (0.102)
Rural	0.003 (0.003)	0.010 (0.008)	0.076 (0.070)	−0.108 (0.091)
Shymkent	−0.001 (0.001)	0.013*** (0.003)	−0.001 (0.002)	0.005 (0.004)
Almaty	0.003 (0.003)	0.008 (0.006)	−0.005 (0.003)	−0.017** (0.008)
Astana	0.002 (0.001)	−0.001 (0.002)	0.003 (0.002)	−0.006 (0.005)
Tenure < 1	−0.007* (0.004)	−0.010** (0.005)	−0.024 (0.022)	0.039* (0.022)
Primary	−0.001 (0.002)	0.001 (0.002)	0.006 (0.047)	0.025 (0.058)

(continued)

Table 5 (continued)

	2019 (explained)	*2022 (explained)*	*2019 (unexplained)*	*2022 (unexplained)*
Tertiary	−0.002 (0.006)	0.004 (0.008)	0.052 (0.075)	0.152 (0.106)
Constant	0.625 (0.676)		0.998 (0.804)	
N	4,759	4,329	4,759	4,329

***$p < 0.01$, **$p < 0.05$, *$p < 0.1$

By 2022, university education contributed 0.038 log points, or 41% of the explained component, reflecting its growing concentration among formal workers. Vocational education was no longer significant. Differences in unskilled occupations accounted for −0.023 log points and skilled agricultural work was no longer statistically significant. Nevertheless, occupational contributions remained broadly similar between 2019 and 2022: craft and trades, as well as plant and machine, continued to contribute positively to the explained component. In 2022, gender differences became more relevant. That is, variation in the share of female workers across sectors explained −0.014 log points of the gap, slightly narrowing the observed earnings difference. The contribution of short job tenure to the explained component increased slightly after the pandemic. Among regions, only Shymkent had a statistically significant contribution (−0.013 log points) to the explained part of the gap.

Overall, we find that the overall gap rose almost fivefold between 2019 and 2022. And although the explained component also increased, it accounted for a much smaller share of the overall gap. On the other hand, the unexplained component made a much larger impact in driving this rise. Education and occupation continued to contribute to the earnings gap in both years, but their relative importance changed. In particular, university education accounted for a larger share of the explained earnings gap in 2022, contributing 0.038 log points, almost double from 0.016 in 2019. While occupational patterns remained broadly stable, this shift highlights the growing role of university education in differentiating formal and informal self-employment earnings.

7.3 Informality Choice

Table 6 presents probit coefficient estimates (Columns 2 and 3) and corresponding average marginal effects for the likelihood of informal self-employment in 2019 and 2022 (Columns 4 and 5). Our estimates show that informality is less likely among the educated and the effect is stronger after the pandemic. Those with a vocational degree were 4.8% percent less likely to be informal in 2019, rising to 9.9% percent in 2022. The effect for university education is 3.8% in 2019 and 13.1% in 2022. Broadly, our results show that education has an important role in shaping informal self-employment outcomes.

There seems to be little evidence of gender differences in informality from our estimates. Marital status, however, has a modest but significant effect, where married individuals were 1.8 percentage points less likely to be informally self-employed in both years. We also observe that several occupations are positively associated with informal self-employment when compared to managerial and professional occupations (our reference category). Skilled agricultural workers, for example, display the highest likelihood of being informal in 2019 (12.9 percentage points). Among plant & machine operators, the probability of informal self-employment rose from 10.9 percentage points in 2019 to 15.4 percentage points three years later. Craft and trades workers, as well as technicians and service and sales workers, also showed statistically significant positive associations with informality in both years. In contrast, the effect for clerical workers was significant in 2019 but not in 2022.

Self-employed workers in Shymkent were 8.9 percentage points less likely to be informal in 2019, but this association disappeared by 2022. Tenure was another important determinant, with workers who had been employed for less than one year being more likely to be informal in both waves. This effect decreased slightly over time, from 5.2 percentage points in 2019 to 3.7 percentage points in 2022. Sectoral differences also played a role, with employment in the primary and tertiary sectors reducing informality. The negative impact of the primary sector on informality grew from 4.3 percentage points in 2019 to 7.6 percentage points in 2022, while the tertiary sector reduced informality by 2.5 percentage points in 2019 and 6.6 percentage points in 2022.

Overall, our empirical findings underscore the growing importance of education in reducing informal self-employment, while tenure, occupations, and sectoral characteristics continue to influence informality in

Table 6 Informality choice

	Informality 2019 (probit)	*Informality 2022 (probit)*	*Informality 2019 (marginal effects)*	*Informality 2022 (marginal effects)*
Age	0.022	0.002	0.003	0.0003
	(0.019)	(0.020)	(0.002)	(0.003)
Age^2	−0.0003	−0.00002	−0.0004	-3.22×10^{-6}
	(0.0002)	(0.0002)	(0.0003)	-3×10^{-5}
College	−0.223*	−0.679***	−0.028*	−0.094***
	(0.123)	(0.143)	(0.016)	(0.020)
Vocational	−0.382***	−0.719***	−0.048***	−0.099***
	(0.070)	(0.095)	(0.009)	(0.013)
University	−0.303***	−0.951***	-0.038***	−0.131***
	(0.096)	(0.109)	(0.012)	(0.015)
Female	−0.050	−0.044	−0.006	−0.006
	(0.067)	(0.069)	(0.008)	(0.010)
Married	−0.140**	−0.127*	−0.018**	−0.018*
	(0.067)	(0.067)	(0.009)	(0.009)
Unskilled	0.645***	0.498***	0.081***	0.069***
	(0.162)	(0.154)	(0.021)	(0.021)
Technicians	0.686***	0.691***	0.087***	0.096***
	(0.215)	(0.205)	(0.027)	(0.029)
Clerical	0.682***	0.233	0.086***	0.032
	(0.242)	(0.449)	(0.031)	(0.062)
Service/Sales	0.351**	0.584***	0.044**	0.081***
	(0.169)	(0.160)	(0.021)	(0.022)
Agricultural	1.021***	0.873***	0.129***	0.121***
	(0.200)	(0.193)	(0.026)	(0.027)
Craft/Trades	0.984***	0.601***	0.124***	0.083***
	(0.175)	(0.166)	(0.022)	(0.023)
Plant/Machine	0.862***	1.114***	0.109***	0.154***
	(0.169)	(0.155)	(0.022)	(0.022)
Rural	−0.114	−0.071	−0.014	−0.010
	(0.070)	(0.067)	(0.009)	(0.009)
Shymkent	−0.705***	−0.392	−0.089***	−0.054
	(0.240)	(0.250)	(0.030)	(0.035)
Almaty	−0.162	0.157	−0.021	0.022
	(0.255)	(0.206)	(0.032)	(0.028)
Astana	−0.236	−0.108	−0.030	−0.015
	(0.338)	(0.356)	(0.043)	(0.049)
Tenure < 1	0.410***	0.269***	0.052***	0.037***
	(0.083)	(0.096)	(0.011)	(0.013)

(continued)

Table 6 (continued)

	Informality 2019 (probit)	*Informality 2022 (probit)*	*Informality 2019 (marginal effects)*	*Informality 2022 (marginal effects)*
Primary	-0.339^{**}	-0.553^{***}	-0.043^{**}	-0.076^{***}
	(0.149)	(0.160)	(0.019)	(0.022)
Tertiary	-0.198^{**}	-0.480^{***}	-0.025^{**}	-0.066^{***}
	(0.101)	(0.108)	(0.013)	(0.015)
Constant	-1.906^{***}	-0.863^{**}		
	(0.414)	(0.432)		
N	4,759	4,329	4,759	4,329
Pseudo R^2	0.091	0.098		

$^{***}p < 0.001$, $^{**}p < 0.01$, * p < 0.05

nuanced ways. The effects of education on informality appear stronger in the post-pandemic period, suggesting increased formalisation among more educated workers. However, informality remains a challenge across all occupational groups, with the exception of clerical workers, whose likelihood of being informal after the pandemic is no longer statistically different compared to that of managerial and professional workers.

7.4 *Decomposition of Informality Choice*

We apply a non-linear decomposition method proposed by Yun (2004) to examine changes in the likelihood of being informal. As shown in Table 7, the mean predicted probability of informality rose from 7.25% in 2019 to 8.25% in 2022. However, this slight increase masks opposite effects. On one hand, changes in observable characteristics would have led to a 2.6 percentage point decline in informality (Table 7). This negative endowment effect suggests that the composition of the workforce in 2022 became more associated with formal employment. On the other hand, the coefficient effect contributed a 3.6 percentage point increase in informality. This implies that characteristics that are generally associated with lower informality had a weaker association in 2022 compared to 2019. The net result was a small increase in informality despite favourable compositional changes. These findings suggest that policies which only focus on improving workers' qualifications and level of education are limited unless accompanied by policies that aim to affect how the labour market rewards these attributes.

The detailed Yun decomposition results, presented in Table 8, show that university education was the most influential factor explaining the change in the predicted probability of informal self-employment between 2019 and 2022. Moreover, the coefficient effect was also negative and statistically significant, suggesting that the effect of university education on informality strengthened between 2019 and 2022. In other words, by 2022, holding a university degree was more effective at reducing the likelihood of informal self-employment than it had been in 2019. We also find that other educational and occupational categories, as well as demographic or geographic factors, played a limited role in accounting for the change, whether through shifts in worker characteristics or through changing returns to those characteristics.

Overall, our empirical results suggest that the modest rise in the predicted probability of informal self-employment was not driven by a deterioration in observable characteristics. Instead, it reflects changes in how the labour market valued those attributes over time. Additionally, we find that university education emerged as the most important factor against informality among the self-employed workers after the pandemic.

Table 7 Summary of the Yun decomposition results

Reference Group Means (2022)	0.0825
Comparison Group Means (2019)	0.0725
Endowments	−0.026***
	(0.004)
	−260%
Coefficients	0.036***
	(0.007)
	+ 360%
Raw Gap	0.010*
	(0.005)
	100%
N	9,088

Notes Standard errors are in parentheses. Percentages represent each component's share of the raw gap. ***$p < 0.01$, **$p < 0.05$, *$p < 0.1$

Table 8 Detailed Yun decomposition

	Due to difference in Characteristics	*Due to difference in Coefficients*
Age	0.0003 (0.0027)	−0.1570 (0.2143)
Age^2	−0.0002 (0.0018)	0.0945 (0.1140)
College	−0.0005*** (0.0001)	−0.0050** (0.0024)
Vocational	−0.0051*** (0.0009)	−0.0331** (0.0148)
University	−0.0232*** (0.0034)	−0.0247*** (0.0079)
Female	0.0003 (0.0005)	0.0006 (0.0082)
Married	−0.0003* (0.0002)	0.0018 (0.0131)
Unskilled	0.0007*** (0.0002)	−0.0064 (0.0094)
Technicians	−0.0002*** (0.0001)	0.0000 (0.0021)
Clerical	−0.0006 (0.0011)	−0.0017 (0.0019)
Service/Sales	−0.0082*** (0.0022)	0.0110 (0.0117)
Agricultural	0.0032*** (0.0008)	−0.0029 (0.0053)
Craft/Trades	0.0017*** (0.0005)	−0.0078* (0.0045)
Plant/Machine	0.0048*** (0.0007)	0.0065 (0.0066)
Rural	0.0006 (0.0005)	0.0056 (0.0126)
Shymkent	0.0005 (0.0004)	0.0024 (0.0026)
Almaty	0.0003 (0.0005)	0.0011 (0.0011)
Astana	−0.0001 (0.0004)	0.0004 (0.0014)
Tenure < 1	−0.0018*** (0.0006)	−0.0030 (0.0027)
Primary	0.0002*** (0.0001)	−0.0076 (0.0081)

(continued)

Table 8 (continued)

	Due to difference in Characteristics	*Due to difference in Coefficients*
Tertiary	0.0013***	−0.0367*
	(0.0003)	(0.0210)
Constant	0.1984*	
	(0.1151)	
N	9,088	

***$p < 0.01$, **$p < 0.05$, *$p < 0.1$

8 Policy Recommendations

We begin this section by noting that addressing informal self-employment will require a broad array of policy solutions. Our policy recommendations are detailed below.

First, the government should continue to invest in education at the primary, secondary, and tertiary levels. Both our research and other studies demonstrate that education is key towards reducing informality and increasing the probability of getting a formal job (see: Natarajan et al., 2023). Furthermore, higher levels of education are strongly associated with "upward transitions into better-paying work status groups" (Fields et al., 2023: 364). For example, Strokova et al. (2016) found that the educational attainment gap in Kazakhstan between the bottom 40% and top 60% of workers has expanded in recent years, and targeted educational initiatives could empower the bottom 40% to secure higher-paying jobs with higher productivity rates.

Second, the government should prioritise policies aimed at increasing workers' entrepreneurial skills and help raise labour productivity among those who are currently self-employed. We argue that it is important to distinguish between initiatives targeting those workers, particularly more mature individuals, already working in the informal sector. To reduce informality, the government should focus on training current workers by helping them navigate the regulatory environment, registration rules, and digital tools. Continued investment in public infrastructure, including institutions as well as physical infrastructure such as roads and digital tools, can help facilitate this transition (Loayza, 2018).

Moreover, the government should continue to reduce or remove barriers to entering the formal economy. Such measures include minimising and simplifying registration protocols and requirements and easing access to financing (see: Ohnsorge & Yu, 2022). In this respect, the government could also consider reinstating SAP or a SAP-like regime. SAP was in effect during the pandemic, which means that it was probably not fully "tested" to the same extent it would have been had the economy operated without COVID-era restrictions.

Finally, insofar as digital tools, such as electronic payment systems and e-banking mobile services, are critical to the economy as a whole, the government should continue to invest in digital infrastructure in order to reduce informality (Ohnsorge & Yu, 2022: 164). Such investment initiatives could include expanding the geographic reach of cellular and broadband services, expanding bandwidth, and upgrading coverage.

9 Conclusion

This research provides updated empirical evidence on informal self-employment in Kazakhstan, documenting the evolution of informality and earnings in the context of the COVID-19 pandemic. It highlights that both the likelihood of being informal and the gap in earnings between formal and informal increased between 2019 and 2022. In 2019, a substantial portion of the earnings gap was explained by differences in characteristics. By 2022, the gap had grown by nearly five times, driven by the unexplained component. This indicates that a larger portion of the gap could not be attributed to observable characteristics in 2022 compared to 2019. This could potentially be interpreted as the effect of COVID-19 and the resulting uncertainty in the labour market. Next, university-level education contributed more to the explained component of the earnings gap in 2022 than in 2019, indicating that differences in educational attainment accounted for a larger share of the observed earnings differential in the post-pandemic period.

Our estimates also show that the predicted probability of informal self-employment increased slightly between 2019 and 2022. This increase was not driven by changes in observable worker characteristics such as education, age, gender, or sector of employment. The distribution of these characteristics remained relatively stable over the period. We find that changes in the likelihood of informal self-employment over the period are attributable to changes in the returns to these characteristics or other unobserved factors.

Our empirical results have important policy implications. It can be argued that improving educational outcomes remains central to reducing informality and narrowing the earnings gap between formal and informal self-employed workers in Kazakhstan. In sum, this chapter contributes to the broader literature on informality in Turkic states by providing empirical evidence from a middle-income country, in which the sharp increase in the formal–informal earnings gap and the resilience of informality suggest that self-employed workers are vulnerable to external shocks.

Appendix

See Table 9.

Table 9 Descriptive statistics

	Formal 2019	*Informal* 2022	*Formal* 2019	*Informal* 2022
Hourly Earnings (Log)	5.232	5.150	5.690	5.266
	(0.778)	(0.754)	(0.984)	(1.053)
Age	40.46	39.33	40.99	41.12
	(11.76)	(11.84)	(10.96)	(11.33)
Age^2	1775.03	1686.98	1800.90	1818.42
	(959.01)	(941.70)	(903.67)	(926.80)
College	0.057	0.072	0.061	0.070
	(0.231	(0.260)	(0.239)	(0.256)
Vocational	0.526	0.383	0.547	0.560
	(0.499)	(0.487)	(0.498)	(0.497)
University	0.205	0.142	0.328	0.160
	(0.404)	(0.350)	(0.469)	(0.367)
Female	0.456	0.348	0.423	0.305
	(0.498)	(0.477)	(0.494)	(0.461)
Married	0.728	0.646	0.737	0.689
	(0.445)	(0.479)	(0.440)	(0.464)
Unskilled	0.230	0.226	0.240	0.193
	(0.421)	(0.419)	(0.427)	(0.395)
Technicians	0.037	0.029	0.035	0.034
	(0.190)	(0.168)	(0.185)	(0.180)
Clerical	0.020	0.023	0.009	0.003
	(0.139)	(0.151)	(0.092)	(0.053)
Service/Sales	0.257	0.119	0.188	0.123
	(0.437)	(0.324)	(0.390)	(0.329)

(continued)

Table 9 (continued)

	Formal 2019	*Informal* 2022	*Formal* 2019	*Informal* 2022
Agricultural	0.100	0.157	0.119	0.146
	(0.300)	(0.364)	(0.323)	(0.353)
Craft/Trades	0.097	0.235	0.112	0.207
	(0.296)	(0.424)	(0.315)	(0.406)
Plant/Machine	0.132	0.191	0.147	0.266
	(0.338)	(0.394)	(0.354)	(0.443)
Rural	0.682	0.710	0.644	0.678
	(0.466)	(0.454)	(0.479)	(0.468)
Shymkent	0.042	0.009	0.036	0.008
	(0.201)	(0.093)	(0.186)	(0.091)
Almaty	0.018	0.012	0.029	0.020
	(0.134)	(0.107)	(0.168)	(0.139)
Astana	0.016	0.006	0.022	0.006
	(0.126)	(0.076)	(0.147)	(0.075)
Tenure < 1	0.104	0.203	0.074	0.143
	(0.306)	(0.403)	(0.262)	(0.350)
Primary	0.185	0.209	0.184	0.193
	(0.388)	(0.407)	(0.388)	(0.395)
Tertiary	0.693	0.545	0.681	0.552
	(0.461)	(0.499)	(0.466)	(0.498)
N	4,414	345	3,972	357

Note Standard deviations are in parenthesis

References

Blunch, N. H. (2015). Bound to lose, bound to win? The financial crisis and the informal-formal sector earnings gap in Serbia. *IZA Journal of Labor & Development, 4*(1), 13. https://doi.org/10.1186/s40175-015-0035-5

Dell'Anno, R. (2021). Inequality and informality in transition and emerging countries. *IZA World of Labor*. https://doi.org/10.15185/izawol.325.v2

Elgin, C., Kose, M. A., Ohnsorge, F., & Yu, S. (2021). *Understanding informality* (No. 16497, CEPR Discussion Papers). https://doi.org/10.2139/ssrn.3916568

Fields, G. S., Gindling, T. H., Sen, K., Danquah, M., & Schotte, S. (Eds.). (2023). *The job ladder: Transforming informal work and livelihoods in developing countries*. WIDER Studies in Development Economics. Oxford University Press. https://doi.org/10.1093/oso/9780192867339.001.0001

Gasparini, L., & Tornarolli, L. (2009). Labor informality in Latin America and the Caribbean: Patterns and trends from household survey microdata. *Desarrollo y sociedad, 63*, 13–80. https://doi.org/10.13043/dys.63.1

Gimpelson, V. E., & Kapeliushnikov, R. I. (2015). The Russian labour market model: Trial by recession. *Journal of the New Economic Association, 2*, 249–254. https://www.econorus.org/repec/journl/2015-26-254-259r.pdf. Accessed 17 August 2025.

Government of Kazakhstan (GoK). (2023a). *Digital Kazakhstan*. https://egov.kz/cms/en/digital-kazakhstan. Accessed 17 August 2025.

Government of Kazakhstan (GoK). (2023b). *Ob utverzhdenii Koncepcii razvitija rynka truda Respubliki Kazahstan na 2024–2029 gody* [Concept for the development of the labor market of the Republic of Kazakhstan for 2024–2029]. https://adilet.zan.kz/rus/docs/P2300001050. Accessed 17 August 2025.

Government of Kazakhstan (GoK). (2025). *Sustainable development goals in the Republic of Kazakhstan*. https://kazstat.github.io/sdg-site-kazstat/en/8-3-1/. Accessed 29 June 2025.

Henley, A., Arabsheibani, G. R., & Carneiro, F. G. (2009). On defining and measuring the informal sector: Evidence from Brazil. *World Development, 37*(5), 992–1003. https://doi.org/10.1016/j.worlddev.2008.09.011

ILO. (2023). *World employment and social outlook: Trends 2023*. International Labour Office, Geneva. https://www.ilo.org/publications/flagship-reports/world-employment-and-social-outlook-trends-2023. Accessed 17 August 2025.

Kahyalar, N., Fethi, S., Katircioglu, S., & Ouattara, B. (2018). Formal and informal sectors: Is there any wage differential? *The Service Industries Journal, 38*(11–12), 789–823. https://doi.org/10.1080/02642069.2018.1482877

Kanbur, R. (2011) Avoiding informality traps. In E. Ghani (Ed.), *Reshaping tomorrow: Is South Asia ready for the big leap?* (pp. 260–278). Oxford University Press. https://documents.worldbank.org/pt/publication/documents-reports/documentdetail/311391468101989889/reshaping-tomorrow-is-south-asia-ready-for-the-big-leap. Accessed 17 August 2025.

Kanbur, R. (2017). Informality: Causes, consequences and policy responses. *Review of Development Economics, 21*(4), 939–961. https://doi.org/10.1111/rode.12321

Karymshakov, K., Sulaimanova, B., & Bergolo, M. (2023). Employment vulnerability and earnings in Kyrgyzstan. *The Journal of Development Studies, 59*(7), 1076–1091. https://doi.org/10.1080/00220388.2023.2191780

Kim, Y. S., Matytsin, M., & Freije-Rodriguez, S. (2019). *Informal employment and worker's well-being in the Russian Federation* (World Bank Policy Research Working Paper, 8989). https://ssrn.com/abstract=3440365

KPMG. (2019, February). *NewsFlash: Tax and legal*. https://assets.kpmg.com/content/dam/kpmg/kz/pdf/NF-Employment-Formalization-Eng.pdf. Accessed 17 August 2025.

Loayza, N. (2018, December 19). *Informality: Why is it so widespread and how can it be reduced?* (World Bank Research and Policy Briefs No. 133110). https://ssrn.com/abstract=3360124. Accessed 17 August 2025.

Mussurov, A., & Arabsheibani, G. R. (2015). Informal self-employment in Kazakhstan. *IZA Journal of Labor & Development, 4*(1), 9. https://doi.org/10.1186/s40175-015-0031-9

Mussurov, A., Sholk, D., & Arabsheibani, G. R. (2019). Informal employment in Kazakhstan: A blessing in disguise? *Eurasian Economic Review, 9*(2), 267–284. https://doi.org/10.1007/s40822-018-0117-1

Natarajan, R. R., Schotte, S., & Sen, K. (2023). *Moving up or down the job ladder in India: Examining informality-formality transitions*. Oxford University Press. https://doi.org/10.1093/oso/9780192867339.003.0004

National Bureau of Statistics. (2023). *The number of informally employed population in Kazakhstan*, Astana. National Bureau of Statistics.

National Bureau of Statistics. (2025). *Main labour market indicators*, Astana. National Bureau of Statistics.

Oaxaca, R. L., & Ransom, M. R. (1994). On discrimination and the decomposition of wage differentials. *Journal of Econometrics, 61*(1), 5–21. https://doi.org/10.1016/0304-4076(94)90074-4

Ohnsorge, F., & Yu, S. (Eds). (2022). *The long shadow of informality: Challenges and policies*. World Bank. http://hdl.handle.net/10986/35782

Powers, D. A., Yoshioka, H., & Yun, M. S. (2011). Multivariate decomposition for nonlinear response models. *The Stata Journal, 11*(4), 556–576. https://doi.org/10.1177/1536867X1201100404

Rutkowski, J. (2011). *Promoting formal employment in Kazakhstan: Challenges and policy options*. The World Bank. http://conference.iza.org/conference_files/InfoETE2011/rutkowski_j1928.pdf. Accessed 17 August 2025.

Slonimczyk, F. (2022). *Informal employment in emerging and transition economies* (IZA World of Labor). https://doi.org/10.15185/izawol.59.v2

Staneva, A. V., & Arabsheibani, G. R. (2014). Is there an informal employment wage premium? Evidence from Tajikistan. *IZA Journal of Labor & Development, 3*(1), 1. https://doi.org/10.1186/2193-9020-3-1

Strokova, V., Elzir, A., & Margolis, D. (2016). *Kazakhstan labor market outcomes: Achievements and remaining challenges* (No. 27641968). The World Bank. https://doi.org/10.1596/27479

UN. (2024a, June). *The sustainable development goals report 2024*. United Nations Department of Economic and Social Affairs. https://unstats.un.org/sdgs/report/2024/. Accessed 17 August 2025.

UN. (2024b). *Policy brief: Transforming the informal economy to leave no one behind*. https://www.un.org/sites/un2.un.org/files/2024/04/unen_policy_brief_march_2024.pdf. Accessed 17 August 2025.

WDI. (2025). *Kazakhstan*. https://data.worldbank.org/country/kazakhstan. Accessed 17 August 2025.

World Bank. (2024). *More, better and inclusive jobs in Kazakhstan*. Washington, DC. http://documents.worldbank.org/curated/en/099030724012521561. Accessed 17 August 2025.

World Bank. (2025). *Kazakhstan poverty and equity assessment 2024*. World Bank. http://hdl.handle.net/10986/42616

Yun, M. S. (2000). *Decomposition analysis for a binary choice model*. Available at SSRN 233897. https://ssrn.com/abstract=233897. Accessed 17 August 2025.

Yun, M. S. (2004). Decomposing differences in the first moment. *Economics Letters, 82*(2), 275–280. https://doi.org/10.1016/j.econlet.2003.09.008

CHAPTER 5

Shadow Economy in Kyrgyzstan: Analyses and Tackling Policies

Kanat Tilekeyev

1 Introduction

In the last period of the Kyrgyz Republic's modern history, economic informality has become a recognized economic phenomenon observed by the national government and also by researchers. A shadow or informal economy is defined as economic activity based on economic operations in which economic actors carry out operations in the areas of unregistered (businesses) and informal (households) production and service provision. The primary goals of shadow economic operations are to lessen the tax burden and state authority. According to official estimates, the shadow economy (excluding the agricultural sector) accounted for at least 23–24% of GDP in 2014–2018. From 2019, it gradually decreased to 20%, with the lowest estimate in 2023 being 19.2% (NSC, 2024a).

Only 34% of the workforce is employed under labor contracts, while the rest work on oral or without any labor contracts (NSC, 2024b). In

K. Tilekeyev (✉)
Institute of Public Policy and Administration, University of Central Asia, Bishkek, Kyrgyzstan
e-mail: kanat.tilekeyev@ucentralasia.org

E. Bagirzadeh and O. Gokcekus (eds.), *Shadow Economies in Turkic Republics*, https://doi.org/10.1007/978-3-032-12872-0_5

terms of income and productivity levels, rights and recognition, voice and representation, and social protection coverage, labor markets that largely operate in the shadow economy are characterized by severe deficiencies in decent employment. The COVID-19 pandemic and the ensuing shocks from Russia's conflict in Ukraine brought home once more how urgent it is to solve issues of informality. Since many individuals are still unprotected by social security programs, broad access to social security systems is crucial to averting ongoing problems among the poor in Kyrgyzstan.

The chapter gives an overview of Kyrgyzstan's shadow economy, including methods used to study the economic phenomenon, an evaluation of studies on informality conducted for the Kyrgyz Republic, an analysis of informality in labor markets, a description of the tax system and social security system, and a policy landscape analysis that impacts the country's shadow economy. Reviewing possible policy initiatives to lower Kyrgyzstan's degree of shadow economy concludes the chapter.

2 Country's Economic and Institutional Profile

The Kyrgyz Republic is one of the least developed countries in the Europe and Central Asia region, with a gross national income per capita of US$2,150 in 2024 (Atlas method). The economy of Kyrgyzstan shows rapid growth from 2022 to 2024, with an average annual GDP growth of 9% during this period. In the previous period (2014–2019), the average economic growth rate was significantly lower at 4.2%, followed by a decline (−7.1%) in 2020 due to the COVID-19 pandemic. Remittances peaked at one-third of GDP, averaging 30% in 2015–2021, and then declined in 2022–2023 to 26.5% and 18.8%, respectively (World Bank, 2025b). The rapid economic growth observed in recent years is associated with increasing consumption, trade, and investment flows in Kyrgyzstan. The main drivers of economic development were manufacturing, construction, services, and agriculture, respectively (World Bank, 2025a).

The country's tax system is regulated by tax legislation (Tax Code adopted in 2022) and regulatory legal acts (GKR, 2022). The State Tax Service under the Government of the Kyrgyz Republic is the authorized body that monitors compliance with tax legislation, timeliness, and completeness of tax payments. Since taxes accounted for more than 70% of total revenues between 1995 and 2024, an overview of the trends of tax revenues emphasizes the significance of taxes as a significant source of budget income in Kyrgyzstan. Since joining the Eurasian Economic Union (EAEU) in 2015, import taxes have played a bigger role in tax revenues. This sum, which is determined by Kyrgyzstan's share of the customs taxes imposed on all EAEU nations, includes a sizable payment from the EAEU organizations to Kyrgyzstan's budget. In 2020, these taxes accounted for 16.2% of total tax receipts; however, by 2024, they had dropped to 12%. Income taxes, international trade taxes, and national consumption taxes are the primary levies required to serve as the foundation for the state budget. The nation's budget is less affected by other taxes, such as municipal taxes and levies from special tax regimes.

The current tax system creates significant opportunities for different types of taxation for businesses in certain sectors. For example, if you start a trading business, you must pay VAT on sales, corporate income tax on profits, personal income tax for your employees' wages, and social security contributions for your workers. Meanwhile, you as a business owner may register multiple individual entrepreneurs as your employees to avoid many taxes and only pay a single tax on turnover. The same situation appears in construction, hospitality, and food service industries, as well as many manufacturing plants. It is easy to see how such businesses can quickly shift to informal economic activities based on personal ties rather than on official tax compliance.

The foundation of Kyrgyzstan's social security system is the system of social insurance contributions, commonly recognized as social taxes, and social deductions. All payments made by payers for social insurance contributions are sent to the Kyrgyz Republic's Social Fund. In parallel, the Kyrgyz Republic's Ministry of Labor and Social Protection and the Social Fund divide the costs of social insurance. Regardless of their organizational and legal structure, state social insurance contributions are paid by legal entities and also by business entities working under special tax regimes. Farmers, the textile and apparel sector, and special tax regimes—patents, simplified tax regimes, and tax contracts—are subject to different social security tax regimes than registered legal companies (GKR, 2004). It implies that several social taxation systems may apply to commercial entities operating in the same economic sector. Similarly to the different tax regimes, different social contribution rates create incentives to decrease payments. Rationally, it makes it very hard for companies to operate in the sectors where social taxation motivates business fragmentation with the parallel different tax regimes.

Small business owners benefit from a favorable tax structure created by these differences in social security, taxes, and special tax regimes. It lowers the tax burden and operating costs for family-run businesses, individual entrepreneurs, and subsectors with advantageous tax regimes, such as the IT cluster, the casino industry, and the apparel industry.

Reduced domestic and foreign investment flows in the key industries of the national economy that depend on industrial activities may also be a direct result of the unequal tax burden. Except for some industries such as mining, state-supported enterprises, and infrastructure monopolies or industries with advantageous tax regimes, Kyrgyz economic development is hindered by the country's current tax system.

The Social Fund's primary budget source for social disbursements is derived from social security contributions. The demands of the social security system are not entirely met by the social levies that are collected, though. Consequently, there is a discrepancy between the amount of money collected and the demands that the state budget can provide. It is evident that the proportion of social payments from the Social Fund that the state budget covers has grown over time. It contributed 15% of the Social Fund's total income in 1995. It peaked at 39–40% in 2015–2020. Transfers reach 34% in 2024.

The rise in state budget contributions shows that the bulk of the nation's social payments are funded by the Social Fund's earnings, which is unsustainable. The entire strategy of the social protection system has to be reevaluated to be more sustainable because the money collected for social security has been insufficiently stable over the last 25 years. Over the previous ten years, the overall amount of social benefits disbursed through the Social Fund has increased, ranging between 7 and 10% of GDP. The whole tax burden, which ranges from 25 to 27% of GDP, includes all tax receipts as well as social security payments.

3 Review of Estimations of Shadow Economy of Kyrgyzstan

The shadow economy is a common economic phenomenon. According to the standard definition, it would include all currently unregistered economic activity that, if counted, would contribute to the official national output (Schneider & Williams, 2013). Unregistered shadow economic activity hinders business growth, contracts, labor rights protection, violent actions, and tax burden. Such activities also include underground, illegal industries and domestic activities for ultimate purposes, which were overlooked due to the national statistics' lack of primary data collection. The importance of the first type of operation is based on the high influence on the labor market's structure and operations. It is difficult to measure the shadow sector, as it involves estimating economic activity that is concealed from official transactions. The proportion of the European shadow economy ranges from 10% in the UK to 15% to 20% in Southern European countries. Tax burden (including social security), tax morale, the quality of governmental institutions, and labor market legal restrictions are the primary drivers of shadow economic observations (Schneider & Williams, 2013).

A distinct body of research examines the phenomenon of the shadow economy from several angles, including how it operates and how it affects the economy and society. There are a few ways to estimate the extent of the shadow economy: direct, indirect, and a combination of both. To assess the shadow economy, direct methodologies employ surveys, sampling, voluntary replies, tax audits, and other compliance techniques. Because surveys are sensitive to the quality of research techniques, they tend to underestimate the extent of the shadow economy. The size of the shadow economy is estimated using indirect techniques, also known as indicator approaches, which modify the procedure by employing many factors (Abdih & Medina, 2013). Consequently, estimations of the size of the shadow sector are supported by statistical modeling approaches employing various econometric models that include the estimation of the shadow economy as an omitted variable. Among the techniques employed are measurements based on the currency demand approach alone or in conjunction with the multiple indicator multiple cause (MIMIC) process (Schneider & Williams, 2013). The literature is examination of the MIMIC method's applicability (Feige & Urban, 2008).

The United Nations Economic Commission for Europe prepared a variety of the estimation practices of the shadow economy at the national level in 2008. It was adopted by the national statistical office and presented in the following section. It contains a variety of point estimates as well as explanations of the estimation processes. It does not, however, provide information on evaluating the accuracy of the data or show how the shadow economy's approach has changed over time. Ignorance of the shadow economy at the country level may lead to incomplete data and methodologies, which can hinder economic performance assessment (Feige, 2016).

Various researchers have estimated the shadow economy in a number of nations, including the Kyrgyz Republic (Table 1), with a range of methods used with varying outcomes. The lowest estimate, which is 17%, is within the average range for OECD nations. Other estimates mostly fall between 26 and 46%. The estimating techniques and structural shifts in the national economy may account for the discrepancy between them. The repetition of the similar type of studies potentially may have brought us to the similar type of conclusions. Usually, informality studies covering the Kyrgyz Republic articulate the persistence of the shadow economy as an established economic reality, and among the main incentives described are the basic persuading factors: avoidance of tax burden, prevalence of weak tax morale among business entities, and overall low institutional development in the country.

Table 1 Shadow economy estimations in the Kyrgyz Republic in 1990–2018

#	*Research studies*	*Estimation methods*	*The size of shadow economy, % of GDP/ estimation period*
1	Lacko (2000)	Electricity consumption	35%/1989–1995
2	Feige and Urban (2008)	Electricity consumption, currency deposit	46.2–49.5%/2000
3	UNECE (2008)	NIPA method	17%/2003
4	Schneider (2012)	MIMIC model	40.4%/1999–2007
5	UNDP (2006)	Electricity Survey	33.5%/2004 46.3%/2004
6	Akimkanov (2014)	Electricity consumption	39.5%/1995–2013
7	Abdih and Medina, (2013)	MIMIC model	26.3%/2008
8	Medina and Schneider (2017)	MIMIC model	37.9%/1999–2015
9	Putniņš and Sauka (2019)	Phone survey of businesses	46.1 and 44.5%/ 2017–2018
10	SIAR (2019)	Survey	28.1 and 29.8%/ 2017–2018
11	Balabushko et al. (2024)	MIMIC model and Dynamic General Equilibrium (DGE) model	35.5–36.7%/ 2018–2022

(*Source* Author's representation)

4 Analysis of Shadow Economy and Informal Employment in Kyrgyzstan

The National Statistical Committee of the Kyrgyz Republic (NSC) regularly provides an official estimation of the country's shadow economy (Fig. 1). By official estimation, the shadow economy level (including hidden and informal activity) was quite stable in the period of 2016–2023, with approximately 18–20% of GDP.[1] From 2014, it started to increase to a maximum of 24.5% in 2016 and then again slowly declined to approximately 20% after 2020.

In Kyrgyzstan, the non-observed economy encompasses hidden, informal, and illegal activities. Hidden economic activity refers to legal economic activities hidden or reduced by entities to evade taxes, social security contributions, labor protection regulations, sanitary standards, and compliance with administrative forms or statistical questionnaires, often resulting in decreased registered economic activity. Informal economic activity is primarily legal, involving individual producers or unincorporated enterprises owned by individuals or households. This activity is based on informal commercial relations and often involves secondary employment and non-professional activities. Many entrepreneurs, including those engaged in trade, car repair, personal

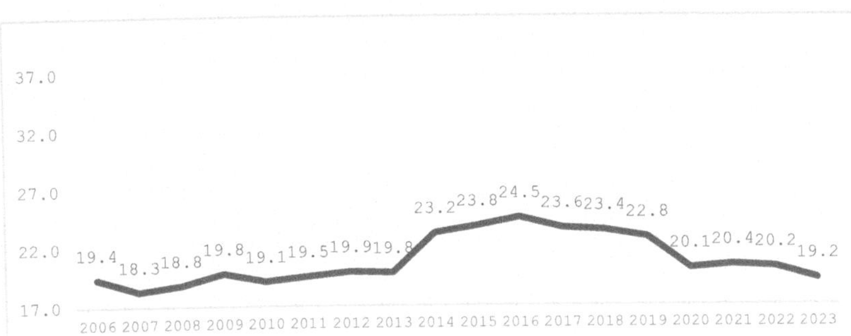

Fig. 1 Shadow economy in Kyrgyzstan in 2006–2023, % of GDP (*Source* NSC)

[1] Estimations does not include agriculture. Such an excusion of agriculture based on the situation when there is almost no direct taxes implies on agricultural production. More details provided later in the separate section devoted to the tax regimes in the country.

transportation, sewing, flour milling, and baking, are considered individuals under existing legislation, belonging to the "Households" sector or informal sector. Illegal economic activity includes activities related to the production, circulation, and use of goods and services prohibited by the legislation of the Kyrgyz Republic. The volume of the non-observed economy in 2023, estimated from the production side, is 19.2% of GDP. The share of the hidden economy in GDP is estimated as 4.5% of GDP, and the share of informal production activities amounted to 14.7%. The illegal economic activity is not estimated by NSC (NSC, 2024c).

Most active sectors where shadow economic activity is observed in Kyrgyzstan include trade and services, construction, transport and logistics, and processing industries production (Fig. 2). The biggest sector where most of the estimated official shadow activity is concentrated is trade and services. 65–68% of all shadow operations in Kyrgyztsan's economy concentrated in that sector. During the last few years, the share of informal unregistered activities in the sector declined, and it mainly causes the overall decline of the shadow economy level in the country. Transport and logistics and processing industry sectors also demonstrated decline of the unobserved economic operations in the country, while the construction sector shows an increase of informality.

The changing demographic situation in Kyrgyzstan determines the development of the labor market. Between 2010 and 2023, the labor

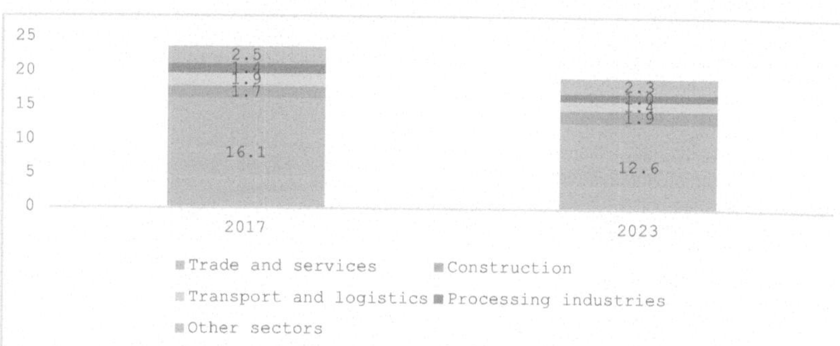

Fig. 2 Shadow economy's sectoral pattern change in Kyrgyzstan, 2017 and 2023, % of GDP (*Source* NSC)

force[2] increased by 12.7%, reaching 2.77 million people. As of 2023, 61% of Kyrgyzstan's labor force is men. Over the observed period, the share of women in the labor force decreased from 42 to 39%. In 2023, 61% of the labor force lived in rural areas. However, the urban labor force increased from 35 to 39% over the same period. The number of working laborers[3] increased by 18.4% between 2010 and 2023, reaching 2.65 million people. The gender distribution and composition of employed people in urban–rural strata reflects the structure of the labor force.

From a 2.65 million working labor force in 2023, 1.75 million of them were employed in the informal sector. Only 901.6 thousand people are employed in the formally registered sector, i.e., have labor contracts and pay social security contributions (NSC, 2024b). The labor market in Kyrgyzstan provides few main options for employment (officially and informally): (a) hired laborers working on enterprises and companies, (b) peasant farmers, (c) individual entrepreneurs, (d) laborers hired by individual entrepreneurs (including peasant farmers), and (e) laborers working on household farms (including paid and unpaid family workers). Between 2014 and 2023, the structure of the officially registered and informal labor market changed toward higher formalization (NSC, 2015). Between 2014 and 2023, the level of formalization increased from 28 to 34% due to an increase in formal employment by peasant farms and individual entrepreneurs (Fig. 3). Share of workers hired by companies slightly declines from 28 to 27%. At the same time, visible restructuring of the employment occurs in the informal sector—the share of jobs provided by individual entrepreneurs increased from 24 to 39%. This type of employment is the biggest job provider in the country and is fully informal. Employment as peasant farmers or laborers on household farms declined during the observed period. Those sectors lost 13% of their share of the overall labor market in the observed period. It is also worth noting that the number of informal workers employed by enterprises decreased by 1% during the last decade.

The difference in access to jobs for women in Kyrgyzstan is visible but mostly concentrated in the informal market (Fig. 4). In the formal jobs market in 2014, the number of women slightly exceeded the number of

[2] The labor force (economically active population) is a part of the population aged 15 years and over, providing the supply of labor for the production of goods and services. The labor force includes employed and unemployed people.

[3] Working labor refers to the employed population aged 15 years and over.

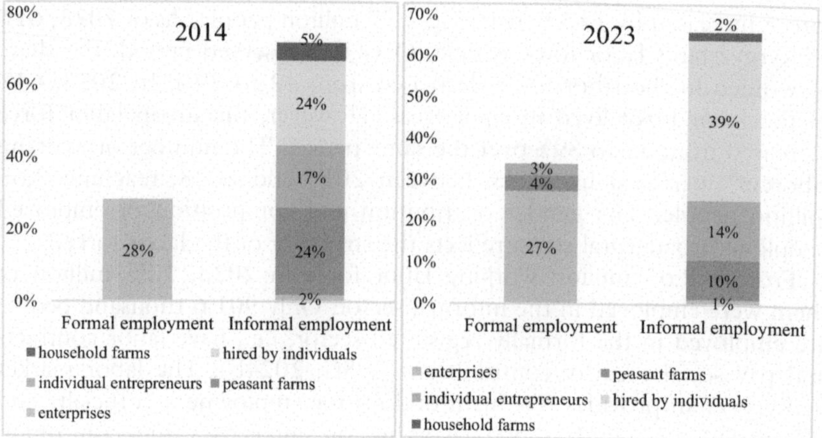

Fig. 3 Formal and informal employment by type of employment structure in Kyrgyzstan in 2014 and 2023, % (*Source* NSC)

men, while in 2023, the balance moved toward the prevalence of men—54% vs. 46% for women. In the informal labor market, the prevalence of men increased from 63% of jobs occupied by males in 2014 to 65% in 2023. In total, from 353.5 thousand new jobs, only 93 thousand go to women. However, from that amount of newly created jobs, 71% were in the formal sector.

Another interesting aspect presents data on how the labor market has changed in rural and urban areas of Kyrgyzstan (Fig. 4). The labor market grew by an average of 15% during the observed period, with most of that growth happening in urban areas—32% compared to 7% in rural areas. The formalization of jobs was mostly focused in rural regions—the number of formal jobs increased by 211.5 thousand, while informal jobs decreased by 112 thousand. It is noticeable that most of the new jobs created in urban areas are in the informal labor market (213.4 thousand jobs), while only 40.4 thousand new formal jobs were added in cities over the last decade. Most of the jobs created in Kyrgyzstan's formal labor market from 2014 to 2023 are related to peasant farm formalization and the official registration of individual entrepreneur-type employment (Fig. 3).

The sectoral structure of the labor market reflects the overall growth and shows changes in employment across different sectors from 2014 to

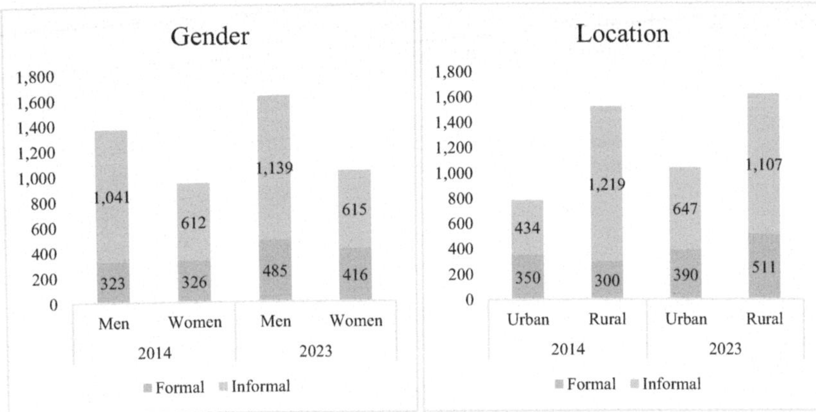

Fig. 4 Formal and informal employment by gender and location in Kyrgyzstan in 2014 and 2023, thousands of workers (*Source* NSC)

2023 (Table 2). Employment in all main sectors increased except agriculture, whose share in employment declined from 32% in 2014 to 17% in 2023.

Employment in sectors with high informality grew—namely trade and services, construction, transport and logistics, and the processing industry (Fig. 2 and Table 2). Informality in trade and services decreased slightly over the last decade—from 89 to 86%. However, it increased in three other sectors—construction (from 82 to 93%), transport and logistics (from 78 to 86%), and the processing industry (from 61 to 80%).

A significant decrease in informal employment was seen in agriculture, which is not included in the official shadow economy assessment (from 99 to 76%). Some sectors displayed high levels of formalization, such as education, healthcare, and public sector organizations. Conversely, other sectors that are relatively small in employment but more prominent in economic performance also experienced increases in informality—hotels and restaurants (from 71 to 87%), the finance and banking sector (from 16 to 36%), and IT and communication (from 26 to 41%).

The labor market informality demonstrates a number of key characteristics that public policy stakeholders should take into account in their analysis of the shadow economy:

Table 2 Sectoral employment structure (formal and informal) in Kyrgyzstan in 2014 and 2023, thousand people and %

	2014			*2023*		
	Employment, thousand people	*Formal, % to row*	*Informal, % to row*	*Employment, thousand people*	*Formal, % to row*	*Informal, % to row*
Agriculture	727	1%	99%	454	24%	76%
Processing industry	160	39%	61%	290	20%	80%
Construction	254	18%	82%	332	7%	93%
Trade and services	348	11%	89%	419	14%	86%
Transport and logistics	146	22%	78%	223	14%	86%
Hotels and restaurants	85	29%	71%	178	13%	87%
Education	177	94%	6%	262	94%	6%
Healthcare	80	87%	13%	118	86%	14%
Public sector, social services, defense	95	100%	0%	110	98%	2%
Finance and banking	25	84%	16%	48	64%	36%
IT and communica-tion	27	74%	26%	37	59%	41%
Other sectors	179	36%	64%	185	52%	48%
Total	2303	28%	72%	2,656	34%	66%

(*Source* NSC)

- The labor market increases following the country's population growth. It will continue further and consequently will increase pressure on the labor market. Creation of new jobs thus became one of the highest priorities for the Kyrgyz government.
- The level of informality on the labor market exceeds the level of shadow economy assessed by the Kyrgyz Government and researchers (66% in 2023). Part of the reason lies in the structure of the labor market—most of the jobs in the country are created by micro-SMEs—individual entrepreneurs, farmers, and self-employed entrepreneurs (Fig. 3). It creates a high self-employment level with the numerous jobs created in the specified sectors of the economy.

It contributes to the national economy and creates most of the jobs in the economy, but at the same time creates a highly fragmented structure of the economy that is highly costly to administer by tax service.

- Positive change in the formalization of the labor market occurs mainly due to improved performance and formalization of rural areas. Urban areas don't demonstrate good results in the formalization of labor relations (Fig. 4).
- Participation of women in the labor market is low (39% in 2023) and has worsened during the last decade. In general, it demonstrates an overall decline in women's empowerment in the country. Measures on improved access to jobs for women may bring positive results in women's employment.
- A few major sectors of the economy in Kyrgyzstan where informality is prevalent in the labor market are construction, trade, agriculture, processing industry, and transport. Those sectors (except agriculture) are also assessed as the main sectors responsible for the shadow, unregistered economic operations in Kyrgyzstan (Fig. 2).

National Policy on the Shadow Economy in Kyrgyzstan

Within the policy landscape of Kyrgyz legislation, there is no clear policy describing the attitude of the Kyrgyz government toward the shadow economy. Moreover, there is no clear distinction between the shadow and informal economies, and often both terms are used interchangeably in the official programs.

However, this distinction has been formulated in the global development agenda, such as the definition provided by the ILO. The informal economy means any economic activity of workers and economic units that are not covered at all or not fully covered by formal relationships (ILO, 2015). This term does not include illegal activities. Therefore, informal activity in ILO interpretation includes underground production and informal household production but does not include illegal production and activity that is forbidden by legislation, e.g., production and trade in drugs or illegal gambling. The differentiation of informal activity allows for the decriminalization of at least half of the labor market and most of the micro- and small-business activity in the world and includes them in the sustainable development agenda.

A legislative framework developed in Kyrgyzstan regarding shadow economic activity is mainly driven by the fiscal vision of the state. Most of the notations in the laws and state programs are oriented toward eradicating the shadow (or informal) economy. The Ministry of Economic Development and Trade, in October 2007, approved the Plan on Measures to Legalize the Shadow Economy in Kyrgyzstan for 2007–2010 (MEC, 2006). The plan proclaims the strengthening of the role and share of the formalized business community in the public policy area, reducing the cost of doing business, increasing the attractiveness of formal business, and balancing the use of incentives and restrictions. The core activities include a national information campaign on the importance of legalization of the shadow economy, the introduction of the formal business registration service, an inventory of legal acts to decrease state regulation, and measures to fight corruption with a focus on public authorities. Most of the measures proposed in this plan were not implemented.

The National Strategy for Sustainable Development of the Kyrgyz Republic for 2013–2017 describes the informal economy (instead of the shadow economy) as a serious barrier to economic growth and a phenomenon driven by the high corruption and high tax burden in the country. The necessity of measures to decrease the informal economy was declared in the program (GKR, 2013). The national state body responsible for the decrease of the shadow economy is the Ministry of Economy and Commerce (GKR, 2016). In 2018, the National Bank declared and implemented measures to decrease the shadow economy and support the formalized economy through improved control of the flow of cash transfers and decrease of cash transactions in the economy (NBKR, 2017). According to the National Bank's opinion, a decrease of cash transactions may lead to the decrease of informal economic operations.

In 2019–2021, the Kyrgyz Government and Parliament produced the series of policy documents and decisions on the necessity of the measures to decrease the shadow economy in the country (PKR, 2019, 2020a, 2020b; GKR, 2020, 2021a). The overall tone regarding informality in the economy in the policy documents is mostly negative, although it acknowledges the importance of the shadow economy in job creation, decreasing the poverty rate in the country, and supporting SMEs. The logic of policy documents is driven primarily by the desire to increase budget revenues. The terms 'shadow economy' and 'unobserved economy' are also used interchangeably in the policy documents. It should be stressed again that there is no officially fixed definition and no difference between the 'shadow economy' and 'informal economy' in the Kyrgyz legislation.

The national long-term country development strategy outlines that it is necessary to develop a set of measures to transform and legalize the shadow sector of the economy. Most of the efforts concentrated around a better business environment guaranteeing the private capital protection and increasing non-cash transactions in the economy. The main declared goals are an improved business environment, increasing budget revenues, and private investments (GKR, 2018).

From 2017 to 2025, a number of programmatic documents were produced by the Kyrgyz Government that form public policy regarding shadow economy policy:

- Medium-term forecast of socio-economic development of the Kyrgyz Republic for 2022–2024 (MEC, 2021)
- The national development program of the Kyrgyz Republic up to 2026 (GKR, 2021a)
- Program on support and development of women's entrepreneurship in the KR for 2022–2026 (GKR, 2021b)
- National Program of the Kyrgyz Republic up to 2030 (GKR, 2025).

All four documents use the terms 'informal economy' and 'shadow economy' interchangeably. The term 'shadow economy' is used in the sections of the fiscal reform devoted to increasing the tax service's controlling role or decreasing the informal economic operations. The 'informal economy' term is used to describe its role in the labor market, including the role of women and the necessity to decrease their share in the economy. It also stresses limited access to social services and pensions due to the high share of workers, primarily women, in the informal economy. The dual approach of the state concerning the shadow economy creates tension in the business environment, as it is easily transformed into an increase in the control functions of the state apparatus. However, discussions about this in the public space are very limited. The lack of public consensus on the shadow economy leads to a contradiction between the public wealth and the private interest of businesses and employees. The need to pay taxes will reduce the profitability of the businesses and the real income of workers in the clothing sector. This gap in the policy might bring a high chance of future conflicts between the state and numerous micro-SMEs in Kyrgyzstan.

5 Conclusions and Policy Recommendations

The current business climate is favorable for the development of new jobs. Low taxes also contribute to the preservation of the populace's living level. A larger tax burden may also result in an increase in the price level. Minimal startup costs, high manufacturing process flexibility, and minimal transaction costs are further advantages for businesses. However, the drawbacks of the shadow economy include a high degree of job insecurity, a lack of incentives for workers to improve their skills, the need to have access to new technologies, difficulties meeting quality standards, and constrained investment and business expansion due to different tax regimes.

The implementation of the fairness principle for taxpayers is a compelling case against the existing state of affairs. For instance, taxpayers with the same income or capital should be taxed equally. This implies that taxes on various taxpayers should be equitable. Because of the lower tax rates, microbusinesses frequently gained from the present tax and social security system, according to observation. Such unjust taxes currently impede investment, workers' rights, and the growth of industrial sectors in Kyrgyzstan.

The complexity of tax administration is another issue with low tax rates for micro and small firms, since administrative expenses may outweigh tax revenue. Because there is a high chance of tax evasion under such circumstances, tax discipline is severely undermined, which encourages tax evasion, which becomes a widespread corporate practice and damages the state's reputation.

One of the primary goals of properly designed tax reform for Kyrgyzstan is the elimination of the shadow economy. As the main steps required for raising tax monitoring collections, ensuring that different businesses applied the same tax rates, bolstering law enforcement, and enhancing labor regulations, notably those of occupational health and safety, and sick pay.

To create comprehensive strategies to lessen the shadow economy, policymakers must, nevertheless, keep in mind to perform a cost–benefit analysis. Otherwise, the policy's advantages will be outweighed by the expenses to the government and general social welfare. One such expense is the loss of an atmosphere that encourages entrepreneurship and boosts economic expansion. Therefore, in order to promote more effective policies that benefit all stakeholders, all programs aimed at reducing the shadow sector should be supported with pertinent analysis, policy debates, and consultations.

The government should employ strategies to encourage entrepreneurs as well as to compel the economy to become less formalized. The approach of increased control requires better detection techniques in addition to a rise in penalties and consideration of risk factors. More efficient data processing and comparison, as well as collaboration between different government agencies and business parties, are examples of more effective detection techniques. The shadow economy will eventually decline as a result of stricter penalties for businesses and greater public knowledge of the new penalties.

The motivation approach for businesses is aimed primarily at reducing the difficulties for new businesses: simplification of requirements, tax incentives, and support for the development of micro-enterprises—training and consultations. This approach offers measures to support businesses operating in the shadow sector of the economy in the process of their formalization. It may include the development of direct and indirect tax regimes for sectors with a high degree of informality, voluntary disclosure of information, and amnesties. In addition, support is required for businesses operating in the formal sector of the economy by equalizing tax rates to ensure tax fairness, promoting formal employment, promoting mutual training of business circles, and promoting tax justice.

References

Abdih, Y., & Medina, L. (2013). *Measuring the informal economy in the caucasus and Central Asia*. IMF Working Paper Series WP/13/137. Retrieved August 11, 2025, from https://www.imf.org/external/pubs/ft/wp/2013/wp13137.pdf

Akimkanov, R. (2014). Уровень Теневой Экономики в Кыргызстане. Reforma, *2*(62), 32–37. Retrieved August 11, 2025, from https://dergipark.org.tr/en/pub/reforma/issue/40502/533305

Balabushko, O., Gyulumyan, G., Dubashov, B., Vujovic, D., & Burns, L. (2024). *Review of the tax system in the Kyrgyz Republic (English)*. World Bank Group. Retrieved August 11, 2025, from http://documents.worldbank.org/curated/en/099060624221026206

Feige, E. (2016). Reflections on the meaning and measurement of unobserved economies: What do we really know about the "Shadow Economy"? *Journal of Tax Administration, 2*(1). Retrieved August 11, 2025, from https://jota.website/jota/article/view/136

Feige, E., & Urban, I. (2008). *Measuring underground (unobserved, non-observed, unrecorded) economies in transition countries: Can we trust GDP?* William Davidson Institute Working Paper # 913. Retrieved August 11, 2025, from https://deepblue.lib.umich.edu/handle/2027.42/64384

GKR. (2004). *Law of the Kyrgyz Republic "On the rates of insurance contributions for state social insurance"*. No. 8 of 24 January 2004.

GKR. (2013). *National strategy for sustainable development of the Kyrgyz Republic for 2013–2017*. Approved by the Decree of the President of the Kyrgyz Republic of 21 January, 2013, No. 11, Retrieved August 11, 2025, from https://cbd.minjust.gov.kg/61542/edition/473771/ru

GKR. (2016). Budget Code of the Kyrgyz Republic. 16 May, 2016, No. 59, Retrieved August 11, 2025, from https://cbd.minjust.gov.kg/111338/edition/7319/ru

GKR. (2018). *National strategy of the development of Kyrgyz Republic on 2018–2040.* Retrieved August 11, 2025, from https://www.gov.kg/ru/programs/8

GKR. (2020). *Decree of the government of the KR on main directions of the fiscal policy of the KR for 2021–2023.* 14 Sept 2020. No. 483.

GKR. (2021a). *National development program of the Kyrgyz Republic up to 2026.* Approved by the Decree of the President of the Kyrgyz Republic. 12 October 2021. No. 435. http://cbd.minjust.gov.kg/act/view/ru-ru/430700

GKR. (2021b). *Program on support and development of women's entrepreneurship in the KR for 2022–2026.* November 17, 2021. No. 270. Retrieved August 11, 2025, from http://cbd.minjust.gov.kg/act/view/ru-ru/158749

GKR. (2022). *Tax code of the Kyrgyz Republic*, No. 3 of 18 January 2022.

GKR. (2025). National Program of the Kyrgyz Republic up to 2030, approved by the Decree of the President of the Kyrgyz Republic. 5 June 2025. UP No. 178. Retrieved August 11, 2025, from https://www.gov.kg/files/news/froala/dd08061311362a4faa610d681b49a92ae4f73a55.pdf

ILO. (2015). International Labour Conference. Recommendation 204, concerning the transition from the informal to the formal economy. *Geneva, 12 June 2015.* Retrieved August 11, 2025, from https://www.ilo.org/sites/default/files/wcmsp5/groups/public/@ed_norm/@relconf/documents/meetingdocument/wcms_377774.pdf

Lackó, M. (2000). Hidden economy—An unknown quantity? Comparative analysis of hidden economies in transition countries. 1989–95. *Economics of Transition, 8*(1), 117–149. https://doi.org/10.1111/1468-0351.00038

Medina, L., & Schneider, F. (2017). Shadow economies around the world: New results for 158 countries over 1991–2015. *CESifo Working Paper* No.

6430. Retrieved August 11, 2025, from https://www.ifo.de/DocDL/cesifo1_wp6430.pdf

MEC. (2006). *Order of the ministry "On approval of the plan on measures to legalize the shadow economy in the KR for 2007–2010" of 9 October*, 2007, No. 153.

MEC. (2021). *Socioeconomic development forecast of the Kyrgyz Republic on 2022–2024*. Approved by the Decree of the Cabinet of the Ministers of the Kyrgyz Republic. 28 June 2021. No. 47, Retrieved August 11, 2025, from https://mineconom.gov.kg/froala/uploads/file/c02fbcb4e76a3190a4a304eea1f08ab0902ad9f4.pdf

NBKR. (2017). *Resolution of the board of the NBKR on main directions of development of the payment system of the KR for 2018–2022*. No. 2017-ПІ-14-51-7-(ПС). Retrieved August 11, 2025, from https://nbkr.kg/DOC/26122017/000000000048958.pdf

NSC. (2015). *Employment and unemployment. Results of the integrated survey of the households' budget and labour force in 2014*. https://stat.gov.kg/

NSC. (2024a). *Non-observed (hidden and informal) economy in Kyrgyzstan in 2006–2023*. Retrieved August 11, 2025, from https://stat.gov.kg/en/statistics/download/dynamic/855/

NSC. (2024b). *Employment and unemployment. Results of the integrated survey of the households' budget and labour force in 2023*. https://stat.gov.kg/

NSC. (2024c). *National Accounts of the Kyrgyz Republic in 2019–2023*. https://stat.gov.kg/

Putniņš, T., & Sauka A. (2019). Shadow Economy Index for Russia 2017–2018: Comparison with the size of the shadow economies in Ukraine, Kyrgyzstan, Kosovo, Moldova, Romania, Latvia, Lithuania, Estonia, and Poland. *The Centre of Sustainable Business at SSE Riga*. Retrieved August 11, 2025, from https://www.sseriga.edu/sites/default/files/2020-01/Shadow%20Economy%20Index%20for%20Russia%202018%20FINAL.pdf

PKR. (2019). *Resolution of the Jogorku Kenesh of the KR on the Budget Resolution of the KR for 2020 and the forecast for 2021–2022*. 16 May 2019. No. 3057-VI

PKR. (2020a). *Resolution of the Jogorku Kenesh of the KR On measures to reduce negative socio-economic consequences in connection with currency inflation and the spread of coronavirus infection COVID-19*. 1 April 2020. No. 3659-VI

PKR. (2020b). *Resolution of the Jogorku Kenesh of the KR on the Budget Resolution of the KR for 2021*.10 June 2020. No. 3822-VI

Schneider, F. (2012). The shadow economy and work in the shadow: What do we (not) know? *IZA Discussion Paper*, No. 6423. Retrieved August 11, 2025, from https://www.iza.org/publications/dp/6423/the-shadow-economy-and-work-in-the-shadow-what-do-we-not-know

Schneider, F., & Williams, C. (2013). *The shadow economy.* The Institute of Economic Affairs. Retrieved August 11, 2025, from https://iea.org.uk/wp-content/uploads/2016/07/IEA%20Shadow%20Economy%20web%20rev%207.6.13.pdf

SIAR. (2019). *Shadow economy index for Kyrgyzstan. SHADOW: An exploration of the nature ofinformal economies and shadow practices in the former USSR region.* SIAR research and consulting.

UNDP. (2006). *The shadow economy in the Kyrgyz Republic: Trends, estimates and policy options.* https://doi.org/10.13140/RG.2.1.4648.0087

UNECE. (2008). *Non-observed economy in national accounts. Survey of country practices.* Retrieved August 11, 2025, from https://digitallibrary.un.org/record/630778?v=pdf

World Bank. (2025a). *Economic overview of Kyrgyz Republic.* Retrieved August 11, 2025, from https://www.worldbank.org/en/country/kyrgyzrepublic/overview#3

World Bank. (2025b). *World development indicators.* DataBank. Retrieved August 11, 2025, from https://databank.worldbank.org/source/world-development-indicators

CHAPTER 6

The Effect of Shadow Economy, Public Debt, and Energy Efficiency Measures on Ecological Quality in Türkiye

Mustafa Kızıltan and Ahmet Burçin Yereli

1 Introduction

The World Health Organization (WHO) reports that 9 out of 10 people worldwide are exposed to polluted air, and that approximately 7 million deaths occur annually due to pollution-related health issues. Notably, 90% of these deaths are concentrated in low and middle-income countries (WHO, 2018). As a developing country, Türkiye is profoundly affected by these challenges. Türkiye is in a critical situation regarding environmental pollution, as highlighted in the Guardian newspaper's headline: "*8 out of 10 most polluted cities in Europe are in Turkey*" (Health and Environment Alliance [HEAL], 2017). This alarming level of pollution contributes

M. Kızıltan (✉) · A. B. Yereli
Faculty of Economics and Administrative Sciences, Department of Public Finance, Hacettepe University, Beytepe, Ankara, Türkiye
e-mail: mustafa.kiziltan@hacettepe.edu.tr

A. B. Yereli
e-mail: aby@hacettepe.edu.tr

E. Bagirzadeh and O. Gokcekus (eds.), *Shadow Economies in Turkic Republics*, https://doi.org/10.1007/978-3-032-12872-0_6

to mortality in Turkey. It is argued that a reduction in pollution could prevent many of these deaths (Varol et al., 2021). Furthermore, the control and health costs resulting from environmental pollution also lead to significant fiscal burdens for Türkiye, which faces resource limitations (Ara Aksoy et al., 2021).

Additionally, Elgin et al. (2021) estimated that the shadow economy in Türkiye accounted for approximately 30% of the official gross domestic product (GDP) between 1990 and 2020. Both pollution and the shadow economy are global challenges, as the existence of shadow economic activities enables firms to evade environmental regulations (Huynh, 2020). In Türkiye, where the shadow economy is a significant issue, environmental pollution is also a major concern. In this regard, Türkiye is taking various measures aimed at reducing both the shadow economy and environmental pollution. Some measures aimed at reducing environmental pollution are implemented through command-and-control instruments. Additionally, fiscal policy tools, such as environmental taxes, incentives, public spending on pollution control, and regulatory frameworks, are also examined. The intersection of the shadow economy, fiscal policy, and environmental pollution has been explored in several studies (Huynh, 2020). For instance, Dada et al. (2022) assessed the impact of the shadow economy on carbon emissions in West African countries, controlling for institutional factors. Their findings indicate that countries with stronger institutional frameworks are more successful in combating environmental pollution. Moreover, they recommend the use of fiscal policy instruments alongside institutional regulations to mitigate environmentally harmful activities. Similarly, Ahmad and Hussian (2024) conducted an analysis on a larger sample of 127 developing countries between 2002 and 2018, taking corruption into account. They concluded that corruption exacerbates the environmental impact of the shadow economy.

The primary aim of this study is to examine how economic factors, beyond the shadow economy and fiscal policy, have influenced environmental quality in Türkiye between 1990 and 2020. In this study, we first provide a brief economic profile of Türkiye and attempt to descriptively analyze the impact of Türkiye's ongoing economic transformation process on environmental quality. We then examine the scope of the shadow economy in Türkiye and analyze its evolution over time. Additionally, we highlight the government's commitment to promoting a more transparent economy and present the strategic steps taken to address this issue. Finally, we present our research, which measures the impact of the shadow economy and other various factors on environmental quality, while emphasizing the importance of sustainability.

2 Türkiye: Economic and Institutional Profile

The brief/main economic and institutional profile of Türkiye is presented in Table 1. An examination of Table 1 reveals that Türkiye's population increased from 56,015,628 in 1990 to 83,384,680 in 2020, representing a growth of approximately 48.85% over the three-decade period. During the same period, the industrial sector's share in GDP averaged around 27.96%. The lowest share of industry was recorded in 2009 at 24.02%, while the highest was in 1994 at 32.08%. The services sector held the largest share throughout the period, with an average of approximately 52%. In contrast, the agricultural sector accounted for an average share of 10.09%; although occasional minor increases were observed, its overall trend was downward, reaching a relatively low level of 6.67% in 2020. The share of trade in GDP increased from around 30% to approximately 63%. While GDP grew by 251.73% over the same period, per capita GDP rose by 136.29%. When these figures are considered collectively, it becomes evident that Türkiye has undergone a significant economic transformation, accompanied by a substantial population increase and accelerating urbanization. Along with the decrease in the added value of agriculture, urbanization has also accelerated during the analysis period. While 59.20% of the total population lived in cities in 1990, this proportion increased by 28.56%, reaching 76.11% in 2020. It is almost impossible for this economic transformation process not to impact energy use and environmental quality. From these perspectives, the subject requires thorough examination and also represents a highly interesting area of study.

Dynamic processes such as structural changes in the economy, increasing urbanization, and the expansion of the service sector have further complicated the situation in the shadow economy. In this context, examining the evolution of the shadow economy in Türkiye, along with the estimation methods employed in this area, is of critical importance for attaining a more comprehensive understanding of the country's economic transformation.

Table 1 Türkiye's economic and institutional profile between 1990–2020 (based on the World Bank database)

Variable	*Mean*	*Min*	*Max*
Population (total)	69,452,363.06	56,015,628	83,384,680
Industrial Value Added (% of GDP)	27.96	24.02	32.08
Services Value Added (% of GDP)	52.72	48.05	57.16
Agriculture, forestry, and fishing, value added (% of GDP)	10.09	5.79	17.48
Trade (% of GDP)	47.46	30.48	63.19
Urban population (% of total population)	67.82	59.20	76.11
Unemployment, total (% of total labor force) (national estimate)	9.71	6.50	14.03
GDP (constant 2015 US$)	571,254,621,606.57	288,739,518,672.102	1,015,597,272,884.83
GDP Per Capita (constant 2015 US$)	7964.802	5101.207	12,179.66

Source The World Bank (2024b)

3 Shadow Economy in Türkiye: Trends and Estimations

The shadow economy is presented in two ways by Elgin et al. (2021). The Dynamic General Equilibrium (DGE) model is an extremely comprehensive estimation method, both in terms of the countries covered and the time horizon. The MIMIC model, on the other hand, provides a robust estimation in accounting for the underlying causes of the shadow economy (Elgin et al., 2021). Various studies have examined the shadow economy and its influencing factors in Türkiye, resulting in an extensive body of literature on the subject. Notable works focusing specifically on Türkiye include those by Yereli et al. (2007), Karanfil and Ozkaya (2007), Schneider and Savasan (2007), Karanfil (2008), Elveren and Özgür (2016), Bayar and Aytemiz (2017), Ikiz (2017), and Köksal et al. (2020). The main motivation behind the studies in this field is the fact that informality has remained a significant issue in Türkiye, as a developing country, despite the measures taken over many years.

Table 2 descriptively presents the shadow economy in Türkiye for the period 1990–2020. During the analysis period, the shadow economy in Türkiye is estimated at 30.73% of GDP according to DGE estimates and 31.80% of GDP according to MIMIC estimates. Elgin et al.'s (2021) Informal Income Database (World Bank Group) includes 156 countries for the DGE estimates and 158 countries for the MIMIC estimates. According to our calculations for 54 high-income countries in the World Bank income classification (The World Bank, n.d.), based on data from Elgin et al. (2021), the shadow economy in these high-income countries is on average 21.85% in the DGE estimate and 23.14% in the MIMIC estimate for the same period. According to the income classification, Türkiye is categorized as an upper-middle-income country, and informality in Türkiye is considered a significant issue, with rates of 30.73% and 31.80% according to the DGE and MIMIC estimates, respectively, which are notably higher compared to those in high-income countries (Figs. 1 and 2).

Table 2 Shadow Economy of Türkiye—Size (absolute (in $); percent of GDP; relative to formal economy; change over time-trend line, etc.)

Variable	*Mean*	*Min*	*Max*
Dynamic general equilibrium model-based (DGE) estimates of informal output (% of official GDP) (1990–2020)	30.73	24.17	38.45
Multiple indicators multiple causes model-based (MIMIC) estimates of informal output (% of official GDP) (1993–2020)	31.80	30.44	33.06

Source Elgin et al. (2021)

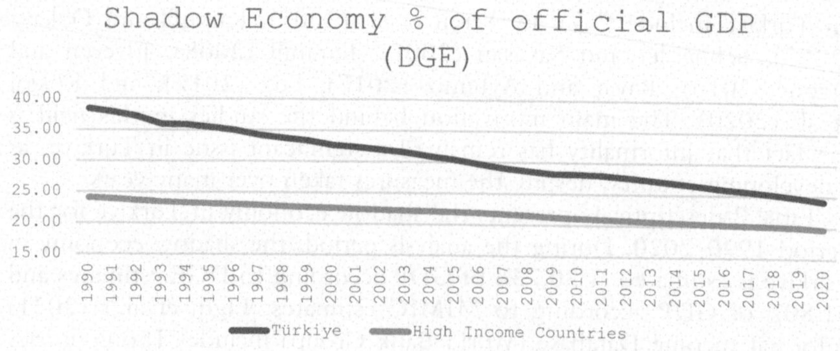

Fig. 1 Shadow economy of Türkiye and high income countries % of official GDP (DGE) (*Source* Authors' calculation based on Elgin et al. [2021])

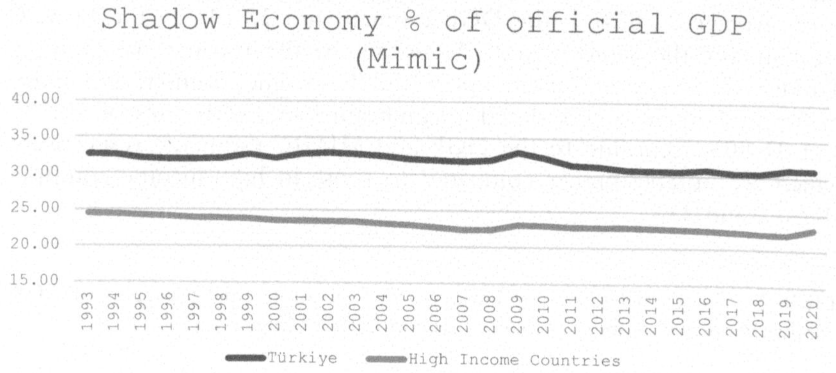

Fig. 2 Shadow economy of Türkiye and high income countries % of official GDP (MIMIC) (*Source* Authors' calculation based on Elgin et al. [2021])

4 Policies and Institutional Responses to Informality

An analysis of Figs. 1 and 2 shows that the informality in Türkiye has decreased for both estimates. The primary reason for this is believed to be related to the economic development of the country, as discussed in the first section. In this section, examples of measures to combat informality in Türkiye are summarized in Table 3. In addition to economic developments, these strong institutional efforts are also considered to have contributed to the decline in informality.

To mitigate the potential environmental impacts of informality, even in the European Union, the need to formalize the informal sector to comply with environmental regulations and use more environmentally friendly technologies is emphasized. It is recommended to develop fiscal mechanisms to encourage this. It is stated that reducing informality will have a positive impact on the environment (Olanrewaju et al., 2025). In this

Table 3 Laws, rules, and regulations regarding informal activities in Türkiye

Responses to informality	*Sources*
Action Plans for the Fight Against the Informal Economy Strategy were prepared within the Revenue Administration of the Ministry of Treasury and Finance of the Republic of Türkiye in the years 2008–2010, 2011–2013, 2015–2017, 2019–2021, 2023–2025	(Republic of Türkiye Ministry of Treasury and Finance Revenue Administration, n.d.)
In 2006, the Fight Against Unregistered Employment (KADİM) Project was launched	(Official Gazette of the Presidency of the Republic of Türkiye, 2006)
The Financial Crimes Investigation Board was established in 1996 within the Ministry of Treasury and Finance of the Republic of Türkiye with Law No. 4208 on preventing money laundering	(Republic of Türkiye Ministry of Treasury and Finance Financial Crimes Investigation Board, n.d.)
The Tenth Development Plan (2014–2018) Unregistered Economy Reduction Program Action Plan was prepared under the coordination of the Revenue Administration of the Ministry of Treasury and Finance of the Republic of Türkiye	(Republic of Türkiye Ministry of Treasury and Finance Revenue Administration, 2014)
The Revenue Administration of the Ministry of Treasury and Finance of the Republic of Türkiye was established	(Republic of Türkiye Ministry of Treasury and Finance Revenue Administration (Gelir İdaresi Başkanlığı), n.d.)
The Tax Inspection Board Presidency was established in 2011 as a service unit affiliated with the Ministry of Treasury and Finance of the Republic of Türkiye	(Republic of Türkiye Ministry of Treasury and Finance Tax Inspection Board Presidency, n.d.)
Measures to combat the informal economy are included in the Medium Term Programs	(Presidency of the Republic of Türkiye Strategy and Budget Directorate (Strateji ve Bütçe Başkanlığı), n.d.)

regard, it can be said that Türkiye still has a long way to go in addressing informality compared to high-income countries. This is considered important both to reduce the negative impact of informality on the economy and to improve the environment.

The environmental impact of fiscal policies in an economy with high informality is unclear and depends on the economic and sectoral dynamics of the country. Taking steps to prevent/reduce informality and protect the environment/reduce environmental damage are important functions of fiscal policies. Fiscal policy plays a crucial role in shaping environmental outcomes, particularly in economies where informality is high; its effects are uncertain and are driven by a country's economic and sectoral dynamics. Designing fiscal policies aimed at reducing informality can also serve as a tool to mitigate ecological degradation (Adekoya et al., 2024).

5 Environmental Implications of the Shadow Economy in Türkiye

5.1 *Background, Context and Motivation*

Studies focusing on ecological quality have attracted traction due to concerns about insufficient economic and fiscal frameworks to tackle global pollution and climate change. The UN's Sustainable Development Goals highlight Goal 7, promoting universal access to clean energy, and Goal 13, focusing on climate-related measures (United Nations Department of Economic & Social Affairs, 2025). Accordingly, academic interest in this area has also intensified as countries take steps toward these goals.

Moreover, country-specific dynamics shape ecological quality, and understanding these dynamics can significantly contribute to better environmental outcomes. Since the 1980s, Türkiye has undergone rapid industrialization and urbanization, leading to a profound economic transformation that inevitably affects the environment. This raises important questions: *Does Türkiye's economic transformation pressure environmental quality? What are the principal determinants of environmental quality?* Investigating these issues is essential for Türkiye. Therefore, this work aims to identify the key factors of ecological quality and provide policy recommendations for sustainable environmental management. Our findings will support policymakers in protecting natural ecosystems for future generations.

This subsection aims to investigate the underlying dynamics of ecological quality in Türkiye. We argue that these dynamics may have economic, fiscal, financial, and social dimensions. To observe the effects of these various dynamics, we first require a variable that accurately represents ecological quality which can be measured in different ways. However, the most widely used indicators in literature have been developed by the Global Footprint Network (2025). For instance, ecological deficit is the gap between a country's biocapacity and ecological footprint. An ecological deficit arises when the ecological footprint exceeds the biocapacity. The biocapacity-to-ecological footprint ratio, the *load capacity factor* (LCF), is the most effective indicator of ecological quality, according to Siche et al. (2010). The ratio below 1 indicates that existing policies are ecologically unsustainable, whereas a ratio above 1 suggests the country can sustainably support its population's lifestyle. This balance is essential for meeting present needs while preserving natural ecosystems for future generations, highlighting the importance of ecological sustainability for a thriving society.

Adebayo and Samour (2024) argue that the LCF is a superior indicator of carbon emissions and ecological footprint, as it allows for considering the environment from both supply and demand perspectives. Similarly, Guloglu et al. (2023) argue that carbon emissions and ecological footprint only reflect the demand side of nature and do not consider the supply side of nature-related issues. From this point of view, the LCF provides a more comprehensive (supply-demand) analysis, making it a better indicator for addressing issues related to the Sustainable Development Goals.

The Republic of Türkiye's Ministry of Development outlines its national environmental vision in the "Sustainable Management of Environment and Natural Resources Working Group Report (Republic of Türkiye Ministry of Development, 2018)" part of the "Eleventh Development Plan (2019–2023)." This report emphasizes the vision advocating for a structured and regionally balanced approach to sustainable resource management to ensure ecological integrity across the country as "*A Türkiye that protects the environment and natural resources, uses resources efficiently, adopts ecosystem-based approaches grounded in innovation and technological developments, utilizes a sustainable development approach, and develops in a human-centered, climate- and environmentally-friendly manner.*" This definition presents a vision addressing nature's supply and demand sides and proposes policies to achieve these goals. The corresponding report aims to establish a low-carbon development model, demonstrate national and sectoral potential in sustainable development, develop environmental research, development and innovation strategies, enhance an effective waste management system, and present national strategies and plans. In this regard, our study will also contribute to developing policy recommendations for sustainable environmental management.

The ecological situation of Türkiye is presented in Fig. 3. Examining Fig. 3 reveals that while there were ecological reserves previously, both in per capita terms (Fig. 3a) and in global hectares (Fig. 3b), an ecological deficit began to emerge after 1984. The LCF was above one before 1984 but fell below one starting from that year. Throughout the analysis period, the average LCF is 0.5914. It reached its highest value of 0.8210 in 1991, whereas the lowest value of 0.4406 was observed in 2017. In summary, economic policies observed particularly since 1984 have created an ecologically unsustainable situation, which has progressively worsened. Türkiye has been in an environmentally unsustainable situation regarding the LCF and ecological deficit indicators between 1990 and 2020, which was chosen as our study period. Investigating the factors influencing this situation is thus of considerable interest.

Extensive research has identified the key factors influencing the LCF in Türkiye, focusing on various influencing factors. However, a research gap exists concerning the impression of the shadow economy and rising public debt as fiscal variables on ecological sustainability. The shadow economy can undermine sustainable practices, while increased public debt may restrict government investment in ecological initiatives. Our study intends to fill this gap by examining how these factors interact and affect ecological sustainability in Türkiye, providing insights for policymakers to enhance environmental strategies.

This subsection addresses the association between fiscal, economic, and financial variables and their influence on ecological sustainability in Türkiye. It includes a literature review, data and methodology, estimation results with discussions, and concludes with actionable policy recommendations.

5.2 *Literature Review on Shadow Economy and Ecological Quality*

Ecological quality should be examined from a multidimensional perspective. Incorporating economic, fiscal, and financial dynamics that influence ecological quality into the analytical framework is essential. The literature

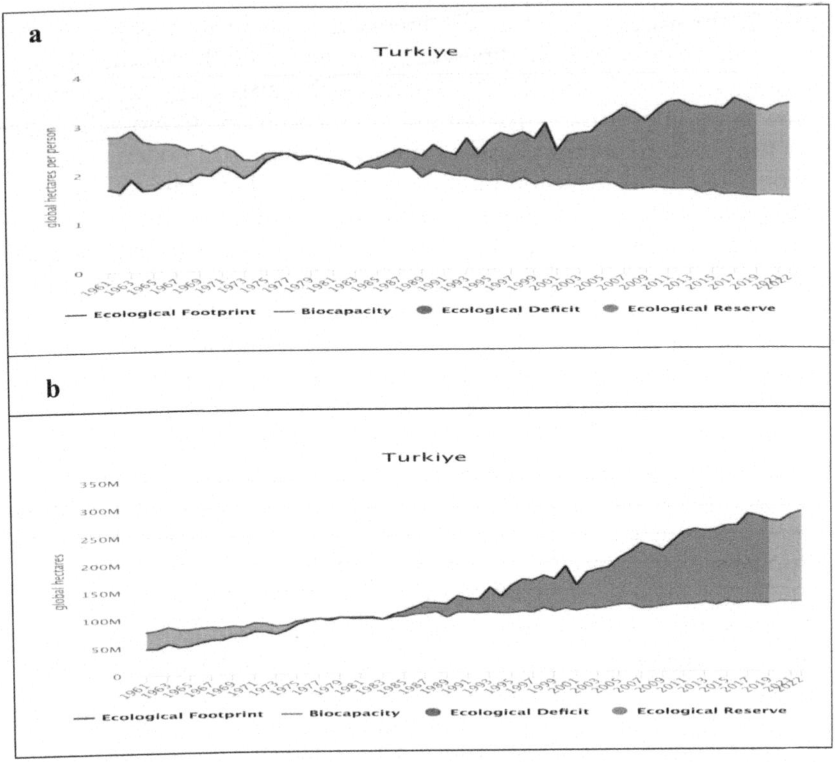

Fig. 3 Ecological situation of Türkiye (1961–2022). (**a**) Türkiye's ecological footprint, biocapacity and ecological deficit in global hectares per person. (**b**) Türkiye's ecological footprint, biocapacity, and ecological deficit in global hectares (*Source* Global Footprint Network [2025])

includes studies investigating ecological quality from different angles and about multiple determinants.

One of the key variables we focus on is the shadow economy, which is considered an important determinant of ecological quality and is therefore specifically included in our analysis. By definition, the shadow economy, also referred to as the informal or underground economy, encompasses economic activities conducted outside formal government regulations. This issue is particularly significant in developing countries and is frequently addressed in the literature. For an in-depth examination of the perspectives of different economic schools on the shadow economy, see Dell'Anno (2022). Stuart et al. (2018) also describe the shadow economy as the "*new normal,*" especially in developing countries. The shadow economy is also closely linked to fiscal policy, especially regarding budget deficits and public expenditures. For example, Vo et al. (2023), who analyzed the influence of public spending and budget deficits on the shadow economy, highlighted a significant link between increased government spending and the growth of the shadow economy, indicating that higher expenditures often lead to more informal economic activities. On the other hand, an investigation of the impact of the shadow economy and corruption on public debt at the regional level in Spain between 2000 and 2012 indicated that higher levels of shadow economy lead to boosted public debt (González-Fernández & González-Velasco, 2014). While corruption perceptions also positively affect public debt, their impact is smaller than that of the shadow economy. An enormous shadow economy contributes to rising public debt through the need for additional public interventions and fiscal policies.

Elgin and Öztunalı (2014b) examine that the shadow economy has an inverse effect on environmental pollution. In other words, environmental pollution is low at low levels of shadow economy activity, peaks at moderate levels, and declines again when it reaches a high level. For the United States, it is explored that the force of fiscal policies on carbon emissions, distinguishing between consumption and production-based sources of emissions (Halkos & Paizanos, 2016). Their findings imply that increased public spending reduces both consumption and production-related emissions, while budget deficit policy increases consumption-related emissions.

Yang et al. (2024) analyze BRICS countries from 1990–2018. Although their study did not specifically aim to assess the validity of the LCF Curve, they observed that globalization and the growth of gross domestic products deteriorate ecological quality. They recommend the implementation of a sustainable energy transition to improve ecological outcomes. In another analysis conducted for BRICS countries, Adebayo and Samour (2024) investigated the impacts of fiscal policies on the LCF between 1990 and 2018 using panel data analysis techniques and second-generation unit root tests. Their estimation results show that the most significant contributors to the deterioration of environmental quality are increased public expenditures, economic expansion, and fossil energy.

They emphasize that fiscal policies should support investment in renewable energy sources to improve ecological quality. The effects of various factors on the LCF have also been examined for OECD countries. Human capital and adopting renewable energy meaningfully enhance, whereas urbanization contributes to degradation (Guloglu et al., 2023). Another study focusing on OECD countries analyzed the effects of the insurance market. The MMQR results exhibit that the insurance sector negatively impacts ecological quality due to its stimulation of economic activity (Pata & Samour, 2023).

Pata and Isik (2021) examined the LCF in China and revealed that human capital is the only variable among those considered that improves environmental quality. Ahmed et al. (2022) analyzed Brazil, a rich country in natural resources, and found a U-shaped link between income and biocapacity, suggesting economic growth begins to have a positive effect on the environment after surpassing a certain threshold, evidence of the U-shaped pattern. According to their findings, rapid urbanization is Brazil's most significant cause of biocapacity loss. In a study of South Korea's economic transformation, the transformation's impact on the LCF was assessed; the results of this study indicate that economic growth, structural change, renewable energy consumption, and trade openness positively affect ecological improvement (Abdulmagid Basheer Agila et al., 2022). In the case of Poland, an analysis was carried out to identify the determinants of the LCF and greenhouse gas emissions. The results confirm that economic growth and fossil fuel consumption have reduced the LCF. But technological innovation, the presence of forested areas, globalization, and the use of renewable energy positively affect the LCF (Raihan et al., 2024).

Yan et al. (2024) investigated the relationship between the LCF and different variables as part of Germany's environmental sustainability goals. Using the wavelet coherence method with quarterly data from 1990 to 2020, their findings argue that efficient energy use, switching to energy sources, will improve environmental quality in the short and medium-term. In a recent study, Ali et al. (2025) examined the effects of nuclear energy, financialization, and public debt on ecological quality in France, using the LCF factor as an indicator. Employing the Augmented ARDL model, their results reveal that nuclear energy and renewable energy use enhance ecological quality, whereas an increase in public debt leads to environmental degradation.

For France, it has been argued that a shift to cleaner energy is critical for achieving ecological sustainability, and that environmentally friendly projects should be supported through public financial instruments. Pata and Samour (2022) focused on nuclear energy, an important variable for France, using Fourier-based co-integration and causality tests. Their findings show that nuclear energy reduces emissions, thereby increasing the LCF. Degirmenci et al. (2025) analyzed the long-run effects of different indicators on the LCF and ecological footprint of the United States. Their results demonstrate that preferring low carbon levels in energy use and investing in R&D of new energy technologies positively contribute to environmental quality.

Our study investigates the impact of economic, fiscal, financial, and social variables on ecological quality in Türkiye. Examining ecological quality will contribute to the sustainable management of the environment in Türkiye. To the best of our knowledge, there is no existing study that simultaneously considers ecological quality, the shadow economy, public debt, and energy efficiency measures for Türkiye. In the existing studies, for example, Karanfil and Ozkaya (2007) tried to estimate shadow and formal economy in Türkiye using environmental variables. Elgin and Öztunalı (2014a) analyzed the relationship between environmental pollution indicators and the shadow economy in Türkiye using annual data from 1950–2009. Their results suggest that the moderate level of shadow economy leads to high pollution levels in the long run. A study investigating the ecological footprint's impact on the shadow economy in Türkiye reveals that the shadow economy plays a significant role in contributing to long-term environmental pollution (Köksal et al., 2020). In another study, Pata and Balsalobre-Lorente (2022) examined the effects of the tourism sector and energy consumption, two important components of the Turkish economy, on the LCF from 1965 to 2017. Their findings indicate that these variables did not affect the LCF. They assert that the most powerful influence on the LCF stems from the dynamics of economic growth. Yavuz et al. (2023) examined the relationship between unemployment and environmental quality in Türkiye within the Environmental Phillips Curve (EPC) framework for 1982–2022. Their findings support the validity of the EPC for Türkiye and indicate that unemployment contributes to environmental degradation. They recommend that governments develop policies promoting renewable energy sources as a policy implication. Examining the effects of financialization, life expectancy at birth, and hydroelectric energy use on the LCF in Türkiye, Yurtkuran and Güneysu (2023) observed that financialization and hydroelectric energy use improve environmental quality.

Unlike previous studies, Dam and Sarkodie (2023) used the inverted version of the LCF as an indicator of environmental quality to examine the Turkish economy between 1965 and 2018. They determined a link between income and the inverted LCF, concluding that Türkiye has not reached high-income levels regarding long-term environmental sustainability. Thus, they recommend taking circular economy measures. Pata et al. (2024) conducted a quantile regression analysis for Türkiye, India, Brazil, and South Africa over the period 1985–2018, exploring the impacts of energy security and geopolitical risks. Their findings indicate that such risks harm environmental quality, and they emphasize that renewable energy sources should be preferred in case risks increase.

5.3 *Methodology and Data*

Using time series data for Türkiye from 1990 to 2020, we perform an empirical analysis to examine the effects of the shadow economy, public debt growth rate, energy efficiency measures, financialization, gross domestic product per capita growth, and unemployment rate on the LCF. The mathematical functional form of the empirical model and its econometric specification are presented below as Eqs. (1) and (2), respectively.

$$\ln \text{lcf} = \text{f}\left(\text{sha, debtgr, enereff, fin, gdppcapgr, unemp}\right) \tag{1}$$

$$\begin{aligned} \ln \text{lcf}_t = {} & \alpha_0 + \alpha_1 \text{sha}_t + \alpha_2 \text{debtgr}_t + \alpha_3 \text{enereff}_t + \alpha_4 \text{fin}_t \\ & + \alpha_5 \text{gdppcapgr}_t + \alpha_6 \text{unemp}_t + \varepsilon_t \end{aligned} \tag{2}$$

Here, α_0 denotes the constant term, ε_t represents the error term, t indicates the period (1990–2020), and $\alpha_1 - \alpha_6$ capture the impacts of the independent variables on the LCF. Descriptive statistics for the variables are presented in Table 4, while the pairwise correlation matrix is provided in Table 5.

The dependent variable used in this study is the LCF (lnlcf), calculated as the ratio of per capita biocapacity to per capita ecological footprint. In addition, the natural logarithm of the variable is taken to express the changes in percentage terms. The shadow economy variable (sha)

Table 4 Descriptive statistics

Variable abbreviation	*Measurement*	*Sources*	*Mean*	*Std. Dev*	*Min*	*Max*
lnlcf	Log of Biocapacity (gha per person) / Ecological Footprint (gha per person)	(Global Footprint Network, 2025)	−0.5443087	0.1977317	−0.8195215	−0.1972023
sha	Relative size of the shadow economy (% GDP)	(Elgin et al., 2021)	30.73475	4.190562	24.16651	38.4483
debtgr	Gross public debt per cent of GDP (% annual growth)	(IMF, n.d.-a)	0.0168377	0.1641116	−0.2294917	0.4713787
fin	Private credit by deposit money banks (% of GDP)	(The World Bank, 2024a)	33.7167	19.91466	14.01065	70.92025
gdppcapgr	GDP per capita growth (annual %)	(The World Bank, 2024b)	3.1408	4.462787	−6.915473	9.579864
unemp	Unemployment (% of total population)	(IMF, n.d.-b)	9.119355	1.99356	6	13.7
enereff	Per capita GDP / Per capita energy consumption (kg of oil equivalent)	(The World Bank, 2024b)	6.014064	0.4835734	5.424545	6.912366

Table 5 Pairwise correlations of the variables

	lnlcf	*sha*	*unemp*	*gdppcapgr*	*debtgr*	*fin*	*enereff*
lnlcf	1.0000						
sha	0.9695	1.0000					
unemp	−0.6534	−0.7543	1.0000				
gdppcapgr	−0.1621	−0.0365	−0.1410	1.0000			
debtgr	0.1951	0.0599	0.0064	−0.8639	1.0000		
fin	−0.8660	−0.8567	0.6658	0.0677	−0.0628	1.0000	
enereff	−0.7748	−0.8044	0.6796	0.0960	−0.0918	0.9008	1.0000

is obtained from the (World Bank Group, n.d.). Elgin et al. (2021) estimate the shadow economy as a percentage of GDP based on the Dynamic General Equilibrium (DGE) model. The shadow economy variable obtained in this way is referred to as the relative value of the shadow economy in the literature (Nguyen, 2022). The analysis period of the study is 1990–2020, as the shadow economy data covers these years. During the analysis period, the average size of it in Türkiye was approximately 30.73% of GDP.

Elgin (2021) emphasizes that the level of environmental pollution relies on the strict implementation of government restrictions, highlighting that the shadow economy should not be neglected in environmental policy analyses. Elgin (2021) states that a larger shadow economy is expected to cause worse ecological quality. However, since the shadow economy is often concentrated in small enterprises and labor-intensive sectors with low capital intensity, a larger shadow economy can also exhibit better environmental performance. The opposite is also true. In other words, a smaller shadow economy can also cause greater environmental pollution. This is an indirect effect because the sectors where the shadow economy is concentrated are labor-intensive. Elgin and Öztunalı (2014b) describe the inverse relationship between the shadow economy and environmental pollution as the scale effect, while the linear relationship is called the deregulation effect. Our study initially considered the effect as uncertain, which aligns with these findings.

The support of fiscal policies for the green shift is of great importance today, when climate change is on the agenda (Wang & Li, 2024). In this context, another explanatory variable in our study is the growth rate of gross public debt to GDP (*debtgr*). This is because the increase in public debt increases economic activity, which in turn causes an increase in energy demand. Expansionary fiscal policies involving increased public spending can increase energy consumption and demand, thereby increasing emissions and causing ecological impacts (Adebayo & Samour, 2024; Halkos & Paizanos, 2016). For this purpose, the debt variable used in the study was obtained from the (IMF, n.d.-a), and we calculated the annual increases in gross public debt. During the analysis period, the average annual public debt ratio in Türkiye was 39.61%. It was at its lowest level of 25.78% in 1990, rising to a peak of 75.51% in 2001 due to the economic crisis.

Türkiye has been implementing energy efficiency measures and enacting various public regulations for many years to achieve the sustainable and efficient use of natural resources (Akcollu Oguz et al., 2015; Official Gazette of the President of the Republic of Türkiye, 2007; Republic of Türkiye Ministry of Development, 2018). For an assessment of the outcomes of these measures and regulations, see (Kiziltan, 2021). To examine the impact of energy efficiency measures on environmental quality, the energy efficiency variable (*enereff*) was added to the model as a proxy variable, as in Özkan et al. (2024). This variable is calculated by dividing per capita GDP (constant 2015 US$) by per capita energy consumption (kg of oil equivalent). This variable is expected to indicate whether Türkiye has been successful in its energy efficiency measures. Since energy efficiency measures aim to reduce carbon emissions, this variable is presupposed to impact the LCF positively and, consequently, on ecological quality. Data for per capita income and per capita energy consumption used for this variable are obtained from the World Bank (2024b).

Apart from these main explanatory variables, the first control variable used in our model is financialization. The ratio of private credit by deposit banks to GDP is used as an indicator of financialization (*fin*). This ratio is obtained from the World Bank (2024a). According to the report "*Global Financial Development Report 2019/2020: Bank Regulation and Supervision a Decade after the Global Financial Crisis*," the data on credit provided by deposit banks is divided by GDP. The other control variables are per capita GDP growth rate (*gdppcapgr*) and the unemployment rate (*unemp*). During the analyzed period, the average per capita income in Türkiye was 7,964.802 USD. The lowest level was observed in 1991 at 5,101.207 USD, while the peak value during the analyzed period was recorded in 2020 at 12,179.66 USD. The per capita GDP growth rate represents economic growth. Unemployment exists to examine the validity of the Environmental Phillips Curve for Türkiye as in Yavuz et al. (2023).

5.4 *Results and Discussion*

Since the pairwise correlation table indicated high correlations for some variables, we performed the VIF test to examine whether our model has multicollinearity, as presented in Table 6. The mean VIF value and the individual VIF values for all variables are below 10, which indicates that our model does not have multicollinearity.

Before model estimation, the time series characteristics of the variables were analyzed by the Augmented Dickey-Fuller (ADF) (Dickey & Fuller, 1979) and Phillips-Perron (PP) tests (Phillips & Perron, 1988), with optimal lag lengths determined by the Schwarz Information Criterion (SIC). In line with the literature, variables are used without log or growth transformations solely for performing unit roots tests. The results, summarized in Table 7, cover both level and first-difference models with specifications for a constant and a constant plus trend. These findings support that all variables are stationary at the first difference, meeting the co-integration requirement. Specifically, the financialization indicator is significant at the 5% level, while all other variables are significant at the 1% level in all deterministic forms. At the level, the LCF is insignificant in the constant model for both tests, but becomes significant at the 5% level in the constant and trend model. The unemployment rate is insignificant in all deterministic forms for the Phillips-Perron test, but significant at the 10% level in the ADF test for the constant and trend model. All other variables are insignificant at the level.

Table 6 VIF Results

Variables	*VIF*
Fin	7.28
Debtgr	4.40
Gdppcapgr	4.76
Sha	4.93
Enereff	5.81
Unemp	2.92
Mean VIF	5.02

Table 7 Unit Root Tests

		ADF		*PP*	
Parameters	*Deterministic*	*At level*	*At first difference*	*At level*	*At first difference*
Lcfpcap	Constant	−1.4416 *0.5487*	−6.0370 *0.0000****	−1.4416 *0.5487*	−9.3190 *0.0000****
	Constant and Trend	−3.6891 *0.0388***	−6.5605 *0.0000****	−3.6476 *0.0424***	−10.7174 *0.0000****
Fin	Constant	1.0291 *0.9958*	−3.5870 *0.0125***	0.8163 *0.9927*	−3.5870 *0.0125***
	Constant and Trend	−1.3162 *0.8643*	−3.9495 *0.0225***	−1.3788 *0.8466*	−3.8874 *0.0258***
Gdppcap	Constant	0.8484 *0.9932*	−4.6795 *0.0008****	0.8446 *0.9932*	−4.6824 *0.0008****
	Constant and Trend	−1.9253 *0.6166*	−4.7758 *0.0033****	−1.9459 *0.6060*	−4.7607 *0.0035****
Sha	Constant	−1.9586 *0.3025*	−4.7581 *0.0007****	−2.8385 *0.0649**	−4.7337 *0.0007****
	Constant and Trend	−2.2703 *0.4363*	−5.1492 *0.0014****	−2.2484 *0.4475*	−5.2709 *0.0010****
Enereff	Constant	−0.5405 0.8694	−5.1435 0.0002***	−0.4589 0.8860	−5.2026 0.0002***
	Constant and Trend	−2.2062 0.4693	−5.2159 0.0012***	−2.1726 0.4868	−6.6765 0.0000***
Unemp	Constant	−1.0492 *0.7222*	−4.8815 *0.0005****	−0.8542 *0.7886*	−6.7553 *0.0000****
	Constant and Trend	−3.2967 *0.0867**	−4.8558 *0.0028****	−1.9807 *0.5878*	−8.3157 *0.0000****
Debt / GDP	Constant	−1.6211 *0.4598*	−4.6595 *0.0009****	−1.8177 *0.3651*	−4.7247 *0.0007****
	Constant and Trend	−2.4021 *0.3706*	−4.6019 *0.0051****	−1.8859 *0.6368*	−4.5938 *0.0052****

To specify the model, it is also necessary to determine whether there is a long-run relationship among the variables. For this, the model should have a co-integration relationship. The investigation of the co-integration relationship began with the selection of the optimal lag length, which shows the effect of a change in the past period on the long-term performance. The appropriate lag length is determined based on the SIC and is consistent with the unit root tests. According to the results, the SIC is 15.61565 at 0 lags, 9.466551 at 1 lag, and 10.61128 at 2 lags. Schwarz's information criterion shows that the optimal lag length should be 1.

Table 8 Roots of the characteristic polynomial

Root	*Modulus*
0.995059	0.995059
0.896584	0.896584
0.636373	0.636373
0.231342 − 0.461931i	0.516623
0.231342 + 0.461931i	0.516623
0.078543	0.078543
−0.011471	0.011471

Therefore, lag length 1 has been selected as the optimal lag order. Table 8 presents the Roots of the Characteristic Polynomials, while Fig. 4 shows the Inverse Roots of the Characteristic Polynomials. Based on these, none of the polynomial roots lie outside the unit circle, and all modulus values are less than 1. This indicates that the model is stable.

Table 9 highlights the results of the Johansen co-integration rank test. It shows three co-integrating equations for trace statistics and two for maximum eigenvalue statistics, both significant at the 5% level (Johansen & Juselius, 1990). These results confirm a long-run relationship between the LCF and the explanatory variables, allowing for estimating a long-run model.

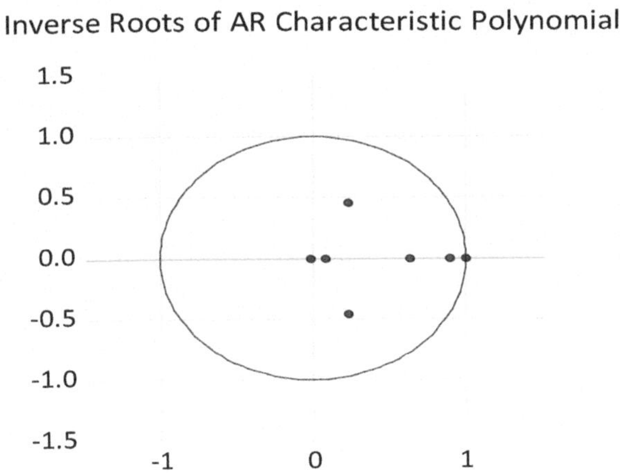

Fig. 4 Inverse roots of the characteristic polynomial

Table 9 Johansen co-integration rank test

Unrestricted Co-integration Rank Test (Trace)				
Hypothesis	*Eigenvalue*	*Trace Statistic*	*0.05*	*Prob.***
R = 0*	0.918572	195.6874	125.6154	0.0000
R = 1*	0.823293	122.9543	95.75366	0.0002
R = 2*	0.667311	72.68970	69.81889	0.0290
R = 3	0.492666	40.77382	47.85613	0.1960
R = 4	0.335069	21.09481	29.79707	0.3518
Unrestricted Co-integration Rank Test (Max-eigenvalue)				
Hypothesis	*Eigenvalue*	*Max-Eigen Statistic*	*0.05*	*Prob.***
R = 0*	0.918572	72.73307	46.23142	0.0000
R = 1*	0.823293	50.26459	40.07757	0.0026
R = 2	0.667311	31.91588	33.87687	0.0842
R = 3	0.492666	19.67901	27.58434	0.3637
R = 4	0.335069	11.83411	21.13162	0.5641

Note *Denotes rejection of the hypothesis at the 0.05 level. **MacKinnon-Haug-Michelis (1999) p-values

The long-run model estimation results are demonstrated in Table 10 for both the FMOLS and CCR estimators, the latter being used as a robustness check. According to the shadow economy estimates, a 1% increase in the shadow economy increases the LCF by 0.047% for FMOLS and 0.046% for CCR. An increase in the LCF indicates a widening gap between biological capacity and ecological footprint, which implies a recovery in ecological quality. Similarly, a 1% growth in public debt increases the LCF by 0.205% according to the FMOLS estimates, and by 0.194% based on the canonical co-integration regression results. In essence, a rise in public debt improves the environment.

The variable representing energy efficiency also positively impacts environmental quality, as expected. This finding shows the success of the steps taken within Türkiye's vision for sustainable environmental management and highlights the need to maintain this vision with determination. The energy efficiency measures taken seem to be successful in ensuring sustainability. Furthermore, the unemployment variable has a positive and statistically significant effect on the LCF. This proves the validity of the Environmental Phillips Curve for Türkiye, as in Yavuz et al.

Table 10 FMOLS and CCR, estimation results—Dependent Variable: lnlcfpcap

Variables	*FMOLS*	*CCR*
Sha	0.047***	0.046***
	(0.001)	(0.001)
Unemp	0.017***	0.016***
	(0.002)	(0.002)
Gdppcapgr	0.002**	0.002
	(0.001)	(0.002)
Debtgr	0.205***	0.194***
	(0.026)	(0.041)
Fin	−0.003***	−0.003***
	(0.000)	(0.000)
Enereff	0.061***	0.060***
	(0.010)	(0.013)
Constant	−2.425***	−2.404***
	(0.071)	(0.075)
R-squared	0.975	0.976

Note Standard errors in parentheses. ***$p < 0.01$, **$p < 0.05$, *$p < 0.1$

(2023). This means that achieving a higher standard of environmental quality may come at the cost of rising unemployment, highlighting the complex trade-offs we face in our pursuit of a sustainable future. Hence, the fight against unemployment should be supported by promoting environmentally friendly production technologies.

The per capita income growth rate is statistically significant and positively impacts the FMOLS estimation, while it is insignificant in the CCR estimation. Financialization causes deterioration in environmental quality in Türkiye, according to the findings of Yurtkuran and Güneysu (2023) and Pata (2018). According to Kartal et al. (2023), the reason behind this is that increased financialization facilitates access to finance for investments, which raises energy consumption and economic activity, causing pollution. We use the share of credits in GDP as the financialization variable. Thus, we argue that easier access to credit causes higher energy consumption, which deteriorates the environment. While income growth contributes positively to environmental quality in accordance with the theory, credit access creates pollution and thus reduces the LCF.

6 Policy Recommendations

The findings of this study provide valuable insights into the determinants of the LCF in Türkiye. Our results indicate that the shadow economy, increasing public debt, increasing per capita income, energy efficiency measures, and unemployment positively affect the LCF. In contrast, financialization and access to credit negatively impact the LCF and environmental quality. Our results allow us to draw the following conclusions:

i. Our findings regarding the shadow economy contradict the approach of Dada et al. (2023), who argue that it worsens the environmental quality in African countries. According to their study, shadow economic activities in Africa are harmful to the environment because they are carried out using non-environmentally friendly technologies. In contrast, our findings align with Elgin (2021) and Elgin and Öztunalı (2014b), showing a strong positive link between the shadow economy and environmental indicators in Türkiye, as well as a correlation between the shadow economy's size and environmental variables. Put differently, there is a linear relationship between the shadow economy and the LCF, which is the result of the deregulation effect as argued by Elgin (2021). In Türkiye, the shadow economy is concentrated mainly in labor-intensive sectors and does not harm the quality of the environment in Türkiye as it does in African countries. Therefore, pollution levels are low due to the widespread shadow economy in these labor-intensive sectors. If shadow economy activities were more concentrated in industrial sectors in Türkiye, a rise in pollution and a negative impact on the LCF would be expected. However, this has not been the case in Türkiye.

ii. The finding that a rise in public debt remediates environmental quality can be explained by the approach of Halkos and Paizanos (2016). According to them, the policy that causes budget deficits and finances these deficits can be due to decreased taxes. Such a decrease in taxes causes an increase in emissions and therefore a reduction in the LCF. This can be exemplified by easing environmental regulations by reducing fuel taxes, causing increased vehicle usage and higher emissions. For this reason, if a budget deficit policy needs to be followed for various economic and fiscal purposes, it is recommended by Halkos and Paizanos (2016) to follow a policy of increasing expenditures rather than implementing a policy of reducing emission taxes, taking emissions into account. The fact that the increase in public debt during the period of analysis in Türkiye increases the LCF creates the impression that Türkiye has followed spending-based budget deficit policies. A similar conclusion was reached by Yousaf et al. (2022) in China. They discover that public spending has a negative effect on the ecological footprint, meaning that higher public expenditures lead to a reduction in it and thus improve environmental quality. Similarly, according to our study results, the increase in public debt increases the LCF.

iii. Our findings regarding energy efficiency indicate that Türkiye, as a developing country, can achieve significant gains through energy efficiency measures. It is emphasized that enhancing energy efficiency initiatives and rising renewable energy consumption are the two most critical solutions for reducing emissions and combating climate change. Efficient use of resources and clean energy can assist in reducing greenhouse gas emissions (Özbuğday & Erbas, 2015). Akram et al. (2020) propose several policy recommendations for reducing carbon emissions in developing countries. They suggest that fiscal and monetary policies that stimulate the economy should be environmentally oriented. They highlight the potential benefits of energy efficiency policies and projects to be implemented in developing countries undergoing industrialization and consuming high amounts of energy. Moreover, it is argued that as incomes rise, both energy efficiency and environmental awareness must be supported by strict environmental standards.

iv. It has been found that income growth has a positive effect. This result has also been demonstrated for Türkiye by Dam and Sarkodie (2023). Pata (2018), examining the structural breaks, income level, and pollution in Türkiye, showed that Türkiye has not yet reached the income threshold necessary to reduce pollution. Similarly, Yurtkuran and Güneysu (2023) confirmed the validity of the LCF *Curve* for Türkiye. Consistent with this hypothesis, when income exceeds a specific point, the LCF is expected to increase and pollution to decrease. Since our study focuses on the effect of income growth, not income level, the finding that income growth positively impacts environmental quality is natural and expected from our perspective.

v. We find that financialization contributes to environmental degradation. As a precaution against this, in Türkiye, the government recommends that the financial sector take steps to provide loans to projects that provide renewable energy and energy efficiency. Within this context, the "*Green Deal Action Plan 2021*" was prepared by the Republic of Türkiye's Ministry of Trade (2021). Within the framework of this action plan, steps were taken toward green finance with the aim of "*identifying steps that can be taken about the national financing system in line with the financing needs of the green transformation and developing an ecosystem that will enable the development of green financing in our country.*" We believe these steps should be continued to alleviate the negative impacts of financialization on the environment. Indeed, energy efficiency and transformation are also highly prioritized during Türkiye's Twelfth Development Plan (2024–2028). Significant targets and policies have been established concerning energy efficiency and energy supply security (Republic of Türkiye Presidency of Strategy and Budget, 2023).

7 Conclusion

This work is motivated by the need to analyze the variables affecting LCF in Türkiye. For this purpose, the FMOLS and CCR estimators were used to analyze the period from 1990 to 2020. Addressing the shadow economy from a sustainability viewpoint is crucial to understanding the relationship between the shadow economy and the problems in developing countries. Considering different aspects, efforts to formalize economic activities provide important advantages for decision makers. Climate change and the exhaustion of natural resources can have undesirable economic impacts and lead to negative fiscal impacts, undermining fiscal sustainability. Hence, sustainable environmental management and preservation of environmental quality must also be monitored from a fiscal perspective (Catalano et al., 2020). Ensuring environmental sustainability, continuing with energy efficiency measures, and ensuring the green transformation of economic activities from the perspective of environmental sustainability and climate change will also prevent government interventions that will be more costly in the future. Fiscal policies and measures will be used in a very active way in the green transition (Wang & Li, 2024). We believe our study can guide policymakers in other developing countries with similar characteristics regarding the necessary actions to be taken in this way.

References

Abdulmagid Basheer Agila, T., Khalifa, W. M. S., Saint Akadiri, S., Adebayo, T. S., & Altuntaş, M. (2022). Determinants of load capacity factor in South Korea: Does structural change matter? *Environmental Science and Pollution Research, 29*(46), 69932–69948. https://doi.org/10.1007/S11356-022-20676-2/FIGURES/1

Adebayo, T. S., & Samour, A. (2024). Renewable energy, fiscal policy and load capacity factor in BRICS countries: novel findings from the panel nonlinear ARDL model. *Environment, Development and Sustainability, 26*(2). https://doi.org/10.1007/s10668-022-02888-1

Adekoya, O. B., Daniel, O. O., Ogunbowale, G. O., & Al-Faryan, M. A. S. (2024). Unregulated economic activities and the environment: The role of fiscal policies. *Journal of Environmental Management, 349*, Article 119533. https://doi.org/10.1016/j.jenvman.2023.119533

Ahmad, W., & Hussain, B. (2024). Shadow economy and environmental pollution nexus in developing countries: What is the role of corruption? *International Economic Journal, 38*(2), 293–311. https://doi.org/10.1080/10168737.2024.2331463

Ahmed, Z., Le, H. P., & Shahzad, S. J. H. (2022). Toward environmental sustainability: How do urbanization, economic growth, and industrialization affect biocapacity in Brazil? *Environment, Development and Sustainability, 24*(10), 11676–11696. https://doi.org/10.1007/S10668-021-01915-X/TABLES/5

Akcollu Oguz, F. Y., Algedik, O., Limaye, D. R., Orucu, A. Y., & Singh, J. (2015). *Turkey - Institutional review of energy efficiency*. Washington, D.C. http://documents.worldbank.org/curated/en/725221468334280649/Turkey-Institutional-review-of-energy-efficiency

Akram, R., Chen, F., Khalid, F., Ye, Z., & Majeed, M. T. (2020). Heterogeneous effects of energy efficiency and renewable energy on carbon emissions: Evidence from developing countries. *Journal of Cleaner Production, 247*, Article 119122. https://doi.org/10.1016/J.JCLEPRO.2019.119122

Aksoy, S., Kiziltan, A., Kiziltan, M., Aydinalp Köksal, M., Öztürk, F., Tekeli, S. E., Aslanoğlu, S. Y., Im, U., Duran, N., Ünal, A., Baykara, M., Ozyurek, N., Dogan, P., Yilmaz, A. G., Koksal, C. E., Gurtepe, I. C., Yereli, A. B., … Güllü, G. (2021). Mortality and morbidity costs of road traffic-based air pollution in Turkey. *Journal of Transport & Health, 22*, 101142. https://doi.org/10.1016/J.JTH.2021.101142

Ali, M., Soomro, S. A., Bakari, H., Samour, A., & Tursoy, T. (2025). Does nuclear energy consumption contribute to load capacity factor? Modeling the effects of public debt and financial development in France. *Nuclear Engineering and Technology, 57*(6), Article 103414. https://doi.org/10.1016/J.NET.2024.103414

Bayar, Y., & Aytemiz, L. (2017). Financial development and shadow economy in Turkey. In S. Koç, A. Orhan, & M. Ç. Gözen (Eds.), *Unregistered employment* (pp. 170–175). IJOPEC Publication. http://ijopec.co.uk/assets/5-unregistered_employment.pdf#page=172

Catalano, M., Forni, L., & Pezzolla, E. (2020). Climate-change adaptation: The role of fiscal policy. *Resource and Energy Economics, 59*, Article 101111. https://doi.org/10.1016/J.RESENEECO.2019.07.005

Dada, J. T., Ajide, F. M., & Adeiza, A. (2022). Shadow economy and environmental pollution in west African countries: The role of institutions. *Global Journal of Emerging Market Economies, 14*(3), 366–389. https://doi.org/10.1177/09749101211049038

Dada, J. T., Ajide, F. M., Arnaut, M., & Adeiza, A. (2023). On the shadow economy-environmental sustainability nexus in Africa: The (ir)relevance of financial development. *International Journal of Sustainable Development and World Ecology, 30*(1), 6–20. https://doi.org/10.1080/13504509.2022.2115576

Dam, M. M., & Sarkodie, S. A. (2023). Renewable energy consumption, real income, trade openness, and inverted load capacity factor nexus in Turkiye: Revisiting the EKC hypothesis with environmental sustainability. *Sustainable Horizons, 8*, Article 100063. https://doi.org/10.1016/J.HORIZ.2023.100063

Degirmenci, T., Bozatli, O., Aydin, M., & Balsalobre-Lorente, D. (2025). Is energy security the missing piece of the environmental puzzle? Fresh evidence from load capacity factor and ecological footprint indicators. *Gondwana Research, 139*, 221–229. https://doi.org/10.1016/J.GR.2024.11.015

Dell'Anno, R. (2022). Theories and definitions of the informal economy: A survey. *Journal of Economic Surveys, 36*(5), 1610–1643. https://doi.org/10.1111/JOES.12487

Dickey, D. A., & Fuller, W. A. (1979). Distribution of the estimators for autoregressive time series with a unit root. *Journal of the American Statistical*

Association, 74(366), 427–431. https://doi.org/10.1080/01621459.1979.10482531

Elgin, C. (2021). *The informal economy measures, causes, and consequences*. Routledge. https://www.routledge.com/The-Informal-Economy-Measures-Causes-and-Consequences/Elgin/p/book/9780367522155

Elgin, C., Kose, M. A., Ohnsorge, F., & Yu, S. (2021). *Understanding Informality* (CERP Discussion Paper 16497). Centre for Economic Policy Research, London.

Elgin, C., & Öztunalı, O. (2014a). Environmental Kuznets curve for the informal sector of Turkey. *Panoeconomicus, 4*, 471–485. https://doi.org/10.2298/PAN1404471E

Elgin, C., & Öztunalı, O. (2014b). Pollution and informal economy. *Economic Systems, 38*(3), 333–349. https://doi.org/10.1016/J.ECOSYS.2013.11.002

Elveren, A. Y., & Özgür, G. (2016). The effect of informal economy on income inequality: Evidence from Turkey. *Panoeconomicus, 63*(3), 293–312. https://doi.org/10.2298/PAN1603293E

Global Footprint Network. (2025). *Home - Global Footprint Network*. Retrieved 26 May 2025, from https://www.footprintnetwork.org/

González-Fernández, M., & González-Velasco, C. (2014). Shadow economy, corruption and public debt in Spain. *Journal of Policy Modeling, 36*(6), 1101–1117. https://doi.org/10.1016/J.JPOLMOD.2014.10.001

Guloglu, B., Emre Caglar, A., & Korkut Pata, U. (2023). Analyzing the load capacity factor determinants in OECD countries: Evidence from advanced quantile panel data methods. *Gondwana Research, 118*, 92–104. https://doi.org/10.1016/J.GR.2023.02.013

Halkos, G. E., & Paizanos, E. A. (2016). The effects of fiscal policy on CO2 emissions: Evidence from the U.S.A. *Energy Policy, 88*, 317–328. https://doi.org/10.1016/J.ENPOL.2015.10.035

Health and Environment Alliance (HEAL). (2017). *HEAL in Turkey: 8 out of 10 most polluted cities in Europe are in Turkey*. Health and Environment Alliance. Retrieved 25 July 2025, from https://www.env-health.org/heal-in-turkey-8-out-of-10-most-polluted-cities-in-europe-are-in-turkey/

Huynh, C. M. (2020). Shadow economy and air pollution in developing Asia: What is the role of fiscal policy? *Environmental Economics and Policy Studies, 22*(3), 357–381. https://doi.org/10.1007/S10018-019-00260-8/TABLES/8

Ikiz, A. S. (2017). Shadow economy and economic growth in Turkey. In M. Bilgin, H. Danis, E. Demir, & U. Can (Eds.), *Regional studies on economic growth, financial economics and management. Eurasian studies in business and economics* (Vol. 7, pp. 269–278). Springer. https://doi.org/10.1007/978-3-319-54112-9_17

IMF. (n.d.-a). *Public Finances in Modern History Database*. Retrieved 17 May 2025, from https://www.imf.org/external/datamapper/datasets/FPP

IMF. (n.d.-b). *World Economic Outlook Database*, April 2025 Edition. Retrieved 4 June 2025, from https://www.imf.org/en/Publications/WEO/weo-database/2025/april

Johansen, S., & Juselius, K. (1990). Maximum likelihood estimation and inference on cointegration - With applications to the demand for money. *Oxford Bulletin of Economics and Statistics, 52*(2), 169–210. https://doi.org/10.1111/J.1468-0084.1990.MP52002003.X

Karanfil, F. (2008). Energy consumption and economic growth revisited: Does the size of unrecorded economy matter? *Energy Policy, 36*(8), 3029–3035. https://doi.org/10.1016/j.enpol.2008.04.002

Karanfil, F., & Ozkaya, A. (2007). Estimation of real GDP and unrecorded economy in Turkey based on environmental data. *Energy Policy*, 4902–4908. https://doi.org/10.1016/j.enpol.2007.04.012

Kartal, M. T., Pata, U. K., Destek, M. A., & Caglar, A. E. (2023). Environmental effect of clean energy research and development investments: Evidence from Japan by using load capacity factor. *Journal of Cleaner Production, 416*, Article 137972. https://doi.org/10.1016/J.JCLEPRO.2023.137972

Kiziltan, M. (2021). Water-energy nexus of Turkey's municipalities: Evidence from spatial panel data analysis. *Energy, 226*, Article 120347. https://doi.org/10.1016/J.ENERGY.2021.120347

Köksal, C., Işik, M., & Katircioğlu, S. (2020). The role of shadow economies in ecological footprint quality: Empirical evidence from Turkey. *Environmental Science and Pollution Research, 27*(12), 13457–13466. https://doi.org/10.1007/S11356-020-07956-5/FIGURES/2

Nguyen, C. P. (2022). Does economic complexity matter for the shadow economy? *Economic Analysis and Policy, 73*, 210–227. https://doi.org/10.1016/J.EAP.2021.12.001

Official Gazette of the Presidential of Republic of Turkey. *Energy Efficiency Law* (in Turkish), Pub. L. No. 5627 (2007). Turkey: 26510. https://www.resmigazete.gov.tr/eskiler/2007/05/20070502-2.htm

Official Gazette of the Presidential of Republic of Turkey. *Fight Against Unregistered Employment (KADİM) Project* (Kayıt Dışı İstihdamla Mücadele (KADİM) Projesi) (in Turkish), Pub. L. No. Circular 2006/28 (2006). https://www.resmigazete.gov.tr/eskiler/2006/10/20061004-13.htm

Olanrewaju, V. O., Uzun, B., Özkan, O., & Adebayo, T. S. (2025). Unveiling the environmental impact of total energy-based shadow economy in high-income EU countries. *Sustainable Futures, 9*, Article 100577. https://doi.org/10.1016/J.SFTR.2025.100577

Özbuğday, F. C., & Erbas, B. C. (2015). How effective are energy efficiency and renewable energy in curbing CO2 emissions in the long run? A heterogeneous panel data analysis. *Energy, 82*, 734–745. https://doi.org/10.1016/J.ENERGY.2015.01.084

Özkan, O., Saleem, F., & Sharif, A. (2024). Evaluating the impact of technological innovation and energy efficiency on load capacity factor: Empirical analysis of India. *Environmental Science and Pollution Research International, 31*(4), 5610–5624. https://doi.org/10.1007/S11356-023-31233-W/METRICS

Pata, U. K. (2018). Renewable energy consumption, urbanization, financial development, income and CO2 emissions in Turkey: Testing EKC hypothesis with structural breaks. *Journal of Cleaner Production, 187*, 770–779. https://doi.org/10.1016/J.JCLEPRO.2018.03.236

Pata, U. K., & Balsalobre-Lorente, D. (2022). Exploring the impact of tourism and energy consumption on the load capacity factor in Turkey: A novel dynamic ARDL approach. *Environmental Science and Pollution Research, 29*(9), 13491–13503. https://doi.org/10.1007/S11356-021-16675-4/FIGURES/1

Pata, U. K., & Isik, C. (2021). Determinants of the load capacity factor in China: A novel dynamic ARDL approach for ecological footprint accounting. *Resources Policy, 74*, Article 102313. https://doi.org/10.1016/J.RESOURPOL.2021.102313

Pata, U. K., Kartal, M. T., Mukhtarov, S., & Magazzino, C. (2024). Do energy and geopolitical risks influence environmental quality? A quantile-based load capacity factor assessment for fragile countries. *Energy Strategy Reviews, 53*, Article 101430. https://doi.org/10.1016/J.ESR.2024.101430

Pata, U. K., & Samour, A. (2022). Do renewable and nuclear energy enhance environmental quality in France? A new EKC approach with the load capacity factor. *Progress in Nuclear Energy, 149*, Article 104249. https://doi.org/10.1016/J.PNUCENE.2022.104249

Pata, U. K., & Samour, A. (2023). Assessing the role of the insurance market and renewable energy in the load capacity factor of OECD countries. *Environmental Science and Pollution Research, 30*(16), 48604–48616. https://doi.org/10.1007/S11356-023-25747-6/FIGURES/2

Phillips, P. C. B., & Perron, P. (1988). Testing for a unit root in time series regression. *Biometrika, 75*(2), 335–346. https://doi.org/10.1093/BIOMET/75.2.335

Presidency of the Republic of Turkey Strategy and Budget Directorate (Strateji ve Bütçe Başkanlığı). (n.d.). *Medium Term Programs*. Retrieved 12 January 2025, from https://www.sbb.gov.tr/orta-vadeli-programlar/

Raihan, A., Voumik, L. C., Zimon, G., Sadowska, B., Rashid, M., & Akter, S. (2024). Prioritising sustainability: How economic growth, energy use, forest area, and globalization impact on greenhouse gas emissions and load capacity in Poland? *International Journal of Sustainable Energy,*

43(1). https://doi.org/10.1080/14786451.2024.2361410;PAGE:STRING:ARTICLE/CHAPTER

Republic of Turkey Ministry of Treasury and Finance Revenue Administration. (2014). *Tenth Development Plan (2014–2018) Action Plan for the Reduction of Unregistered Economy Program* (in Turkish). Retrieved 22 February 2025, from https://www.sbb.gov.tr/wp-content/uploads/2018/10/9Kayitdisi_Ekonominin_Azaltilmasi_Programi.pdf

Republic of Turkey Ministry of Treasury and Finance Revenue Administration (Gelir İdaresi Başkanlığı). (n.d.). *Republic of Turkey Ministry of Treasury and Finance Revenue Administration* (Gelir İdaresi Başkanlığı). Retrieved 16 January 2025, from https://www.gib.gov.tr/

Republic of Turkey Presidency of Strategy and Budget. (2023). *Twelfth Development Plan (2024–2028) Energy Efficiency and Security of Supply Specialist Commission Report (in Turkish).* Ankara. https://www.sbb.gov.tr/wp-content/uploads/2025/06/Enerji-Verimliligi-ve-Arz-Guvenligi-Ozel-Ihtisas-Komisyonu-Raporu.pdf

Republic of Turkiye Ministry of Development. (2018). *Republic of Turkiye Ministry of Development Eleventh Development Plan (2019–2023) Sustainable Management of Environment and Natural Resources Working Group Report (in Turkish).* Ankara. https://www.sbb.gov.tr/wp-content/uploads/2020/04/Cevre_ve_DogalKaynaklarinSurdurulebilirYonetimiCalismaGrubuRaporu.pdf

Republic of Turkiye Ministry of Trade. (2021). *Green Deal Action Plan 2021* (Yeşil Mutabakat Eylem Planı 2021) (in Turkish). Ankara. Retrieved from https://ticaret.gov.tr/data/60f1200013b876eb28421b23/MUTABAKATYEŞİL.pdf

Republic of Türkiye Ministry of Treasury and Finance Financial Crimes Investigation Board. (n.d.). *Republic of Türkiye Ministry of Treasury and Finance Financial Crimes Investigation Board.* Retrieved 26 February 2025, from https://masak.hmb.gov.tr/gorev-ve-yetkiler

Republic of Türkiye Ministry of Treasury and Finance Revenue Administration. (n.d.). *Transition to Formal Economy* (Kayıtlı Ekonomiye Geçiş) (in Turkish). Retrieved 26 February 2025, from http://kayitliekonomiyegecis.gov.tr/tr/eylem-plani

Republic of Türkiye Ministry of Treasury and Finance Tax Inspection Board Presidency. (n.d.). *Republic of Türkiye Ministry of Treasury and Finance Tax Inspection Board Presidency.* Retrieved 26 June 2025, from https://vdk.hmb.gov.tr/

Schneider, F., & Savasan, F. (2007). Dymimic estimates of the size of shadow economies of turkey and of her neighbouring countries. *International Research Journal of Finance and Economics* (9), 126–143. http://www.eurojournals.com/finance.htm

Siche, R., Pereira, L., Agostinho, F., & Ortega, E. (2010). Convergence of ecological footprint and emergy analysis as a sustainability indicator of countries: Peru as case study. *Communications in Nonlinear Science and Numerical Simulation, 15*(10), 3182–3192. https://doi.org/10.1016/J.CNSNS.2009.10.027

Stuart, E., Samman, E., & Hunt, A. (2018). *Informal is the new normal Improving the lives of workers at risk of being left behind*. London. https://media.odi.org/documents/11993.pdf

The World Bank. (2024a). *Global Financial Development Database (GFDD)*. Retrieved 8 October 2024, from https://www.worldbank.org/en/publication/gfdr/gfdr-2016/data/global-financial-development-database

The World Bank. (2024b). *World Development Indicators (WDI)*. Retrieved 8 October 2024, from https://data.worldbank.org/indicator

The World Bank. (n.d.). *WDI - The World by Income and Region*. Retrieved 29 March 2025, from https://datatopics.worldbank.org/world-development-indicators/the-world-by-income-and-region.html

United Nations Department of Economic and Social Affairs. (2025). *THE 17 GOALS*. Sustainable Development. Retrieved 31 May 2025, from https://sdgs.un.org/goals

Varol, G., Tokuç, B., Ozkaya, S., & Çağlayan, Ç. (2021). Air quality and preventable deaths in Tekirdağ, Turkey. *Air Quality, Atmosphere and Health, 14*(6), 843–853. https://doi.org/10.1007/S11869-021-00983-2/TABLES/3

Vo, D. H., Tran, N. P., Tran, T. P. K., Le, Q. T. T., & Nguyen, P. V. (2023). Government expenditure, budget deficit and shadow economy. *Journal of Economic Policy Reform, 26*(4), 442–460. https://doi.org/10.1080/17487870.2023.2268250

Wang, R., & Li, S. (2024). Research on the influence mechanism of fiscal and tax policy on green economic transition: From the perspective of industrial structure conduction effect. *Environment, Development and Sustainability, 26*, 16129–16148. https://doi.org/10.1007/s10668-023-03290-1

World Health Organization (WHO). (2018). *9 out of 10 people worldwide breathe polluted air, but more countries are taking action*. Retrieved 26 July 2025, from https://www.who.int/news-room/detail/02-05-2018-9-out-of-10-people-worldwide-breathe-polluted-air-but-more-countries-are-taking-action

Yang, M., Magazzino, C., Awosusi, A. A., & Abdulloev, N. (2024). Determinants of Load capacity factor in BRICS countries: A panel data analysis. *Natural Resources Forum, 48*(2), 525–548. https://doi.org/10.1111/1477-8947.12331

Yan, Y., Khan, K. A., Adebayo, T. S., & Olanrewaju, V. O. (2024). Unveiling energy efficiency and renewable electricity's role in achieving sustainable development goals 7 and 13 policies. *International Journal of Sustainable*

Development and World Ecology, 31(5), 497–522. https://doi.org/10.1080/13504509.2023.2300006

Yavuz, E., Kilic, E., & Caglar, A. E. (2023). A new hypothesis for the unemployment-environment dilemma: Is the environmental Phillips curve valid in the framework of load capacity factor in Turkiye? *Environment, Development and Sustainability, 26*(11), 29475–29492. https://doi.org/10.1007/S10668-023-04258-X/FIGURES/2

Yereli, A. B., Seçilmiş, İE., & Başaran, A. (2007). Shadow economy and public debt sustainability in Turkey. *Economic Annals, 52*(173), 85–104. https://doi.org/10.2298/EKA0773085B

Yousaf, U. S., Ali, F., Syed, S. H., Aziz, B., & Sarwar, S. (2022). Exploring environment sensitivity to fiscal and monetary policies in China: Using ecological footprints as a contemporary proxy. *Environmental Science and Pollution Research, 29*(24), 36412–36425. https://doi.org/10.1007/S11356-021-18085-Y/TABLES/8

Yurtkuran, S., & Güneysu, Y. (2023). Financial inclusion and environmental pollution in Türkiye: Fresh evidence from load capacity curve using AARDL method. *Environmental Science and Pollution Research 2023, 30*(47), 104450–104463. https://doi.org/10.1007/S11356-023-29766-1

CHAPTER 7

Shadow Economy of a Nation in Shadows: The Case of TRNC

Tufan Ekici and Mustafa Besim

1 Introduction

Studies that focus on informal economies are controversial due to the very nature of the topic. Calculating the size of something that cannot be properly measured is bound to be problematic. Academics have made significant progress on this topic and have used various methods to measure it and offer evidence-based policy recommendations. This task is even more difficult when the economy in question belongs to an informal (de-facto) nation which is not recognized internationally and cannot be influenced by international regulations.

Turkish Republic of Northern Cyprus (TRNC) is a breakaway state that was established in 1983. Since then, this republic has operated without international recognition and is only officially recognized by

T. Ekici (✉)
Ramapo College of NJ, Mahwah, USA
e-mail: tekici@ramapo.edu

M. Besim
Eastern Mediterranean University, TRNC, Famagusta, Northern Cyprus
e-mail: mustafa.besim@emu.edu.tr

E. Bagirzadeh and O. Gokcekus (eds.), *Shadow Economies in Turkic Republics*, https://doi.org/10.1007/978-3-032-12872-0_7

Republic of Türkiye. Although the economic activities of TRNC are monitored by international institutions (such as the World Bank) and other interested parties (such as the EU and the USA), there is not any possibility of direct enforcement of regulations. Unrecognized status of the nation has been a key cause of sheer size of its shadow economy.

One main issue in this line of research is lack of consensus on the definition of shadow economy. One approach is to consider unrecorded income (or value generated) from all the economic activities that are not reflected in national accounts and controlled by the government. Another approach is to focus on the unreported income to the tax authorities which is more of a fiscal perspective. There is also another approach which concentrates only on the magnitude of illegal activities, and yet another definition focuses on the contribution of illegal or unregistered employment to the macroeconomy. Besim et al. (2013) uses a variety of definitions and obtains different estimates for the case of TRNC which we will report in detail in the following sections. However, readers of this volume should be careful when they compare the estimates of 'shadow economy' across different countries and be aware that the terms shadow economy and informal economy will be used interchangeably in this chapter.

Although economists have used a variety of quantitative methods trying to estimate the size of shadow economy (regardless of how it is defined), there is much less work on understanding the behavioural aspects of this outcome. Whether one is interested in income underreporting, involvement in illegal activities, or unregistered employment, the psychology of the participants should be of utmost importance. After all, there are many, albeit inadequate, government regulations designed to prevent participation of people in activities that will contribute to shadow economy. We then need to ask what some of the driving factors for the consumers could be when they decide to take a risk and participate in such activities. We explore in this chapter some of these issues as they pertain to TRNC.

In this chapter we talk about estimates of shadow economy in TRNC and suggest policies that can be used to reduce it. Because of lack of international recognition, official statistics are only available through TRNC's State Planning Organization (SPO). Thus, contrary to the rest of the countries in this volume, we cannot report any estimates from the World Bank but rather we will show calculations done by researchers using these official data. In the main part of the paper, we update our previous estimates of income underreporting for different employment groups and then introduce our approach in analyzing the psychology of shadow economy for our case study. Our chapter concludes with some policy recommendations to reduce the size of shadow economy in TRNC.

2 TRNC's Economic Profile

TRNC economy with 476 thousand *de jure* population has a per capita income of about 12 thousand USD that makes it to be in the upper-middle-income category according to the World Bank classifications. The output value is around 5.5 billion USD in GDP yearly (Table 1) (Statistical Institute, 2015 and State Planning Organization, 2025). TRNC economy uses Turkish Lira as a legal tender and is highly integrated with Turkish economy since Türkiye is the only country that officially recognizes this de-facto state. This makes the economy to be very much affected by the economic policies applied in Türkiye and especially the monetary policy of the Central Bank of Türkiye, i.e. instability in prices and high cost of funds. Some of the key macroeconomic indicators are presented in Table 1.

This micro-sized economy generates as much as 70% of its total value added from services sector (Table 2). Being a service-based micro-economy, TRNC has a large tourism sector and is a popular tourist destination that produced 1.7 billion USD revenues in 2023. Trade, transportation, business, and personal services are the other leading services in TRNC economy. As a developing economy, public service also plays an important role and contributes 15.5% on the average from 2019 to 2023, though declining, to the TRNC economy (Table 2). Higher education with over 60 thousand students from abroad has also been an area that contributes significantly, as much as 8% on the average, to the TRNC in the last two decades. Given the fact that it has limited natural resources and manufacturing sector, TRNC economy meets most of its final and intermediate goods from imports. This causes a huge balance of trade deficits. It is so high that import duties makes up nearly 10% of the gross domestic product (Table 2). On the other hand, revenues from tourism and other exports of services enables TRNC to finance its goods trade deficits (SPO, 2025). The current account balance of TRNC has fluctuated between surplus of 11% to deficit of 9.5% between the years of 2019–2023. There are also light manufacturing and agriculture sectors as complementary to the other sectors comprising about 13% of GDP on average from 2019–2023 (Statistical Institute, 2025).

Table 1 Basic macroeconomic indicators of TRNC, 2019–2023

Indicators	*2019*	*2020*	*2021*	*2022*	*2023*
GDP (million, TRY)	21,395	21,407	30,143	73,938	132,350
GDP (million $)	3,767	3,049	3,386	4,456	5,557
Growth (%)	0.2	−16.2	4	13.3	7.3
GDP per capita ($)	9,9.88	7,976	8,767	11,298	11,874
Inflation rate (%)	11.7	14.1	46.1	94.5	83.6
Budget deficit, % of GDP	−1.3	−5.2	−4.8	−7.0	−0.9
Bank deposits (million, $)	5,781	5,951	7,433	6,288	7,839
Bank deposits, % of GDP	1.5	2.0	2.2	1.4	1.4
Reserves (million $)	3,756	4,348	5,715	5,037	6,583
Current account balance, million $,	416.1	−289.3	−74.8	123.1	412.1
Current account balance, % of GDP	11.0	−9.5	−2.2	2.8	7.4
Incoming tourists (million)	1.7	3.8	5.5	1.4	1.8
Net Tourism revenues, million $	954	165	305	876	1,707
Labour force	147,755	147,835	136,385	147,949	156,199
Labour participation rate (%)	51.3	51.1	43.8	49.1	50.1
Employment	138,438	132,883	125,739	138,609	148,213
Employment rate (%)	48.1	45.9	40.4	46.0	48.3
Unemployment rate (%)	6.3	10.1	7.8	6.3	5.1
Population	382,230	382,836	390,745	399,727	476,214

Source TRNC Statistical Institute (2025) and TRNC State Planning Organization (2025)

In terms of its labour force, the latest household labour surveys (HLS) reports that working age population (aged 15 and above) amounted to 306 thousand, of which only around 50.1% is in the labour force (Table 1). Employment rate is reported to be 45.7% on the average for the last five years and increased to 48.4% in 2021 with the recovery from the COVID-19 pandemic (Statistical Institute, 2025). This implies that, less than half of the total population works to provide for the rest—for children and for those of working age who are unemployed and inactive. The situation is even worse for women. Employment rates for women are significantly lower than the men in the TRNC. This is because of lower participation rate and higher unemployment rate, being 38.2% and 9.6% respectively on the average for the last five years. Labour force participation rates overall are also well below the European Union average where for men it is 75% and 65% for women (Eurostat, 2022). Low labour

Table 2 Sectoral distribution of gross domestic product in TRNC

	2019	*2020*	*2021*	*2021*	*2022*	*2023*
1. Agriculture	5.5	6	8.3	8.3	6.6	5.3
2. Industry	7.8	9.6	7.5	7.5	5.4	5.6
3. Construction	5.8	9.6	7.5	7.5	5.8	6.0
4. Trade – Tourism	22.2	12.8	13.8	13.8	30.7	25.8
4.1. Wholesale and Retail Trade	10.5	10.3	10.4	10.4	11.0	11.9
4.2. Hotels and Restaurants	11.7	2.5	3.4	3.4	19.7	13.9
5. Transport and Communication	7.3	6.4	9.2	9.2	9.3	10.4
6. Financial Institutions	8	7.9	8.9	8.9	7.1	9.1
7. Ownership of Dwellings	5.2	6.3	7.3	7.3	5.0	5.7
8. Business and Personal Services	13.2	12.9	14.2	14.2	10.3	10.2
9. Public Services	16.1	19.4	15.5	15.5	11.5	12.9
10. Import Duties	9	9.1	7.8	7.8	8.3	9.0
GDP	100	100	100	100	100	100

Source: TRNC Statistical Institute (2025)

participation rate is an indication of informal employment, which does not appear in labour force statistics. This is supported by empirical findings report that informal employment is around 20% of the labour force and also the size of the shadow economy is estimated to be 29% of GDP in TRNC (Besim et al., 2015).

There is considerable number of immigrant workers which increase the possibility of informal economy in the labour market. The increase in the mobility of foreign labour force in the world and the regional developments have also affected the composition of the labour force in TRNC. Official statistics reports that there are over 55 thousand immigrant workers with work permit in TRNC (Employment Office, 2022). The same source shows that Turkish workers continue to hold the highest share (around 40 thousand workers) of foreign workers with work permits which is 68% on the average for the last three years. Work permit holders are from 120 different countries including Pakistan, Turkmenistan, Bangladesh, Kyrgyzstan, Philippines, Ukraine, Iran, Uzbekistan, Kazakhstan, and Nepal in the top ten. Foreign workers' work permit applications are for all sorts of occupations though mainly for elementary occupations that does not require many skills. In summary, TRNC labour market has high inactivity rate due to unemployment (especially among young), low participation rates, and significant informal employment. There is also the fact that a significant portion of the labour force comprises migrant workers, who tend to work informally (Besim et al., 2015; Employment Office, 2022).

Public finance, and by extension the state budget, plays a significant role in the economic development of TRNC with around 30% of GDP (Table 3). When the structure of the budget is evaluated in terms of revenues and expenditures, it becomes evident that budget revenues have consistently been insufficient to cover expenditures. This fiscal deficit has hovered at a high level, amounting to between 4 and 11% of GDP. Under the current public finance structure, only about 80% of the budget is financed through revenues, while the remaining portion is funded by domestic borrowing and loans and grants from Republic of Türkiye. This external support, which accounts for approximately 10% of the budget renders TRNC economy dependent and aid driven. As we will discuss more in detail later, such a high level of dependence on foreign aid is also likely to cause domestic policy makers to relax and thus allow more room for engagement of the public in activities that contribute to shadow economy.

The fundamental problem behind this unsustainable fiscal structure lies on two fronts:

on one hand, structural issues in the expenditure side of the budget; on the other hand, the inefficiency of the tax system due to weak policy design, legal framework, and institutional capacity. This unsustainable

Table 3 TRNC budget (2019–2023)

	2019	*2020*	*2021*	*2022*	*2023*
Budget Revenues	**31.9**	**30.5**	**25.1**	**22.6**	**25.0**
Tax Revenues	23.1	22.6	19.5	18.0	20.2
Direct taxes	11.5	11.7	9.4	7.6	8.7
Indirect taxes	15.8	15.4	13.1	13.2	14.1
Other revenues	4.6	3.3	2.6	1.7	2.2
Budget Expenditure	**35.9**	**40.6**	**34.4**	**28.1**	**29.2**
Current expenditures	14.9	17.0	14.0	10.8	12.0
Transfers	15.1	17.0	13.7	13.2	13.1
Defence	0.8	2.6	2.2	1.6	1.3
Investments	2.8	0.7	4.5	2.5	0.9
Budget balance	**−4.0**	**−10.1**	**−9.3**	**−10.5**	**−4.2**

Source: TRNC State Planning Organization (2025), https://www.devplan.org/index-en.html

structure hinders the fair taxation of generated income and leads to the implementation of tax and fee policies aimed at generating quick revenue, which in turn results in inefficient allocation of resources, distorts market conditions, and contributes to rising costs and inflation. While the share of direct taxes in GDP are low and declining, indirect taxes has performed well being around 15% of GDP. This indicates that the tax base could not be expanded to the desired extent, and revenue collection has become increasingly reliant on consumption. The insufficient taxation of individuals and corporations, along with the concentration of the tax burden on specific segments of the population, has created regressivity, contributed to the erosion of the system, and the proliferation of informality. The ratios of direct and indirect taxes to GNP are shown in Fig. 1.

In TRNC, businesses are generally small, and the economy is a service-based economy, where a large portion of economic activity is carried out by individuals or small-scale businesses. These activities in general involve transactions that require low capital, are labour intensive and involve limited documentation. Naturally, it is more difficult for the public authorities to audit and regulate such activities. All these pave the way for the formation of an unrecorded, unreported, and shadow economy.

Macroeconomic assessments concerning TRNC's economy indicate that the evolving and diversifying economic activities have not effectively

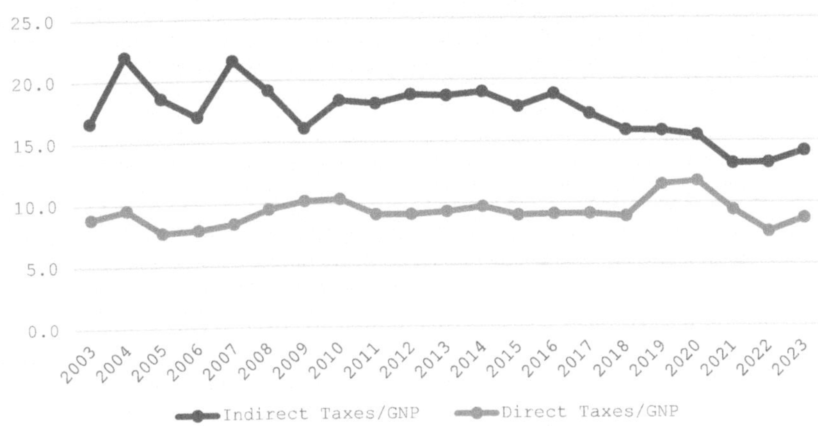

Fig. 1 Ratio of direct and indirect taxes to GNP (2003–202) (*Source*: SPO Economic and Social Indicators 1977–2023, Table 19)

been monitored by the relevant public bodies. The unsustainable nature of public finance, the widening deficit in the social security system, indicators of untapped tax potential, and employment data all point to the persistence of a shadow economy in the country. All this combined with the internationally unrecognized status of the country and its dependence on foreign aid make it an interesting case study for this topic. We talk about the research that estimates the size of shadow economy in TRNC in the next section.

3 A Brief History of TRNC's Shadow Economy

TRNC's shadow economy is a hotly discussed topic among domestic circles but a data-driven analysis on this topic is scarce. Besim et al. (2013) includes the most comprehensive calculation of the size of informal economy in TRNC using multiple methods and we will present a summary of their findings in this section. We also introduce some of our recent estimates of different aspects of informal economy in the next section.

Table 4 below shows the size of shadow economy in TRNC that was calculated by Besim et al (2013) using different methodologies. The details of the methodologies can be obtained from the cited references. The first set of methods calculates the amount of unrecorded national income that is generated through legal means. This amount should be used to adjust official GNP statistics. There are several different ways for this kind of unrecorded income to be generated such as through unregistered employment, unreported household income, and other indirect (monetary) approaches. The final method in this set includes MIMIC approach that is also consistent with the World Bank's calculation for other countries.

The second set of methods focus on unrecorded tax base and calculates the value of economy that should have been taxed by the governments. One way is to compare the salaries reported directly by the employees and the salaries actually recorded by the tax and social security authorities. This should not be a consideration for a developed country where there is full compliance by the employers, but in TRNC it is widely known that many of the private sector employees earn salaries more than what is actually reported to the tax authorities (usually legal minimum wages). These methods revealed that, during 2001–2011 period, the lost income for the fiscal authorities as a result of legally earned but unreported income

Table 4 Size of shadow economy in TRNC

Methods	*Period*	*Ratio of Shadow Economy to GNP*
Unregistered Employment	2006 & 2011	9.1% & 13.6%
Unreported National Income	2008	8.6%
Monetary Methods:	2001–2011	23.2%
Fixed Ratio Method	2001–2011	42%
Currency Ratio Method	2001–2011	24.9%
Tanzi Econometric Method		
Energy Method	1977–2011	24.6%
MIMIC	1990–2011	30.5%

Source: Besim et. al (2013)

in TRNC ranged between 50–60% of official GNP. Such high levels of unrecorded income also have serious implications for the social security system of the country.

Another approach to calculating the size of shadow economy is to look at the value added generated by informal employment. Informal employment includes those who are working in the informal sector, illegal immigrants, workers in formal sector but not registered to social security system, and those who hold a second job. Besim (2003) calculates the ratio of income generated by informal employment to GNP for 1996 and 2000, respectively, as 17.5% and 16.2%. In Besim et al. (2015), we update the numbers for 2006 and 2011 as, respectively, 9.1% and 13.6%. These estimates for 2006 and 2011 also implies respectively, 15.1% and 22.2% lost social security revenues (as a ratio of total social security revenues).

The next set of estimates use the seminal approach of Pissarides and Weber (1989) (PW henceforth). PW introduced a new method to analyze the degree of underreported income by households working in different types of employment groups. The underreported income is assumed to be not subject to taxes thus using these values, one can potentially calculate the amount of lost tax revenues for the government, as well as the amount of shadow economy. PW show that, under the assumption of households having the same marginal propensity to consume (MPC) food out of their permanent income,[1] the income of different groups classified by their working conditions (public sector vs private sector) can be calculated

[1] Those working in the agricultural sector is deleted from the analysis since they may be consuming their own food produce.

accordingly. Any discrepancies between reported income and calculated income can be classified as income underreporting. Many authors have used PW method to estimate income underreporting in various countries (See Engstrom and Hagen 2017 for recent-related literature).

This method has also been applied to TRNC. In Besim and Jenkins (2005), and Ekici and Besim (2016), we have extended PW work to include three groups, namely public, private, and self-employed households. This is especially important for a country like TRNC where lack of regulations give rise to flexibility to the people in the private sector to underreport their earnings. One issue with this extension, however, is the difficulty in classifying households who have a mixture of people working in these three groups in the same household. For example, if the head of household works in the public sector, but the spouse works in the private sector, how should they be classified? PW classified households belonging to private sector if 25% or more of total household income was received from that sector, but they only had two groups. In Ekici and Besim (2016) we only focus on households where both working members received income from the same group, and thus we estimate lower bounds for income underreporting using TRNC household budget survey (HBS) of 2008. The percentage of income underreporting for those working as salaried private sector employees and self-employed are, respectively, 12.2% and 20.2%. Based on these estimates, we find that this is equivalent to a shadow economy of 8.6% (as a ratio of GNP) and 11.1% loss of tax revenues (as a ratio of total tax revenues). In the next part, we introduce and compare the results obtained from HBS 2015 but calculated using a different classification.

4 New Estimates for TRNC's Shadow Economy

The other countries analyzed in this volume reports on the size of informal economy using World Bank's informal economy database. Unfortunately, TRNC is not included in that list. In the previous section, we reported estimates of informal economy for TRNC that were calculated by previous researchers using various approaches. In this subsection, we report some findings that are obtained by similar approaches to the World Bank's informal economy database.

4.1 MIMIC (Multiple Indicators Multiple Causes) Approach

The MIMIC approach has been the standard approach to calculating the size of shadow economy. Although this model has been updated and extended over the years, the basic structure of the model is still a useful point of origin to estimate the size of shadow economy. Besim et al. (2013) used this method to calculate the size of shadow economy for 1990–2011 period and we reported their findings in Table 4 above. In this part, we provide an updated evidence that uses the MIMIC method. Figure 2 shows the results for 2011–2023 that are obtained from Besim (2025). The average value of the ratio of the size of the shadow economy to GDP during this period is around 31.37%. With the exception of 2020 (which could be due to the lack of reliable data collection during COVID period), the ratio has been consistent over the last 18 years. This suggests the failure of the governments in their efforts to combat the underground economy in TRNC.

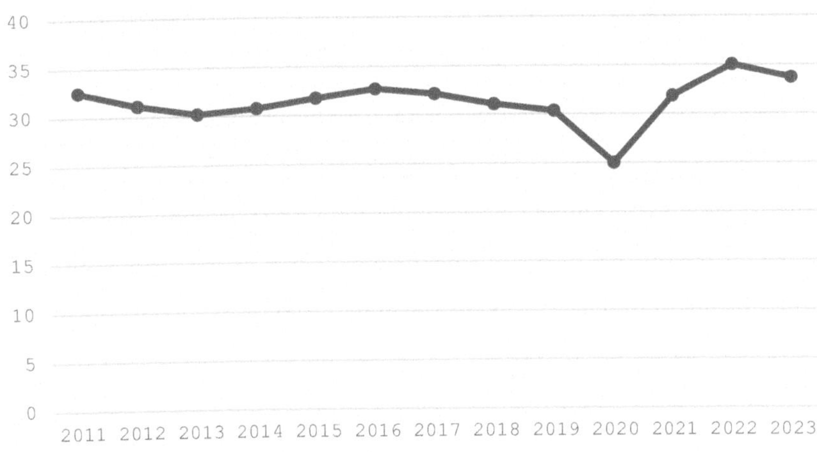

Fig. 2 Ratio of shadow economy to GDP using MIMIC approach (2011–2023) (*Source*: Besim, 2025)

Table 5 Response to the WVS question of whether *cheating is justifiable* (answer categories range from 1 = Never Justifiable to 10-Always Justifiable)

Year	*Average Value*	*% Never Justifiable (=1) (%)*
2006	1.33	88.0
2011	1.52	81.33
2019	1.75	78.27

Source: Author's own calculations

4.2 *Responses to WVS*

Another measure available in World Bank's database is households' response to a question from the World Values Survey (WVS). The question asks the respondents whether cheating on taxes is justifiable (1 is 'never justifiable' and 10 is 'always justifiable') where a higher country average suggests that the country is more tolerant towards the informal sector. Cyprus has been included in WVS in the last three waves and the survey was conducted on both sides of Cyprus. So in Table 5 below we report the TRNC averages for the years 2006, 2011 and 2019 as well as percentage of people who choose 'never justifiable' (value of 1) in the same survey. The latter value should indicate the percentage of the country that is absolutely against shadow economy (does not necessarily imply that these people will not engage in shadow economy). The average value shows a small number which indicates a lot of people are less likely to justify cheating on taxes,[2] but this number has been on the rise over the years (and percentage who never justifies has been declining), which should be alarming for the policymakers in TRNC.

4.3 *Self-employment (% of total employment)*

Next, we report the ratio of self-employment to total employment in Fig. 3 below. This information is obtained directly from TRNC Social Security Office and is also used in MIMIC calculations. The average value is around 10% which is a low number compared to other comparable economies. In previous sections, we have talked about the possibilities

[2] The respective percentages for those years for entire Cyprus are 1.9, 1.6 and 1.6 (Elgin et. al. 2021) which indicates that Northern part of the island justifies cheating on taxes less than their southern counterparts.

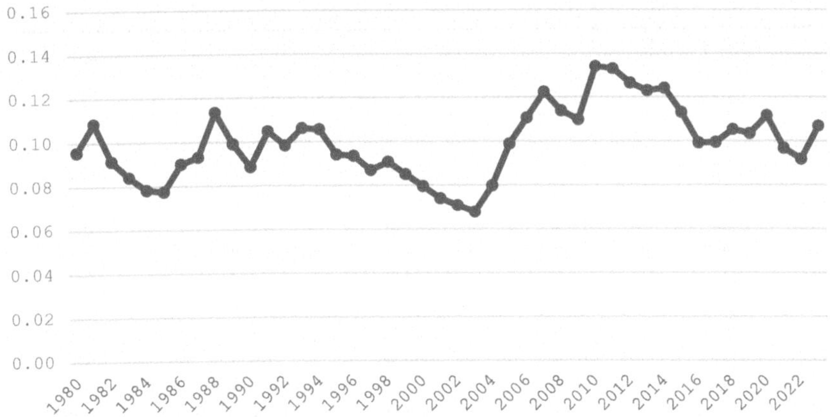

Fig. 3 % of Self-Employment to Total Employment (1980–2023) (*Source*: TRNC Social Security Office, 2025)

of income underreporting and tax evasion by those working as self-employed. The fact that this ratio is small in TRNC is good news for reducing the size of shadow economy, but if the small number of self-employed contributes large amounts to shadow economy, then the problem still exists.

4.4 Unregistered employment

'Informal employment' in World Bank database is defined as 'all workers in the informal sector and informal workers outside the informal sector'. Elgin et al. (2021) notes that 'Almost all persons employed in the informal sector are in informal employment. But not all informal employment is in the informal sector (p. 13)'. Unfortunately we do not have historical data to calculate this distinction for TRNC but instead we offer an alternative aggregate measure, namely percentage of unregistered employment to total employment. Unregistered employment, defined as people who are working without any contribution to a pension system, is only a lower bound estimate for total informal employment defined according to the World Bank.

TRNC Household Labour Force Surveys ask individuals whether they are registered to any of the social security schemes. Percentage of people

Table 6 Percentage of Workers that are unregistered in different employment groups (2014–2023)

Year	*Salaried/ part-time (%)*	*Self-employed (%)*	*Unpaid family business (%)*	*Employer (%)*	*Total (%)*
2014	3.2	17.0	66.9	5.9	6.6
2015	3.7	17.4	75.7	3.6	6.8
2016	3.6	10.2	81.5	3.7	5.4
2017	3.9	15.8	77.6	4.4	6.6
2018	3.1	11.8	74.8	1.3	5.1
2019	3.6	15.9	71.4	4.9	6.5
2020	2.4	14.4	30.0	4.7	4.8
2021	3.1	14.2	66.6	3.4	6.0
2022	2.2	10.0	81.4	6.1	4.7
2023	5.2	17.6	54.9	3.5	7.6

Source: TRNC Statistical Institute, Household Labor Force Survey Reports, 2014–2023, https://istatistik.gov.ct.tr/

by different working status (as well as total) who are not registered are shown in Table 6 for 2014–2023 period.[3] The average value for this period is 6%, but the value for self-employed (14.4%) is much larger than this average. Given that self-employed also earn more than the rest of the population and have more flexibility in reporting their earnings (it is based on income declaration rather than 'pay as you earn' system), the large percentage of unregistered employment by this group could potentially contribute significantly to the size of shadow economy.

5 Some of the Laws, Rules, and Regulations Regarding Informal Activities

Many of the laws and regulations in TRNC have not been updated properly since 1975. There are occasional amendments to the laws, but many of the old adopted regulations from colonial period are still in existence. The laws regulating informal activities are no exception in this case. For example, the law regulating income tax has been in effect since 1982 and it has been amended more than 30 times, but the modifications have been

[3] The values for 2004–2012 are available in Besim et. al (2015), Fig. 2.2, page 28.

very minor. Currently, there are five income tax brackets (10%, 20, 25, 30, 37) and it is argued that the law is very complex (Besim et al., 2013).

Another issue with this tax law is the procedure for tax declarations of the self-employed. For salaried employees, income tax is taken directly out of their paychecks (Pay as you earn, PAYE) but self-employed and businesses are required to declare their own income for tax purposes which is standard in many countries. Tax office could then adjust (with a reason) the amount and potentially ask for more tax to be paid. Unique problem to TRNC is that a taxpayer who was asked to pay more taxes has the option to go and 'negotiate' with the tax official or their manager, or even with the corresponding minister, regarding the amount of tax to be paid. It is at this stage that *clientelism* starts to show its face and tax evasion becomes a reality. We expand on this issue further later in this chapter.

TRNC governments have extended amnesties very often over the years which could have contributed to the rise of informal economy. Firms and households involved in informal economy (tax evasion, informal employment etc.) continued doing so expecting that an amnesty might be forthcoming. In TRNC, amnesties typically manifest as income tax, social security premium liabilities, and immigration amnesties. These amnesty practices have been implemented at various times and we list some of the recent ones below.

Some amnesties give an opportunity to taxpayers who were avoiding payment to come out of shadows without much penalty. An amnesty begun in 2021 allowed taxpayers to restructure certain tax liabilities and submit reduced payments. This regulation allowed taxpayers to restructure and resolve their tax obligations from previous periods under certain situations until June 30, 2021. There was another tax liabilities amnesty from 2022, and prior years was introduced, as per the regulation issued in the Official Gazette on September 6, 2024. Amnesties for outstanding social insurance premium payments have also been implemented (April 10, 2017) that established a waiver for premium commitments accrued from January 1, 2000, to December 31, 2018. This was succeeded by new legislation enacted in 2022, which pertains to premium commitments incurred from January 1, 2000, to December 31, 2019.

Another domain of amnesties closely associated with informal employment pertains to immigration amnesties. The Immigration Amnesty (3/2016) enacted in August 2016 provided various benefits for foreign nationals residing in the country illegally. In order to take advantage of this, illegal residents had three months to apply. An additional immigration amnesty was implemented from November 4, 2021, to January 31, 2022, in accordance with Law No. 18/2021 on Aliens and Immigration (Amendment). This regulation has permitted foreign nationals residing in the country illegally to obtain legal status under certain conditions. In accordance with the regulation implemented on August 5, 2024, foreign nationals who acquired penal status post-January 1, 2021, are granted an amnesty option subject to the payment of one minimum wage. Such frequently granted amnesties raises public's expectations for the future and could nudge them into engaging in shadow economy.

6 Other Aspects of the Shadow Economy

Although many of the laws and regulations in TRNC need to be updated, there are already many relevant regulations in effect designed to deter informal activities. The problem is not necessarily the lack of or outdated laws, but rather the 'loose' application of those. In a survey in 2014, when asked about the methods taxpayers choose to use when they receive audit for inaccurate taxes or additional interest/penalty payments, tax office workers said that 69% of the recipients of such a notice chooses to 'talk to a Minister or another politician', and another 15% 'talks to a high-level public servant' whereas only 10% choose to follow the legal channels (Besim et al., 2015). This is made possible by the clientelism culture that has been fostered in TRNC since 1974. This culture unfortunately contributes tremendously to shadow economy and overall corruption in the nation.

Corruption, which is the enabler of shadow economy, has been a serious problem in TRNC. Using the methodology of Transparency International, Gokcekus and Sonan (2025) have been calculating Corruption Perception Index (CPI) for TRNC since 2017. The methodology involves asking business owners about their perceptions regarding bribery and corruption in TRNC in general, and among different segments of the economy. Overall CPI score for TRNC places the nation at 140 among 180 nations which indicates a very poor performance. According to Gokcekus and Sonan (2025)'s report, about 75% of the respondents in 2024 believe that 'bribe and corruption' is 'Very Common' in TRNC, and more than 50% believe that it is 'very common' for policymakers, members of the parliament and upper-level public servants to be involved in corruption. Another interesting result from the same report is that more than 60% think that TRNC Parliament or the government is 'not at all successful' in preventing corruption in TRNC. Household level corruption perception measures are available for TRNC in the latest wave of WVS which we will explore in the next section.

Given the high level of corruption perception by the public (both households and businesses) and a relatively large size of shadow economy, it is natural to wonder why non-governmental organizations or public in general is not able to fight against it. One possible explanation is the existence of high levels of political clientelism in TRNC. Sonan (2014) provides a good overview of the roots of clientelism in TRNC, and Ekici (2019) explores the more recent years. Broadly defined, political clientelism refers to those in political circles using their position to extend rents to the people in the hope of getting votes in order to maintain their political position for an extended time. In TRNC, this has been practiced by many of the politicians in the form of public employment placement, special treatment on government projects, tax forgiveness and other unfair privileges either directly or indirectly provided. It is no wonder than that the perception of the public about the engagement of politicians in corrupt activities is very high, but it is because the public also reaps benefits of such activities, thanks to clientelism, that they are not making a big deal out of it.

Relations with Türkiye is also another contributor to shadow economy. Since 1974, TRNC has been reliant on foreign aid coming from Türkiye. It is without a doubt that aid has helped the economy to lessen the effects of non-recognition at the international levels. However, with the amount of aid coming into the country, we would have expected much better economic development. Unfortunately, the economic growth has not been consistent with the level of aid coming from Türkiye (Ekici & Özdemir, 2020). This is not surprising since most of the aid has been utilized for clientelistic purposes (such as increasing the size of public sector employment) instead of efficient government spending (Ozdemir & Ekici, 2025). TRNC governments also did not worry about the size of shadow economy because they were always able to finance their budget deficits through the grants and loans (never paid back) from Türkiye.

There is also the existence of illegal economic activities in TRNC. Due to its lack of recognition, international laws are not applicable on this part of the island. This raised the possibility of conducting illegal businesses in the country such as gambling, prostitution, drug and human trafficking and money laundering. Although government regulations exist against doing some of these, over the years the policymakers passed certain laws that allowed these illegal businesses to be conducted freely. And thanks to corruption and clientelistic instincts of the policymakers, illegal and thus informal economy has not been minimal. We are not discussing the amount of shadow economy due to these illegal activities, but the readers are cautioned to interpret the empirical estimates of the size of shadow economy in TRNC due to the existence of illegal activities.

7 The Size of and the Psychology behind Income Underreporting in TRNC

The case of TRNC is rather unique in the shadow economy literature. One the one hand, its small size (geographically and economically) and unrecognized status should make it easier to monitor economic activities easier and enforce laws and regulations easily without outside interference. On the other, this requires local policymakers and law enforcers to have the appropriate will and interest to do that. That has not been the case in TRNC.

Previous literature finds a high degree of shadow economy in the country. In the first part of this section, we calculate the level of income underreporting for different employment groups using a similar approach as Besim et al. (2015). We utilize the data from 2015 Household Budget Survey (HBS) of TRNC that has not been explored before. In the second part of this section, we talk about some of the likely reasons behind income underreporting. In particular, we focus on the relationship between households' trust towards various public institutions and their justification of activities that might contribute to shadow economy. This allows us to understand psychological aspects of consumer behaviour. We propose a new explanation on our findings.

This section is organized as follows. In the first part of this section, we calculate and update the degree of underreporting using TRNC household budget survey from 2015. In doing so, we also raise awareness of potential methodological issues. The second part focuses on behavioural aspects of income underreporting. We analyze the relationship between public opinion towards various government institutions (that are expected to enforce rules and regulations to reduce the size of shadow economy) and public's own views on activities that are known to increase the magnitude of shadow economy in a nation. We utilize different waves of the World Values Survey (WVS) for this exercise.

7.1 Income Underreporting in TRNC

In this subsection, we look at the degree of income underreporting in TRNC using household level data. Income underreporting has been a huge problem exacerbated by lack of confidence, monitoring and accountability. The work in this section is comparable to the work of Besim et al. (2015) but with two main differences. First, we use more recent data on household expenditure patterns, namely 2015 Household Budget Survey (HBS2015).[4] Secondly, as we discuss below, we classify the households differently and focus on the difference between labour income and household income. The last point is also unique in income underreporting literature.

There is also another problem in this line of research. Permanent income is considered a significant piece of information in this type of analysis, but we cannot observe permanent income in cross-sectional surveys, so researchers have used instruments or other proxies for this critical variable. Engstrom and Hagen (2017) shows that using incorrect instruments that does not take transitory income component of permanent income accurately may overestimate the degree of underreporting by 40%. It is also a concern about what type of income to use. Survey measures ask about the labour income but consumption may very well depend on total income from other sources (rent, transfers, etc.). And if a member of the household is currently not working but receive other capital income, labour income will not capture these additional earnings. This is especially important in TRNC since households tend to have additional earnings from other sources.

Compared to Besim et al. (2015), we identify employment groups differently. Group 1 includes everyone who receive labour income only from public sector, Group 2 are those where the labour income comes only from private sector, and group 3 includes mixture of those. Private sector in this paper refers to salaried private sector employees and self-employed. We combined these two groups so that we can have better

[4] We would like to thank Sevda Özsaygin at TRNC Statistical Institute for providing us with HBS2015 micro data.

estimates. In a working paper, we are trying to estimate different models for these different groups.

Since all groups can potentially have non-labour income, we assume that the tendency to lie about these in the surveys should be the same across different groups. However, public sector labour income cannot be underreported. We also have the standard assumption that all these three groups of households should have the same marginal propensity to consume (MPC) food out of their permanent income. We experiment with current disposable labour income and current disposable total income as two proxies for permanent income. Table 7 below compares monthly expenditures on food and annual labour and total household income for different employee groups. We also add a fourth category just to compare the income and spending habits of non-working population with the three groups we created (Table 7).

One interesting feature of this table is the difference between labour income and total income for all of the groups. This is especially important for public sector employees. Although they cannot underreport their labour income from the government, they can potentially underreport their other earnings. So we estimate the following equation using both of the measures.

$$\text{Ln}\ foodi = \beta_0 + \beta_1 D_i + \beta_2 lny_i + \beta_3 X_i + \varepsilon_i$$

where food measures the monthly spending of the household on food, D is a dummy variable indicating income source of the household (=1 for

Table 7 Expenditure and income comparison of various groups

	Public	*Private*	*Mixed*	*Non-working*
Food Spending (monthly)	886 (436)	723 (397)	845 (387)	727 (450)
Total Spending (monthly)	5901 (4653)	4093 (3451)	7305 (9407)	3784 (3679)
Total Labor Income (annual)	55,408 (29,727)	33,747 (24,475)	66,994 (27,280)	NA
Total Income (annual)	67,096 (33,623)	44,007 (31,717)	77,954 (39,748)	37,234 (25,766
Sample Size	573	1065	190	1028

Source: Author's own calculations using HBS 2015. The values shown are averages (standard deviations) and reported in Turkish Lira (TL)

private, = 0 for public), y is the income measure for the household, and X includes control variables (number of adults and kids, age of household head and dummy variables for gender and education of the head of the household) for household preferences, i refers to the household.[5]

The degree of underreporting based on the estimates of the above equation can then be calculated as (Hurst et al., 2014). We report estimates for two different measures of household income. The results indicate a very high degree of income underreporting at 64% and 46% using, respectively, labour income and total income. These results suggest that the measure of income in this line of research could impact the magnitude of the results. Furthermore, in the case of TRNC, this suggests that TRNC officials have not been able to combat shadow economy very effectively given how the numbers here are much higher than our earlier estimates from 2008 (in the range of 14–20% for private sector employees and self-employed). In the next section, we turn to some of the non-economic aspects of TRNC households' tendency to contribute to shadow economy.

7.2 *Insights into Psychology of Income Underreporting in TRNC*

Previous literature on North Cyprus including our earlier analysis in this section has shown that there is a considerable amount of income underreporting by private sector employees in TRNC. Underreporting is likely in any country's economy even developed ones, but the situation in TRNC is highly problematic for three main reasons. First, the degree is too high (60%). Secondly, this is not only constrained to self-employed individuals, but it also includes those who are salaried in the private sector which is not very possible in developed economies. Finally, although it is illegal to have a second job for those working in the public sector, there are plenty of individuals in TRNC working in public sector and earning additional income from other sources. In this section, we analyze some of the attitudes TRNC households have about certain issues that could explain the high degree of income underreporting.

[5] We eliminate the mixed group from this analysis. The complete OLS estimation results are omitted here but available from the authors upon request.

7.2.1 *Descriptive Statistics*

For this section, we utilize data from WVS. This survey has seven waves and it has been collecting information on household attitudes on many topics across many countries since 1980s. As we discussed in the previous sections, Cyprus as a whole has been included in the last 3 waves of the survey, and the survey was conducted on both sides of the island. So we identify the respondents from TRNC and analyze their responses in this section.

As a first step, we report the percentage of people who justify certain acts that are related to shadow economy. WVS has the following question 'Please tell me for each of the following actions whether you think it can always be justified, never be justified, or something in between' with answer categories ranging from 1 to 10. We focus on five actions that are highly likely to contribute to the size of shadow economy. The answers given by the people living in TRNC for the three waves of WVS are given on Table 8. The numbers in the table are the percentage of people who 'always' justifies (answer = 1). So, it is possible that there are more who 'sometimes' justify and thus these are only the lower bounds for these questions.

'Cheating on Taxes' and 'Accepting a bribe' are the biggest contributors to income underreporting. The percentage of people in TRNC who justify this activity has been on the rise between 2006–2019. 'Avoiding a public fare' is not necessarily going to have a significant impact on the size of shadow economy, but the way people feel about this immoral and illegal behaviour is going to be highly correlated with their other behaviour that might be contributors of shadow economy. It turns out that this ratio has also increased over these three waves and in 2019

Table 8 Percentage of sample who always justifies (= 1) the following behaviour

	2006 (%)	*2011*	*2019*
Accepting a bribe	12.0	19.5	22.3
Cheating on Taxes	12.0	18.7	22.1
Avoiding Public Fare	31.2	39.0	63.2
Stealing	N/A	19.0	18.6
Claiming Government benefits not entitled to	21.6	19.1	18.8

Source: Author's own calculations using WVS (waves 5,6 & 7)

it was 63.2%. Overall this table shows that people in TRNC are highly comfortable with avoiding public fare, and around 20% are comfortable with other immoral and illegal activities.

One of the reasons why people might engage in shadow economy contributing activities is their lack of confidence in the system (Feige, 1997; North, 1994). In Table 9 we report confidence levels of the households towards various institutions whose main responsibilities include reduction of corruption and controlling the size of shadow economy. The lack of confidence is high and has been on the rise. When it comes to confidence towards policy makers (parliament, civil services, government, political parties), more than half of the people do not have confidence. This is a recipe for persistence of shadow economy.

Finally, we report how households perceive the extend of corruption in different sectors of the economy including public and private. This measure is only available for the last wave of the survey. If one lives in a society where you 'perceive' a large portion of the people engaging in corruption, one might be more inclined to follow suit (Ekici & Gokcekus, 2025) or at least do not be bothered by it. Table 10 shows that a lot of people in TRNC believe that there is at least some corruption engaged by policymakers and civil service providers. This is consistent with the corruption perception of the business sector that was reported by Gokcekus and Sonan (2025).

These descriptive statistics give us an idea about the psychology of shadow economy in TRNC. People are in general not trusting towards public institutions whose main responsibility is to enforce and enact laws that will prevent the existence, or at least reduce the size, of shadow economy. People in TRNC are also comfortable with some of the immoral and illegal behaviour that are potentially big contributors to the size of

Table 9 Percentage of respondents who have 'Not very much' or 'None at all' *Confidence* in the following groups in different years

	2006	*2011*	*2019*
Police	0.17	0.23	0.30
Parliament	0.34	0.45	0.53
Civil Services	0.39	0.37	0.49
Government	0.35	0.43	0.52
Political Parties	0.56	0.61	0.69
Justice System	0.16	0.19	0.37

Source: Author's own calculations using WVS (waves 5, 6 & 7)

Table 10 Percentage of respondents in 2019 who think 'NONE OF THEM' in these groups are involved in corruption (other options are 'few of them', 'most of them', 'all of them')

Group	*Percentage (%)*
State authorities	9.3
Business Executives	12.3
Local Authorities	6.9
Civil Service Providers	9.1
Journalists and Media	13.3

Source: Author's own calculations using WVS (wave 7)

the underground economy. Finally, people living in TRNC also believe that there are plenty of public sector employees engaging in corruption in the country. This also increases the possibility that people see it as a norm rather than an exception to be involved in corruptive activities, which once again is a problem for the country.

Theoretical prediction of the effect of confidence in institutions on likelihood of engaging in shadow economy is not straightforward. On the one hand, if households have complete trust and confidence in the institutions whose responsibility is to deter people from engaging in shadow economy, then this might give them an incentive not to engage in shadow economy because of being scared to be caught and penalized, since they believe that the institutions are working properly.

On the other hand however, it is likely to have the opposite effect for two reasons. First, households might think of corruption or shadow economy is only related to the civil services or large corporations and their relationship with government officials. So, if institutions are working properly, they will be busy (and successful) with focusing on the high level activities and thus there will be less incentive for these institutions to come after regular citizens. Hence the citizens will have more flexibility and incentive when it comes to engaging in minor shadow economic activities (such as income underreporting, evading taxes, or unregistered employment). This prediction is consistent with the outcome that has been observed in Italy where an increase in the efforts of national institutions to combat corruption at national level has triggered more corruption by local level public officials and politicians (Woodhouse, 2022).

Another negative channel of high confidence in institutions on shadow economy is through clientelism. If public has high 'confidence' in the politicians or high level civil service officials, then they will feel more comfortable with engaging in informal activities. For example, if someone has good relationship with the Deputy of the Tax office (because they are relatives or neighbors), then obviously they will have a high level of confidence in that institution. But, if this person has an issue with their tax payments, who do you think will they contact first? So it is likely that higher confidence might lead to more involvement in informal economy.

7.2.2 Multivariate Analysis

We investigate some of these claims more formally using multivariate regression analysis in this section. In particular, we analyze the relationship between *justifiability of corruptive behaviour* and *confidence in institutions* using WVS data. We also ask whether the risk of being held accountable in case of getting caught has any influence on justifiability of corruptive behaviour. The risk of accountability measure is only available in the latest wave of the survey, thus in order for our models to be comparable, we use only wave 7 of WVS to test our hypothesis.

Our main dependent variable is justifiability of corruptive behaviour. As we have shown in Table 8, there are multiple variables that capture a similar concept. Thus, we combined some of the responses and created an index measure using Polychoric Principal Component Analysis (PPCA). This method is more appropriate than regular principal component analysis when the variable of interest has ordinal response options and is not normally distributed (Olsson, 1979). Our index of 'justifiability of corruptive behavior' is constructed by taking the first principal component of the four questions inTable 8.[6] The eigenvalue of the first component is 2.27, and the Cronbach's alpha among the four questions is 71.8%.

Our first independent variable is constructed as follows. The answer to confidence questions has four options with 'None at all', 'Not very much', 'Quite a lot' and 'A great Deal'. We code the variables so that higher numbers indicate more trust toward the specific measure of the institution. The institutions we include in our analysis are *Parliament,*

[6] We exclude 'stealing' from this analysis because this behaviour is not directly related to shadow economy generating activities and also can be considered more of a hard crime compared to other behaviour.

Civil Services, Government and Political Parties. We estimate this relationship by using Ordinary Least Squares (OLS) regression where we also control for gender, age group, education group and subjective income category (low, medium, high) of the respondents. Table 11 shows the results separately for each of these institutions.

Then we ask whether *risk of being held accountable* in case of getting caught might have any influence in deterring TRNC households from justifying corrupt behaviour. In order to measure this variable, we use the responses to the question '*How high is the risk in this country to be held accountable for giving or receiving a bribe, gift or favor in return for public service? To indicate your opinion, use a 10-point scale where '1' means 'no risk at all' and '10' means 'very high risk'*'. We experiment

Table 11 Confidence in Institutions and Justifiability of Corrupt Behaviour

	(1)	(2)	(3)	(4)
Confidence	0.229***	0.108*	0.114**	0.215***
	(4.20)	(1.86)	(2.15)	(3.38)
Female	−0.0947	−0.110	−0.0990	−0.0788
	(−0.83)	(−0.97)	(−0.85)	(−0.68)
Age 30–49	−0.0186	−0.0579	−0.0541	−0.0617
	(−0.13)	(−0.43)	(−0.39)	(−0.45)
Age 50 +	−0.167	−0.211	−0.125	−0.172
	(−1.04)	(−1.31)	(−0.73)	(−1.05)
Middle Education Group	0.0440	0.0127	0.0278	0.0392
	(0.20)	(0.06)	(0.13)	(0.18)
Upper Education Group	0.335*	0.248	0.315	0.299
	(1.76)	(1.30)	(1.62)	(1.60)
Medium Income	0.0782	0.160	0.165	0.185
	(0.53)	(1.10)	(1.14)	(1.32)
High Income	0.409*	0.529**	0.449*	0.543**
	(1.66)	(2.07)	(1.83)	(2.21)
Constant	−0.561*	−0.273	−0.328	−0.529**
	(−1.94)	(−0.94)	(−1.15)	(−1.98)
Confidence Measure	Parliament	Civil Services	Government	Political Parties
R-squared	0.079	0.045	0.042	0.067
Observations	384	390	385	381

Notes: Omitted categories are Age 15–29, Low Subjective Income, Lower Education Group. *, **, *** indicate significance at, respectively, 10%, 5% and 1% level. The numbers are OLS estimates with robust standard errors in parentheses

Table 12 Risk of being held accountable and justifiability of corrupt behaviour

	(1)	*(2)*	*(3)*
Risk of Being Held Accountabile	−0.0892***	−0.217***	−0.260***
	(−5.07)	(−2.92)	(−5.61)
Female	−0.0741	−0.0651	−0.0952
	(−0.66)	(−0.57)	(−0.85)
Age 30–49	0.00838	0.00605	0.00313
	(0.06)	(0.05)	(0.02)
Age 50 +	−0.0711	−0.0818	−0.0631
	(−0.45)	(−0.50)	(−0.41)
Middle Education Group	−0.0537	0.0146	−0.0818
	(−0.25)	(0.07)	(−0.38)
Upper Education Group	0.177	0.239	0.158
	(0.95)	(1.27)	(0.87)
Medium Income	0.136	0.146	0.122
	(1.02)	(1.05)	(0.89)
High Income	0.485**	0.447*	0.514**
	(2.03)	(1.83)	(2.15)
Constant	0.663**	0.510	0.727***
	(2.48)	(1.60)	(2.79)
Risk Measure	Continuous (1–10)	Ordered (1–3,4–6,7–10)	Ordered (1–5, 6–7, 8–9,10)
R-squared	0.069	0.043	0.092
Observations	392	392	392

Notes: Omitted categories are Age 15–29, Low Subjective Income, Lower Education Group. *, **, *** indicate significance at, respectively, 10%, 5% and 1% level. The numbers are OLS estimates with robust standard errors in parentheses

with three different classifications of this question. The OLS results for all specifications are presented in the next table.

This time we observe a more intuitive outcome. The higher the risk of being held accountable, the less likely the public is to justify corruptive behaviour. This result is highly significant regardless of how we measure the risk variable. This result suggests that increased accountability in TRNC could discourage public from engaging in informal economy (Table 12).

In this section we have looked at some of the behavioural factors of shadow economy in TRNC. First result is consistent with the view that clientelism might be a significant contributor of informal economy in TRNC, while the second result is more consistent with the general policy recommendations for other countries in this line of research where increased accountability is believed to reduce informal activities. Of course these results should be interpreted cautiously since we only used one wave of data with a relatively small size and limited number of other observable characteristics. However, we believe that our results in this section should spark interest regarding the role of public perceptions and their participation in informal economy.

8 Policy Recommendations

The substantial scale of the shadow economy significantly impedes the attainment of sustainable economic governance in the TRNC. Shadow economic activities distort labour markets, damage public finances, promote unfair competition, and erode the social contract between the administration and its citizens. Policy initiatives aimed at mitigating informality should encompass institutional, fiscal, regulatory, and socio-cultural components.

One significant challenge in TRNC is the disaggregation of responsibilities among entities responsible for tax collection, labour inspection, and migration control. The government should establish a centralized and interconnected information system that connects the Tax Office, Social Insurance Department, Labour Department, and Immigration Authority. This will enhance data exchange, streamline compliance monitoring, and enable real-time identification of anomalies (OECD, 2017). The work of Schneider and Williams (2013) reports that by enhancing the ability and autonomy of enforcement agencies, and also with recruitment and training of specialized auditors and labour inspectors together with the investment in digital tools can have favourable results.

As for taxation, it is observed that high tax rates and complex compliance processes are the main drivers of informality. Simplification of the taxation system and lowering the marginal tax rates, especially for small enterprises and self-employed individuals, can promote formalization (Sokhanvar et al., 2019). Implementing tiered tax regimes or presumptive taxation models for micro-enterprises could also ease the way for informal businesses to formalize their activities (World Bank, 2021). At the same time, incentivized action measures (e.g. low-interest financing options or subsidies) should be adapted whereby providing positive discrimination to registered businesses.

A significant component of the shadow economy in TRNC is informal labour, including both locals and migrants. Minimizing non-wage labour expenses, strict enforcement of minimum wage legislation, the issuance of legal work permits for foreign labourers, and the rationalization of hiring processes can facilitate the formalization of informal employment. Public information efforts regarding workers' rights and company responsibilities are crucial. According to Jütting and Laiglesia (2009) countries like Uruguay and Portugal have shown that harmonizing deterrence with facilitation enhances formal labour market participation. It is continuously found that there is a high correlation between undocumented migration and informality in the labour market. This is very much notable in TRNC where formulation of a comprehensive migration policy that aligns work permits with labour market demands is essential. According to ILO (2022) adapting a system for monitoring entry and exit, alongside biometric registration and coordinated visa management, can very much help alleviate informal employment (ILO, 2022). These policies should be supported by enforcement policies including high penalties.

As we demonstrated in Sect. 5 of this chapter, income underreporting is a serious contributor to the shadow economy in TRNC. Another important policy for increasing compliance is via enhancing transparency and accountability in the administration. There are success stories, such as Estonia and Singapore, whereby digitizing tax administration, employment data, and government disbursements enabled them to have more efficient governance (UNDP, 2020). Digitalization, e-invoicing, e-filing and online transaction, lowers transaction expenses and can help establish digital records.

Informality constitutes not only a technical concern but also a cultural and social one. As we demonstrated in Sect. 5, justifiability of non-compliant and illegal behaviour is at very high levels. Altering public perceptions necessitates ongoing involvement via education, media, and civic platforms. National campaigns promoting the advantages of formalization should be devised in partnership with labour unions, business chambers, and non-governmental organizations, aimed at both employers and employees. Educational curricula ought to integrate financial literacy and civic engagement modules that underscore the importance of contributing to the common good. These sustained endeavours are essential for altering the social norms that perpetuate informality (Torgler & Schneider, 2007).

9 Conclusion

In this chapter we provided an overview of shadow economy in TRNC. Due to its small and highly closed economy and internationally unrecognized status, the case of TRNC is an interesting study for academics. Size of shadow economy is substantial and it creates a lot of government revenue losses which TRNC governments are in dire need of. Different estimates of the size of shadow economy for TRNC have been done by a handful of researchers and we report a summary of these estimates in this chapter. According to MIMIC approach, shadow economy in TRNC is around 30% of GNP. We also estimated using 2015 HBS data that private sector employees (including self-employed) underreport their earnings somewhere between 40 and60%. This number is very large and different than other estimates for TRNC using previous years' data. It is safe to say that the size of shadow economy in TRNC is very large and we do not see much initiative taken by the policymakers.

One key determinant of the size of shadow economy is the level of ability of the public institutions and policymakers to enforce the laws and regulations. Making simple infrastructural changes that we discussed in Sect. 6 and enacting/amending relevant laws to address informal economic activities can easily be carried out. Unfortunately, TRNC parliament and upper-level civil servants have not been able (or willing?) to undertake such initiatives. Although it is required by the TRNC Constitution, TRNC governments have not prepared the government budget according to a 5-year development plan since 1997 (Ekici, 2019).[7] Such lack of long-term planning is a poor indication of their willingness to address economic development, let alone informal economy.

It is no surprise that the public does not have much faith in the TRNC governments regarding measures taken against shadow economy

[7] The last 5-year development plan covered 1993–1997 and since then TRNC governments operated without such a plan. Most recently, the newest 5-year plan is prepared that covers periods 2025–2029. We will wait and see if the policymakers can achieve the plan's objectives. The 5-year plans can be found (in Turkish) at https://www.devplan.org/dpo.html?slug=kalkinma-planlari.

operations and informal economic activities. For example, in 2024, the parliament enacted a law entitled 'Law on the Prevention of the Financing of the Proliferation of Weapons of Mass Destruction, the Financing of Terrorism, and the Money Laundering of Criminal Proceeds,' yet effective measures must be implemented to meet its stipulations (R.G.3 - 04.01.2024). However, a draft law on the 'Repatriation of Offshore money into the Economy' is presently under parliamentary consideration, whereby it is proposed that reputable money may be registered to the system upon the payment of a 3% tax. This is entirely opposed to the legislation implemented in 2024, which was designed to combat money laundering.

There is even more troubling evidence on parliament's willingness to address the issue of shadow economy. On August 6, 2013, TRNC Council of Ministers that was composed of ministers from both sides of the political spectrum has voted unanimously to implement a new action plan that details steps to be taken to combat shadow economy.[8] The action plan included many of the policy recommendations that were suggested in Besim et al. (2013), and we also introduced some of them in Sect. 6. However, when a new government was formed later that year, they did not follow through. It is unlikely that such behaviour will inspire much confidence.

In Sect. 5 we show the relationship between confidence in public institutions and public's perspectives on certain activities that could potentially contribute to the size of shadow economy. The empirical results using 2019 data revealed that more confidence towards parliament, civil services, government and political parties, actually make public more tolerant towards corruptive and illegal activities. This is somewhat counterintuitive, but in TRNC this could be due to the 'endemic clientelism' (Sonan, 2014) between the public and the politicians. More empirical research is needed on this topic since we were constrained by only one wave of WVS, but our results should be of interest to researchers in this line of work.

Lack of political will to address the problem of shadow economy is a serious issue in TRNC. On the contrary, political actors benefit from the status quo as their favors to the businesses and general public come

[8] The council of ministers' decision no (K-1) 251–2013. The decision was also announced in the Official Gazette of the government which makes it a legal binding document.

back as votes in the local and general elections. The clientelistic and selfish practices of the politicians over the years in TRNC has created a culture of rentierism and non-compliance. This has resulted in a vicious cycle of general public engaging in informal economic activities without much fear of being penalized, and politicians, dreading loss of voter support, have not acted on the problem. Addressing the shadow economy in TRNC requires a thorough, collabourative, and determined strategy. Policy reforms must be informed by evidence, legally sound, socially inclusive, and politically endorsed. Effective mitigation of informality can only be succeeded through a comprehensive strategy, institutional integrity, and societal commitment.

References

Besim, M. (2003). *Measuring the Size of Underground Economy in a Small Island: The Case of Turkish Republic of Northern Cyprus* (Doctoral dissertation, University of Birmingham, International Development Department, School of Public Policy).

Besim, M. (2025). Measuring the size of Underground Economy in TRNC using MIMIC approach: Updated evidence, *Eastern Mediterranean University Working Paper.*

Besim, M., Ekici, T., & Jenkins, G. P. (2015). Informality in a micro economy: Measurement, composition and consequences. *International Labour Review, 154*(3), 353–371.

Besim, M., & Jenkins, G. P. (2005). Tax compliance: When do employees behave like the self-employed? *Applied Economics, 37*(10), 1201–1208.

Besim, M., Mungan, Z., Gürpınar, A., & Saydam, G. (2013). *Kuzey Kıbrıs Türk Cumhuriyeti'nde Kayıtdışı ekonomi: Boyutlarının ölçümü, çözüm önerileri ve eylem planı.* Kıbrıs Türk Ticaret Odası.

Ekici, T. (2019). *The political and economic history of North Cyprus: A discordant polity.* Springer International Publishing.

Ekici, T., & Besim, M. (2016). A measure of the shadow economy in a small economy: Evidence from household-level expenditure patterns. *Review of Income and Wealth, 62*(1), 145–160.

Ekici, T. & Gokcekus, O. (2025). Corruption Justification Under the Lens of Religiosity: Exploring Micro-Level Determinants, *Working Paper.*

Ekici, T., & Özdemir, Y. (2021). Turkish foreign aid to Northern Cyprus: A mother's blessing or curse? *Southeast European and Black Sea Studies, 21*(3), 437–455.

Elgin, C., Kose, M. A., Ohnsorge, F., & Yu, S. (2021). *Understanding Informality (CERP Discussion Paper 16497).* CEPR.

Engström, P., & Hagen, J. (2017). Income underreporting among the self-employed: A permanent income approach. *European Economic Review, 92*, 92–109.

Feige, E. (1997). Underground Activity and Institutional Change: Productive. *Protective and Predatory Behavior in Transition.*

Gokcekus, O., & Sonan, S. (2025). *Corruption Perceptions in North Cyprus: 2024 Report*. Friedrich Ebert Stiftung: Nikosia.

Hurst, E., Li, G., & Pugsley, B. (2014). Are household surveys like tax forms? Evidence from income underreporting of the self-employed. *Review of Economics and Statistics, 96*(1), 19–33.

International Labour Organization. (2015). *Transition from the informal to the formal economy recommendation (No. 204).*

International Labour Organization. (2022). *Social protection for migrant workers: A rights-based approach.*

Jütting, J., & Laiglesia, J. R. (2009). *Is informal normal? Towards more and better jobs in developing countries*. OECD Development Centre.

North, D. C. (1994). Economic performance through time. *The American Economic Review, 84*(3), 359–368.

Organisation for Economic Co-operation and Development. (2017). *Enhancing the role of SMEs in global value chains.*

Olsson, U. (1979). Maximum likelihood estimation of the polychoric correlation coefficient. *Psychometrika, 44*(4), 443–460.

Özdemir, Y. & Ekici, T. (2025). Can Foreign Aid Foster Political Clientelism: The case of TRNC, *Working paper*.

Pissarides, C. A., & Weber, G. (1989). An expenditure-based estimate of Britain's black economy. *Journal of Public Economics, 39*(1), 17–32.

Schneider, F., & Williams, C. C. (2013). *The shadow economy*. Institute of Economic Affairs.

Sokhanvar, A., Altiok, H. U., & Jenkins, G. P. (2019). *The Political Economy of the Taxation of Individuals in North Cyprus* (No. 2019-01). JDI Executive Programs.

Sonan, S. (2014). *In the grip of political clientelism: the post-1974 Turkish Cypriot politics and the politico-economic foundations of pro-Taksim consensus* (Doctoral dissertation, Dissertation, Duisburg, Essen, Universität Duisburg-Essen, 2014).

Torgler, B., & Schneider, F. (2007). Shadow economy, tax morale, governance and institutional quality: A panel analysis. *Journal of Economic Psychology, 30*(2), 228–245. https://doi.org/10.1016/j.joep.2007.04.004

United Nations Development Programme. (2020). *Digital governance for development: Case studies from Estonia and Singapore.*

World Bank. (2021). *Improving tax compliance for SMEs: International evidence and lessons from Turkey.*

Woodhouse, E. F. (2022). Accountability and corruption displacement: Evidence from Italy. *Journal of Public Policy, 42*(4), 730–754.

CHAPTER 8

Measuring the Shadow Economy in Uzbekistan Using the Electricity Consumption Model

Aziz Magrupov, Obid Khakimov, and Bahtiyor Eshchanov

1 Introduction

The shadow economy comprises all legal production and income-concealing activities that are unrecorded in official GDP statistics (Schneider & Enste, 2000; Schneider et al., 2010). Such informal economic activity is sizable in many developing countries and can distort macroeconomic policy effectiveness and public revenues (Tanzi, 1999). In Uzbekistan, a transition economy with historically high state control, the shadow economy has long been estimated at a large share of total output, reducing the tax base and hindering development (Donaev, 2019). Measuring the shadow economy is crucial for designing effective reforms in tax policy, governance, and energy management. This study

A. Magrupov · O. Khakimov
Center for Economic Research and Reforms, Tashkent, Uzbekistan

B. Eshchanov (✉)
Economics Department, New Uzbekistan University, Tashkent, Uzbekistan
e-mail: b.eshchanov@newuu.uz

E. Bagirzadeh and O. Gokcekus (eds.), *Shadow Economies in Turkic Republics*, https://doi.org/10.1007/978-3-032-12872-0_8

bridges energy economics and development economics by employing electricity consumption as a proxy to estimate the size of Uzbekistan's shadow economy. The approach builds on the premise that electricity usage is a physical indicator of overall economic activity, including both official and unofficial sectors (Kaufmann & Kaliberda, 1996). We utilize an econometric model and robust tests to derive informal output from energy data, and we compare results with other methods for validation. The analysis is empirically focused, using Uzbekistan's power system data and official GDP, but also discusses theoretical expectations and policy implications. Our findings indicate that while the shadow economy in Uzbekistan remains substantial, it has been on a declining trend in recent years, likely reflecting post-2016 market reforms. The study provides new insights into the scale and dynamics of informality in Uzbekistan and illustrates the usefulness of energy-based measurement approaches for emerging economies.

2 Country's Economic Profile

Since the mid-2010s, Uzbekistan has undergone a significant economic transformation characterized by rapid GDP growth and a sweeping program of market-oriented reforms. Following the change of the political landscape in 2016, the country shifted away from a centrally administered model toward greater openness and liberalization (IMF, 2019). Official GDP growth has consistently averaged between 5 and 7% annually, even during global downturns, reflecting the resilience of domestic demand and a diversified production base. Notably, the economy showed strong recovery after the COVID-19 pandemic and maintained high growth in the post-pandemic years, driven by expansion in services, construction, and export-oriented manufacturing.

Central to Uzbekistan's modernization drive has been the liberalization of its foreign exchange regime in 2017, which eliminated the dual exchange rate system and unified the currency market. This pivotal reform boosted investor confidence, improved monetary policy credibility, and enhanced transparency across sectors. In parallel, structural reforms aimed at improving the business climate—such as simplifying tax codes, removing price controls, reducing state monopoly in key industries, and digitizing government services—have contributed to improved economic efficiency. The energy sector, historically a source of inefficiency due to subsidized pricing and legacy infrastructure, has seen significant change as well. Uzbekistan has initiated tariff reform, expanded renewable energy deployment, and invested in metering and grid modernization. These measures, coupled with economic diversification and improved energy governance, have led to a steady decline in the country's energy intensity—laying the foundation for sustained growth with lower electricity dependence (World Bank, 2022).

However, as Uzbekistan continues to formalize its economy, one critical challenge remains: understanding the full scope of economic activity that occurs outside the official system. Despite reforms, a significant portion of production and labor remains informal—unrecorded in official statistics, untaxed, and loosely regulated. Accurately measuring this shadow economy is essential for designing effective fiscal, regulatory, and energy policies. In this context, energy consumption, particularly electricity use analyzed in this study, offers a promising physical proxy to estimate the scale of shadow economic activities. Given the country's high historical energy intensity and evolving energy profile, the ECM approach provides a uniquely suited method for assessing the trajectory and composition of informality in Uzbekistan's transitioning economy.

3 The Drivers of Uzbekistan's Shadow Economy

Uzbekistan's large shadow economy is closely tied to the country's incomplete transition from a centrally planned system to a fully functional market economy. While significant efforts have been made toward liberalizing the economy in recent years, the state continues to play a central role, with state-owned enterprises (SOEs) maintaining substantial involvement across key sectors such as industry, utilities, and infrastructure. This enduring institutional framework, rooted in the country's historical development model, continues to influence economic incentives and administrative practices in ways that may inadvertently contribute to the persistence of informality.

A core incentive driving the shadow economy in Uzbek economy is the rational pursuit of maximizing disposable income by circumventing formal obligations. Small-scale entrepreneurs, self-employed individuals, and agricultural producers often view formalization not as an opportunity but as a financial burden—associated with taxation, regulatory compliance, license acquisition, and mandatory social security contributions (Spot.uz, 2023).

Despite notable reductions in tax rates and streamlined procedures after 2019, many continue to perceive that the costs of formal participation outweigh its benefits. A key structural issue is that business owners can't assess the benefits of formal status, such as bank credit, government procurement opportunities, or subsidized support services. As a result, informal practices such as envelope wages, underreporting of revenues, and dual bookkeeping systems remain widespread—particularly within micro and small enterprises seeking to preserve liquidity and reduce fiscal visibility.

SOEs often benefit from preferential treatment, soft budget constraints, and implicit guarantees, which distort competition and crowd out private sector development. As a result, many small and medium-sized enterprises (SMEs) find it difficult to operate formally under the same regulatory and financial burden, pushing them toward informal arrangements to remain viable.

Despite accounting for approximately 27% of total employment (2021), the agricultural sector remains heavily reliant on informal arrangements and unpaid family labor (ILO, 2020). This reflects a deeper structural issue: the sector lacks the capacity to productively absorb the rural workforce, resulting in widespread disguised unemployment. Much of the rural population is effectively trapped in low-productivity subsistence farming and informal employment. In the absence of meaningful structural transformation, rural-to-urban migration often shifts labor from one informal setting to another, as rural workers frequently end up in precarious urban informal jobs, perpetuating underemployment and economic vulnerability.

A major contributor to this dynamic is Uzbekistan's public utility and infrastructure model, which relies heavily on budget subsidies to maintain essential services such as electricity and natural gas. Until 2023, tariffs were well below cost-recovery levels, creating chronic deficits in utility companies and discouraging private investment in energy infrastructure. Sharp liberalization of tariffs with strong social protection mechanisms made the transition process more smooth and improved efficiency. Recent studies show that increase in energy tariffs in 2024 reduced the consumption of electricity by the population by 10 percent or 1.3 billion kWh (Kun.uz, 2025). Meanwhile, new infrastructure projects, particularly in transport and urban development, suffer from what economists refer to as "cost disease": rapid increases in construction and maintenance costs without proportional improvements in quality or efficiency. These issues are exacerbated by weak quality control mechanisms, especially in the road construction sector, where substandard delivery and recurring repair needs inflate long-term fiscal costs. Combined, these structural inefficiencies place growing pressure on the national budget, prompting policymakers to raise taxes and tighten enforcement. Yet higher tax burdens often backfire by incentivizing tax avoidance and driving more SMEs into the shadow economy. This fiscal-institutional loop reinforces the persistence of informality, making it essential for policymakers to address the underlying structural and governance failures, rather than relying solely on administrative enforcement to shrink the shadow sector in a sustainable manner.

In parallel, economic inequality is deepening due to imperfect mechanisms of income and opportunity redistribution. Limited job creation outside major urban centers has triggered substantial internal migration, putting pressure on housing demand and driving up property prices in cities like Tashkent and Samarkand. As a result, the construction sector has emerged as a primary engine of economic growth. However, its benefits are highly uneven: capital owners and real estate developers accumulate increasing wealth by supplying housing, while aspiring homeowners face escalating costs and long-term indebtedness. This asymmetric outcome exacerbates social inequality and leads to unevenly distributed welfare improvements, further fueling disillusionment with formal institutions and increasing reliance on informal coping mechanisms.

Adding to the fragility of this economic setup is Uzbekistan's heavy dependence on remittances, particularly from labor migrants working in Russia. Remittances account for a significant share of household income and help finance consumption and housing, but they also signal the mismatch between job creation and population growth. Moreover, this dependence on external labor markets makes the economy vulnerable to geopolitical and cyclical shocks beyond the government's control. Although migration levels have shown a declining trend, they remain relatively high, which may contribute to skill mismatches and pose challenges to social cohesion. Addressing this imbalance requires not only job creation within the formal economy but also improvements in labor productivity, education, and inclusive urban development to create sustainable domestic alternatives to outward migration.

4 Review of Existing Studies on Estimating the Shadow Economy

Multiple methods have been developed to estimate the shadow economy, each with advantages and limitations. Broadly, methods are categorized as direct approaches, indirect (indicator) approaches, and model-based approaches. Direct methods include tax audits and surveys that attempt to directly capture unreported income, but they often underestimate the shadow economy (due to non-response or underreporting) and are typically static, failing to track dynamics over time (OECD, 2002). Indirect methods use macroeconomic indicators as proxies for informality, leveraging their dynamic behavior to infer hidden activity (Feige & Urban, 2003). Key indirect approaches include:

- *National accounts discrepancies*: comparing national expenditure and income to find output not captured by income tax data (Schneider & Enste, 2002).
- *Labor force discrepancies*: comparing official employment to actual labor participation, under the assumption that a gap implies workers in the informal sector (Johnson et al., 1997).
- *Currency demand approach (CDA)*: examining excess demand for cash under the assumption that informal transactions occur in cash. A rise in the currency-to-deposits ratio beyond what formal activity explains is attributed to the shadow economy (Cagan, 1958). This method, pioneered by Cagan (1958) and Tanzi (1983), links increases in tax or regulatory burden to higher cash usage as people hide transactions (Tanzi, 1983). While widely applied, the CDA requires assuming ***no shadow economy in a base year*** and equal velocity of money in both sectors—assumptions heavily criticized as unrealistic (Cagan, 1958; Eilat & Zinnes, 2000).
- *Transactions approach*: comparing total monetary transactions (MV) to recorded GDP (PT) using Fisher's quantity equation; any excess of transactions over official GDP indicates unreported output. However, it too assumes a 'zero shadow' economy in the base year and stable velocity (Medina & Schneider, 2018).
- *Physical input (electricity consumption) approach*: using energy usage (especially electricity) as a proxy for total economic activity (Kaufmann & Kaliberda, 1996). This approach, introduced by Kaufmann and Kaliberda (1996), posits that electricity consumption is the

single best physical indicator of overall GDP, since virtually all sectors require energy. By comparing growth rates of electricity use and official GDP, one can infer the growth of the "true" economy and thereby the shadow portion (Donaev, 2019). If electricity is growing faster than recorded GDP, the difference is attributed to expansion of the informal sector (Lackó, 2000). Conversely, if official GDP grows without commensurate energy growth, it may indicate formalization or efficiency gains.

- *Model-based approaches* like the MIMIC (Multiple Indicators Multiple Causes) model treat the shadow economy as a latent variable influenced by causal factors (e.g., tax burden, regulation, corruption) and reflected in multiple indicators (e.g., currency demand, electricity use, labor participation). MIMIC, essentially a structural equation model, can integrate various data but requires calibration with an external estimate of the shadow economy's absolute level in at least one period (Medina & Schneider, 2018; Schneider & Enste, 2002). This dependence on a base value (often drawn from one of the indirect methods) is a noted limitation common to both MIMIC and the electricity approach (OECD, 2002; Schneider & Enste, 2002).
- *There are few unorthodox methods of measuring the size of the shadow economy*: In line with other studies, a recent study by Abdumavlonov et al. (2023) provides a complementary framework for understanding informality in Uzbekistan by combining employment-based estimates with energy consumption metrics. The authors highlight that informal employment accounts for a significant share of total labor, particularly in rural and service sectors, and show that electricity usage data can uncover unrecorded production, especially when adjusted for seasonal and regional anomalies. Their hybrid approach confirms a sustained decline in the shadow economy's relative size following major market reforms post-2017, corroborating findings from MIMIC and ECMs. Notably, their analysis reinforces the need to correct for structural and technological change when applying electricity-based estimators in transition economies. This paper serves as a national benchmark, supporting the validity of ECM-based shadow economy estimates when calibrated with labor and institutional data.

Uzbekistan's case has been less studied in the international literature, but available estimates confirm a large shadow economy that has started to shrink recently. These estimates often relied on the electricity method and showed relatively flat trends since Uzbekistan's per capita electricity consumption was stagnant for some years. A more recent in-depth study by Donaev (2019) applied a MIMIC model to Uzbekistan for 2007–2018, using a calibration of 50% shadow economy share in an initial year based on official sources. The MIMIC results showed the shadow economy declining from ~ 62% of official GDP in 2007 to ~ 50% by 2018. This downward trend aligns with the narrative that post-2016 reforms have brought more activity into the official realm. In fact, Uzbekistan's official statistics agency recently for the first time published an estimate of the "unobserved economy": according to a 2024 report, the shadow economy generated about UZS 505.7 trillion of output in 2024–roughly 34% of overall GDP (approximately 50% of recorded GDP) (UzDaily.com, 2025). This official recognition underscores the magnitude of the issue. Moreover, the report noted that informality is highest in agriculture (nearly two-thirds of that sector's output) and significant in construction and services (~40%), whereas heavy industry is more fully captured. These sectoral patterns are intuitive and important when interpreting results of the electricity approach, since different sectors have varying electricity intensities.

In summary, the literature offers a menu of methods to triangulate the size of the shadow economy. We focus on the ECM, enhancing it with an econometric framework to accommodate efficiency changes. The next section outlines our data and methodology, which aim to produce a robust time-series estimate of Uzbekistan's shadow economy and to compare it with prior benchmarks from other approaches.

5 Model/Data

ECM—the focus of this study—has been applied in transition economies and developing countries due to often unreliable monetary statistics. Kaufmann and Kaliberda's seminal application to Eastern Europe and the former USSR assumed a unit elasticity between electricity consumption and total GDP. In other words, a 1% GDP increase requires roughly 1% more electricity use, implying constant energy intensity. Under this assumption, the shadow economy's growth rate can be inferred by subtracting official GDP growth from electricity consumption growth

(Lackó, 2000). However, the constant elasticity assumption has been criticized. As Eilat and Zinnes (2002) point out, transition economies undergo structural shifts and efficiency gains that can alter electricity-to-GDP ratios over time. For example, modernization, adoption of energy-efficient technologies, or a shift from heavy industry to services can all *reduce the energy intensity* of GDP (Statista, 2025). Indeed, Uzbekistan is known to have one of the highest energy intensities in the world, but it has been *falling rapidly* (about 6.5% per year since 2000) due to efficiency improvements (World Bank, 2024). This means a unit of GDP today requires much less electricity than in the past, violating the static elasticity assumption.

To address this, researchers have introduced adjustments. Kaufmann and Kaliberda themselves experimented with different elasticity scenarios (grouping countries by energy efficiency) (Kaufmann & Kaliberda, 1996). Johnson, Kaufmann, and Shliefer (1997) proposed using country-specific elasticities for cross-country comparisons. Feige and Urban (2003) modified the method by using regression analysis to predict electricity usage from official GDP and other variables, attributing any excess consumption to the shadow economy. Eilat and Zinnes (2002) recommended regressing electricity on recorded output (and perhaps time trends or structural factors) to capture evolving efficiency, then using the residual (unexplained electricity use) as the part due to unrecorded output. We adopt a similar regression-based approach in this paper. In parallel, Lackó's approach focused on household electricity consumption to infer the informal household economy, assuming constant household energy efficiency over time (Lackó, 2000). Lackó (2000) argued that where a large portion of households engage in informal production (e.g., home workshops, unreported services), high residential electricity use signals a larger shadow economy. This method, however, also assumes no changes in household energy efficiency or electrification rates, which may not hold over long periods.

This study draws on a multi-year dataset combining electricity consumption, national accounts, and macroeconomic indicators to estimate the size of the shadow economy in Uzbekistan from 2000 to 2023. The core variable of interest—total electricity consumption—was obtained from the official records of Uzbekistan's unified power system (Uzbekenergo and its successor National Electricity Grids of Uzbekistan company). The dataset includes hourly and annualized electricity consumption figures, which were aggregated to produce consistent yearly totals measured in terawatt-hours (TWh). These values represent the net electricity delivered to final consumers, excluding technical transmission and distribution losses where possible. For the period 2018–2024, detailed hourly load profiles allowed for validation and seasonal adjustment, while data for earlier years were sourced from annual energy balance reports and statistical bulletins published by the Ministry of Energy and the State Committee on Statistics. According to these records, Uzbekistan's electricity use has grown from about 45.6 TWh in 2000 to about 61.7 TWh in 2021, an increase of ~ 35% over two decades (MinEnergo, 2024; UzStat, 2025). Growth has accelerated in recent years: for instance, consumption rebounded by + 5.6% in 2021 to 61.7 TWh after a slight dip in 2020 (Enerdata, 2025; MinEnergo, 2024). By 2023, total electricity demand was on the order of 78–81 TWh reflecting both economic growth and expanded electrification.

To complement the electricity data, we use official estimates of Gross Domestic Product (GDP) at constant prices, expressed in USD and national currency units, adjusted for inflation using official deflators. GDP figures were sourced from the State Agency on Statistics under the President of the Republic of Uzbekistan, the World Bank's World Development Indicators (WDI) database, and cross-verified with the International Monetary Fund (IMF) and Asian Development Bank (ADB) country reports. For real GDP, we constructed a continuous time series using chain-linked volume indices to account for rebasing and methodological changes over time. This harmonized GDP series enables meaningful year-on-year comparisons and accurate elasticity estimation in the econometric model.

Uzbekistan's recorded real GDP grew robustly during 2000–2023, with official growth rates averaging 5–7% per annum (UzStat, 2024b) and no year of contraction even during the 2008–09 crisis or 2020 pandemic. In nominal USD terms, GDP rose from about $13.8 billion in 2000 to $80 billion in 2021 and $115 billion in 2024 (IMF, 2024; Knoema, 2025), owing in part to a major currency liberalization in 2017. For our purposes, we constructed a consistent real GDP series (index 2000 = 100) based on reported annual growth rates and validated it against available PPP-adjusted GDP data.

To control for changes in structural factors, we also include a time trend variable defined as the number of years since 2000. This trend serves as a proxy for improvements in energy efficiency, technological upgrading, and structural shifts in the economy (e.g., transition from heavy industry to services). Additionally, employment statistics and sectoral breakdowns of economic activity were incorporated for robustness checks and sensitivity analysis, particularly to validate the electricity-based estimates against labor market indicators. These supplementary variables were gathered from national labor force surveys, ILOSTAT, and reports by the Center for Economic Research and Reforms (CERR).

All variables were transformed into natural logarithms where appropriate (e.g., ln(electricity consumption), ln(GDP)) to stabilize variance and interpret the estimated coefficients as elasticities. We performed Augmented Dickey-Fuller (ADF) and Phillips-Perron (PP) tests to confirm the non-stationarity of the electricity and GDP series, validating the use of cointegration methods in the subsequent analysis.

Finally, to ensure internal consistency and transparency, all data cleaning, transformations, and calculations were performed in Stata 17. The data span a period of significant economic transformation in Uzbekistan, including currency liberalization in 2017, tax reforms, and increased electrification, making the dataset uniquely suitable for analyzing trends in formal and informal economic activity using the ECM.

We employ a cointegration analysis and Error-Correction Model (ECM) to link electricity consumption with economic output. This approach allows us to estimate the long-run equilibrium relationship between electricity and GDP while accounting for short-run deviations. The basic theoretical relationship can be expressed as:

$$\ln(E_t) = \alpha + \beta \ln\left(Y_t^{\text{off}}\right) + \gamma t + u_t,$$

where E_t is total electricity consumption in year t, Υ_t^{off} is official real GDP, and t is a linear time trend. The inclusion of a time trend γt captures systematic improvements in energy efficiency or changes in economic structure over time (Eilat & Zinnes, 2000; Statista, 2025). The coefficient β represents the elasticity of electricity usage with respect to GDP holding technology constant. If all economic activity were recorded and efficiency stayed constant, we would expect β approximately 1 in an industrial economy (electricity grows parallel with output) (Lackó, 2000). However, with efficiency gains, we expect $\beta < 1$; a significantly lower β suggests that GDP can grow faster than energy use, as seen in Uzbekistan. We expect a positive trend coefficient $\gamma > 0$ in the log-electricity equation) to reflect that for a given GDP, electricity use tends to be higher in earlier years and lower in later years—consistent with declining energy intensity. Alternatively, one can invert the relationship to predict GDP from electricity:

$$\ln(Y_t^{total}) = \frac{1}{\beta}\ln(E_t) - \frac{\alpha}{\beta} - \frac{\gamma}{\beta}t$$

where $\Upsilon_t^{\text{total}}$ is the *true total GDP* including shadow. This equation, derived from the cointegration, forms the basis for our shadow economy estimates: we interpret Υ_t^{total} as the level of output required to generate the observed electricity consumption given the estimated elasticity and trend. The shadow economy (SE) in year t is then calculated as the difference between this implied total GDP and the official GDP:

$$\text{SE}_t = Y_t^{\text{total}} - Y_t^{\text{off}},$$

and we often express it as a percentage of official GDP for interpretability:

$$\text{SE\%}_t = 100\% \times \left(\frac{Y_t^{\text{total}}}{Y_t^{\text{off}}} - 1\right)$$

To estimate the parameters, we first test for cointegration between $\ln(E_t)$ and Υ_t^{off} including a trend. Both the Engle-Granger two-step method and Johansen's trace test indicate one cointegrating relationship at the 5% level, confirming a stable long-run linkage. We estimate the cointegrating equation via *Dynamic OLS (DOLS)* to account for any serial correlation. The results (detailed in the next section) yield a statistically significant elasticity β and trend γ. We then set up a short-run ECM of the form:

$$\Delta \ln(E_t) = \phi\left[\ln(E_{t-1}) - \alpha - \beta \ln\left(Y_{t-1}^{off}\right) - \gamma(t-1)\right] + \theta \Delta \ln\left(Y_t^{off}\right) + \varepsilon_t,$$

where ϕ is the error-correction term indicating how fast deviations from the equilibrium are corrected, and θ captures short-term coupling between GDP changes and electricity changes. We estimate this ARDL (1,0) type model in levels (since variables are cointegrated) using OLS (which yields a super-consistent estimate of ϕ). The inclusion of only contemporaneous $\Delta\ln(\Upsilon_t^{off})$ in the short-run part is guided by Schwarz

Criterion (lagged differences were insignificant). We also tested for any structural breaks—notably around 2008 and 2017—using dummies; a 2017 dummy (post-liberalization) was marginally significant in the short-run equation, suggesting a slight regime shift in electricity-GDP dynamics after market reforms, but it did not materially change long-run estimates. Therefore, our final model does not include break dummies for parsimony.

Finally, to cross-validate our results, we compare them against other independent measures. Although a comprehensive multi-method comparison is beyond our scope, we reference currency demand approach estimates from prior studies and the aforementioned MIMIC model results (Donaev, 2019). These provide a robustness check on whether the electricity-based estimates seem reasonable in magnitude and trend. All statistical analysis was carried out in Stata 17, and time-series plots were produced in Python for visualization.

6 Empirical Results

Long-Run Elasticity and Model Fit: The estimated long-run equation (standard errors in parentheses) is:

$$\ln(E_t) = \underbrace{0.289\ \ln\left(Y_t{}^{\text{off}}\right)0.289\ \ln\left(Y_t{}^{\text{off}}\right)}_{0.055} + \underbrace{0.0275t}_{0.0045} + \underbrace{5.11}_{0.32}$$

with t measured in years since 2000. All coefficients are significant at the 1% level. The elasticity of electricity with respect to GDP is β approximately 0.29, indicating that a 10% increase in official GDP is associated with only about a 2.9% increase in electricity consumption holding the trend constant. This very low elasticity reflects Uzbekistan's dramatically declining energy intensity: the economy has been growing much faster than its power usage. The positive trend term γ implies that each year, for a given GDP, the required electricity is about 2.75% higher if we go one year backward—equivalently, energy needed for the same GDP has been dropping ~ 2.75% per year on average, which is plausible alongside efficiency improvements and structural change. The cointegrating relationship appears robust: residuals are stationary (ADF test statistic = –4.3, $p < 0.01$) and the error-correction term in the ECM is significant ϕ approximately -0.35, $p = 0.02$, meaning about 35% of any deviation between electricity and GDP is corrected in the next year. The short-run coefficient on GDP change is θ approximately 0.15 ($p = 0.10$), suggesting that in any single year, official GDP growth has a positive but weak contemporaneous effect on electricity growth—again underscoring that short-term GDP fluctuations do not proportionally translate into power usage, likely due to the prominence of low-energy services and the buffering effect of energy efficiency measures. Overall, the model fits reasonably well (adj. $R^2 = 0.64$ for the cointegrating regression) given the simplicity of a two-variable model. These results are in line with expectations: Uzbekistan's energy intensity decline of ~ 6–7%/year reported elsewhere (World Bank, 2024) is captured by the combination of $\beta < 1$ and a time trend.

Estimated Size of the Shadow Economy: Using the estimated parameters, we compute the implied total GDP Υ_t^{total} each year from 2000 to 2023. The shadow economy share is then derived as $(\Upsilon_t^{total} - \Upsilon_t^{off})/\Upsilon_t^{off}$. Our estimates indicate that Uzbekistan's shadow economy was extremely large in the early 2000s, on the order of 50–60% of official GDP (Fig. 1). It appears to have peaked in the mid-2000s: for example, in 2007 we estimate the shadow economy at ~ 60% of official GDP, which aligns well with the MIMIC-based 62% estimate for that year (Donaev, 2019). During the 2010s, there is a clear declining trend. By 2015, the shadow share is about 55%, and by 2018 it is about 50%. This again dovetails with Donaev (2019)'s finding of ~ 50% in 2018. In the most recent years, our model suggests the informal sector has shrunk further: by 2023, we estimate the shadow economy to be roughly 35–40% of official GDP, its smallest share in two decades. This is consistent with the official preliminary estimate of ~ 34% of total GDP for 2024 (which corresponds to ~ 50% of official GDP) (UzStat, 2024a). In absolute terms, given an official GDP of about \$80 billion in 2021, a 40% shadow would mean an additional ~ \$32 billion of unreported output in that year.

It is important to emphasize that while the level of the shadow economy (as % of GDP) is model-dependent, the directional trend of decline is robust across methods. Both our electricity-based approach and the alternative methods (MIMIC, currency demand, and even government's own estimate) show a substantial informal sector gradually contracting in relative size over the past decade. This lends credibility to the result. The shrinking shadow share likely reflects structural reforms: after 2017, Uzbekistan simplified its tax system, liberalized foreign exchange (removing the black-market currency premium), and made it

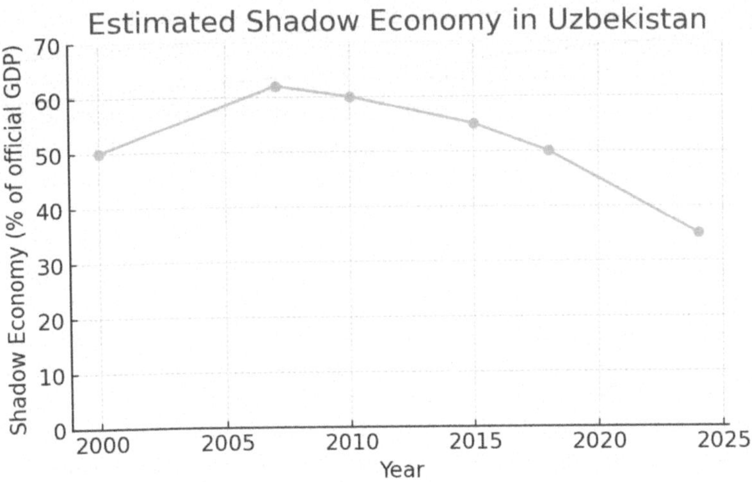

Fig. 1 Estimated size of Uzbekistan's shadow economy (unofficial output) as a percentage of official GDP (*Source* Authors' calculations)

easier for small businesses to operate formally (ADB, 2025; Medina & Schneider, 2018). These changes provided incentives for economic activities to "surface" into the official economy, which is captured as an increasing official GDP without commensurate increases in energy use (since those activities were already happening, just not recorded, or because new formal services are less energy-intensive).

To gauge uncertainty, we conducted a sensitivity analysis. Using a time-varying elasticity, e.g., allowing β to increase in later years or excluding the trend yields a higher inferred shadow in early years and a somewhat lower in later years, but the difference at endpoints is within $\pm$ 5 percentage points. If one naively assumed $\beta = 1$, implying no efficiency gains for the whole period, the method would significantly overestimate the shadow economy in recent years—producing an implausibly large negative shadow, i.e., suggesting over-reporting by 2020, which underscores the necessity of our adjustments. On the other hand, if one assumes a smaller trend improvement, the decline in shadow share would be less steep. Overall, we judge our presented figures to be conservative yet reasonable. For example, in 2023, the electricity method gives ~ 37%

of GDP as informal; a currency demand approach might yield something somewhat higher or lower depending on assumptions, but likely on the order of 30–40%. Notably, in a Central Asia regional study using the currency demand method, Uzbekistan's shadow economy was found to be about 45% of GDP in 2015—higher than our electricity estimate ~ 55% for 2015, possibly because cash usage remained high but declining after 2016, which qualitatively agrees with our findings.

In Fig. 1 (above), we plotted the trajectory of the shadow economy share implied by our estimates, highlighting the peak and recent decline. The figure illustrates that informality in Uzbekistan, while still substantial—roughly one-third of the economy in the 2020s—is lower today than it was 10–15 years ago. The result is encouraging for policymakers, though the shadow economy remains large relative to many other countries. For context, in the 2010s the average shadow economy size worldwide was ~ 27% of GDP and for transition economies around 36% (Medina & Schneider, 2018). Uzbekistan's latest figures are now in line with that regional average, whereas earlier it was an outlier with one of the highest shares.

7 Discussion

The findings have several important implications and insights when interpreted through the lenses of energy and development economics. First, the persistence of a large shadow economy—reaching 30–50% of GDP—in Uzbekistan over the past two decades points to structural and institutional challenges. Key drivers of informality in Uzbekistan likely include high tax burdens and complex regulations which incentivize businesses to hide output, past episodes of foreign exchange controls which drove activities off the official books, and weak enforcement of contracts and property rights in certain periods, prompting reliance on informal arrangements. The sectoral breakdown from official data confirms that agriculture and small trade/services contribute heavily to the shadow economy (UzDaily.com, 2025). These sectors typically have many small transactions, often in cash, and are difficult to monitor. They are also relatively low in electricity usage per unit of value added; for example, trading $100 of produce uses far less electricity than producing $100 of factory output. This underscores a subtle point: the electricity method may underestimate the shadow economy in countries where the informal sector is concentrated in light industries or services. In Uzbekistan, much of the informal activity such as bazaar trading, transport services, home-based workshops, etc. does not proportionally boost national power consumption. Our methodology partly accounts for this via the trend and elasticity, but it is inherently easier to detect “missing” heavy industrial output which would draw noticeable power than missing service output. Thus, our estimate of ~ 35% shadow in recent years might be seen as a lower bound; the true share could be somewhat higher if, for instance, many informal transactions require negligible electricity.

From an energy economics perspective, the dramatic drop in energy intensity in Uzbekistan is both a blessing and a methodological complication. It reflects positive developments—modernization and efficiency gains—but complicates using energy data to track economic activity. Our time-trend approach captures the average efficiency gain, but efficiency improvements are not uniform: for example, the rollout of LED lighting or more efficient motors reduces consumption without reducing output, potentially looking like “shadow economy shrinkage” in the electricity method if not controlled. Additionally, electricity supply constraints—common in Uzbekistan especially in winter peaks of the 2010s—might have capped consumption and forced some informal production to use alternative sources such as diesel generators or simply operate less—meaning our data might miss some off-grid or unserved demand. If anything, chronic power shortages in earlier years could mean we underestimated the shadow economy then, because unmet electricity demand was not recorded, making it appear as if total activity was lower. However, Uzbekistan has been expanding generation capacity and reducing shortages in recent years, so this effect is likely diminishing.

Another interesting angle is that the shadow economy itself can affect energy usage patterns. Anecdotally, when firms operate in the shadows, they may steal electricity or avoid metering, leading to higher transmission and distribution losses. Uzbekistan historically has had high T&D loss rates, reaching 15% or more of electricity output (CEIC Data, 2025; Statista, 2025). Some of these losses include so-called “commercial losses” by enterprises or individuals not reporting their consumption. A campaign to install advanced metering and crack down on illegal connections in 2018–2020 coincided with greater formalization of many small businesses, which may show up as a slight jump in official GDP, as sales are declared, while technical losses in the grid decreased. This interplay between energy policy and informality suggests that investment in grid metering and reliability can support formalization. Businesses are more willing to formalize if electricity supply is reliable and fairly priced, and authorities can better detect undeclared operations via abnormal energy usage.

From a development policy perspective, the shadow economy's large size implies significant foregone tax revenues and social contributions. It hampers the government's ability to fund infrastructure, education, and health—which in turn can perpetuate a cycle where poor public services push more activity into informality. Moreover, a large informal sector can distort competition—in which formal firms are at a cost disadvantage—reduce productivity growth, and limit workers' access to legal protections. Our finding that the informal share is declining is a positive sign: it suggests that recent reforms, i.e., tax cuts, easier business registration, currency convertibility, are building trust in formal institutions. As more entrepreneurs opt into the formal economy, the government should see an expanding tax base, as evidenced by rising tax revenues in 2021–2023. The tax collection grew faster than GDP in real terms during this period, indicating improved compliance.

8 Policy Recommendations

All in all, the battle is not won. With still ~ 40% of output off the books, Uzbekistan needs to continue its reform trajectory. For this purpose, we present policy recommendations in the following areas:

General Recommendations for Reducing Informality:

i. *Simplify tax and regulatory regimes.* High compliance costs and bureaucratic burdens are key drivers of informality. Introducing simplified taxation schemes—such as flat or presumptive taxes for micro and small enterprises—and expanding digital tools for tax filing and registration can lower entry barriers into the formal economy. Broader legal reforms to reduce arbitrary inspections and discretionary enforcement would enhance trust in state institutions and encourage voluntary compliance.

ii. *Expand digital financial inclusion and limit cash transactions.* Informal activities are often cash-based, making them harder to track. Expanding access to bank accounts, mobile money, and e-payment systems—especially in rural areas—can help formalize transactions. Mandating non-cash payments for salaries or high-value purchases can shrink the cash-based shadow economy while improving transparency.

iii. *Rationalize subsidies and strengthen procurement governance.* Many public goods and infrastructure projects in Uzbekistan are delivered through non-transparent channels that inflate costs and create incentives for corruption. A phased transition to cost-reflective utility pricing, paired with targeted subsidies for vulnerable groups, would reduce distortions and fiscal pressure. At the same time, enhancing procurement oversight—especially in sectors like road construction—through digital bidding, independent auditing, and results-based contracting can reduce leakage and cost overruns that indirectly fuel informality.

iv. *Develop inclusive urban policy and job creation outside major centers.* Internal migration and unequal spatial development have driven up housing costs and fed informality in the construction sector. A more balanced regional development policy—investing in job creation, services, and infrastructure in secondary cities—would reduce migratory pressure and promote equitable growth. Measures to curb speculative real estate investments and expand affordable housing would also help formalize the housing and construction value chain.

8.1 ECM-Specific Recommendations Based on Model Findings

i. *Institutionalize the ECM within statistical systems.* The ECM has demonstrated its utility in estimating the scale and evolution of Uzbekistan's shadow economy. To mainstream its application, the State Committee on Statistics and the Ministry of Energy should integrate ECM-based diagnostics into routine monitoring. Regular updates based on high-frequency electricity and GDP data can help policymakers detect trends in informality and assess the real impact of structural reforms.

ii. *Enhance energy data transparency and granularity.* The accuracy of ECM estimates depends heavily on the quality and granularity of electricity consumption data. To improve measurement precision, disaggregated consumption data by sector (industrial, residential, commercial) and region should be made publicly available. Real-time metering data from smart grid infrastructure could further refine estimates of informal activity, especially in service-oriented sectors with low electricity intensity.

iii. *Improve targeting of enforcement using energy-consumption anomalies.* One practical application of ECM findings is the use of electricity consumption as a red flag for underreporting. For example, firms that consume disproportionately high levels of electricity relative to declared output or employment could be flagged for audits. Developing energy-financial benchmarks across sectors could assist the tax authority and anti-corruption agencies in better risk profiling and targeting enforcement.

iv. *Link energy reforms with formalization strategies.* Declining energy intensity, as observed in the ECM results, reflects efficiency gains but can mask persistent informal activity if not properly accounted for. Ongoing energy reforms—such as tariff adjustments and grid modernization—should be paired with pro-formalization policies, such as offering formal enterprises access to preferential electricity pricing, financing for energy-efficient upgrades, and faster connection services. This dual-track approach can incentivize informal actors to register and benefit from modernization.

9 Conclusion

This research set out to measure the size of Uzbekistan's shadow economy using an energy-based proxy approach, contributing to both the energy economics and development economics perspectives. We employed an ECM enhanced with econometric modeling, allowing us to account for changing energy efficiency over time. The results indicate that Uzbekistan's shadow economy is large but has been shrinking—from on the order of ~ 60% of official GDP in the early-to-mid-2000s down to ~ 35–40% in the mid-2020s. These figures align with estimates from other methods (currency demand, MIMIC) and even official statistical releases (Donaev, 2019; UzStat, 2024a), bolstering confidence in our approach.

Methodologically, the inclusion of a time trend and cointegration framework was crucial. A naive application of the electricity method (assuming a fixed one-to-one link between electricity and GDP) would have yielded misleading results in Uzbekistan's case, given the rapid decline in energy intensity (Donaev, 2019). By estimating an elasticity of about 0.3, we capture the reality that the Uzbek economy has grown through diversification and efficiency gains—meaning less extra electricity is needed per unit of GDP. This highlights a general lesson: energy-based estimates of the shadow economy should be tailored to each country's context, incorporating technological and structural changes. For researchers and practitioners, our approach provides a template for integrating energy data with time-series analysis to gauge informality, which could be applied to other countries with improving energy efficiency, for example, the vast majority of the transition and emerging economies.

There are several limitations to acknowledge. Data quality is always a concern when dealing with both electricity statistics and GDP figures in developing countries. We assumed the electricity data fully captures consumption, but if there were unrecorded generation or significant outages, our estimates might be off.

We also treated the relationship as linear in logs; non-linear effects, such as saturation of electricity access, were not modeled but could be relevant in the future. Another limitation is that we did not explicitly model other drivers of the shadow economy, such as tax rates or unemployment, which are included in MIMIC models (Schneider & Enste, 2002). Including such variables in a multivariate cointegration might improve the estimates or allow decomposition of causes, which is a potential area for further research.

Future research could extend this work in several directions. One avenue is to integrate additional physical indicators—for example, gasoline consumption or nighttime light intensity alongside electricity to capture informal activity in transportation and commerce that electricity alone might miss. Another direction is a sectoral analysis: using data on industrial vs residential electricity use to separately estimate informal industrial production, which would reflect in industrial electricity, versus informal services/households, which might correlate with residential electricity and gas usage. Such granularity could inform targeted policy, for example if most informal activity is in retail and uses little power, other approaches are needed to measure and formalize it. Furthermore, as more data become available, one could examine the impact of specific reforms on the shadow economy—for instance, did the 2019 tax reform or the COVID-19 pandemic cause any structural break in our series? Initial signs suggest formalization accelerated after 2017, but quantifying the effect of each policy would require a longer post-reform time series or panel data across regions.

In conclusion, measuring the shadow economy remains a challenging but essential task for development policy. Our study demonstrates that electricity consumption can serve as a revealing window into the hidden part of the economy, especially when combined with rigorous empirical methods. For Uzbekistan, the findings are cautiously optimistic: the shadow economy, while still significant, is gradually being brought into the light. Sustained reforms and investments—in both the economic and energy sectors—are likely to reinforce this positive trajectory. As Uzbekistan continues to modernize, one can expect the gap between official statistics and reality to further narrow, ultimately delivering more transparent and inclusive economic growth for the country.

References

Abdumavlonov, Kh., Eshchanov, B., and Khakimov, O. (2023). The dynamics of parallel economies: Measuring the informal sector in Uzbekistan. *AIP Conference Proceedings, 2812*, 020011.

ADB. (2025). *Uzbekistan Member Fact Sheet,* 2024 (Online). https://www.adb.org/sites/default/files/publication/27811/uzb-2024.pdf. Accessed: July 2025.

Cagan, P. (1958). The demand for currency relative to the total money supply. *Journal of Political Economy, 66*(4), 303–328. https://doi.org/10.1086/258056

CEIC Data. (2025). Uzbekistan GDP and energy data. [Online]. https://www.ceicdata.com/en/uzbekistan/energy-production-and-consumption/uz-electric-power-transmission-and-distribution-losses--of-output. Accessed: July 2025

Donaev, F. (2019). *Estimating the size of the shadow economy in Uzbekistan with MIMIC model*. M.A. thesis, Central European University. https://www.etd.ceu.edu/2019/donaev_farkhod.pdf. Accessed: July 2025.

Eilat, Y., & Zinnes, C. (2000). *The Evolution of the Shadow Economy in Transition Countries: Consequences for Economic Growth and Donor Assistance*. CAER II Discussion Paper No.83, Harvard Institute for International Development, Available at: https://citeseerx.ist.psu.edu/document?repid=rep1&type=pdf&doi=39d1e895838565e095d0ec5ceec38eb137f8711a. Accessed: July 2025.

Eilat, A., & Zinnes, C. (2002). The shadow economy in transition countries: Friend or foe? A Policy Perspective. *World Development, 30*(7), 1233–1254. https://doi.org/10.1016/S0305-750X(02)00036-0

Enerdata. (2025). Uzbekistan energy report (Online). https://www.enerdata.net/estore/country-profiles/uzbekistan.html. Accessed: Jul. 2025.

Feige, E. L., & Urban, I. (2003). Estimating the size and growth of unrecorded economic activity in transition countries: A re-evaluation of electric consumption method estimates and their implications. *William Davidson Institute Working Paper* No. 636. https://deepblue.lib.umich.edu/handle/2027.42/40022. Accessed: July 2025.

ILO. (2020). *Women and the world of work in Uzbekistan—Towards Gender Equality and Decent Work for All*. International Labour Organization, 2020. 2nd edition. https://www.ilo.org/publications/women-and-world-work-uzbekistan-towards-gender-equality-and-decent-work-all. Accessed July 2025

IMF. (2019). *Republic of Uzbekistan: 2019 Article IV consultation - Press release and staff report*. IMF Country Report No. 19/129. May 2019. https://www.imf.org/en/Publications/CR/Issues/2019/05/09/Republic-of-Uzbekistan-2019-Article-IV-Consultation-Press-Release-and-Staff-Report-46884. Accessed: July 2025.

IMF. (2024). Uzbekistan macroeconomic statistics, 2024 (Online). https://www.imf.org/external/datamapper/profile/UZB. Accessed: July 2025.

Johnson, S., Kaufmann, D., & Shleifer, A. (1997). The unofficial economy in transition. *Brookings Papers on Economic Activity, 1997*(2), 159–239. https://www.brookings.edu/wp-content/uploads/1997/06/1997b_bpea_johnson_kaufmann_shleifer_goldman_weitzman.pdf. Accessed: July 2025.

Kaufmann, D., & Kaliberda, A. (1996). Integrating the unofficial economy into the dynamics of post-socialist economies. *World Bank Policy Research Working Paper* No. 1691. https://documents.worldbank.org/en/publication/documents-reports/documentdetail/145671468771609920/integrating-the-unofficial-economy-into-the-dynamics-of-post-socialist-economies-a-framework-of-analysis-and-evidence. Accessed: July 2025.

Knoema. (2025). *GDP current USD (Uzbekistan)* (Online). https://knoema.com/atlas/Uzbekistan. Accessed: July 2025.

Kun.uz. (2025). *Tariff hikes in Uzbekistan drive households to cut energy use*. March 8, 2025. Online material: https://www.kun.uz/en/news/2025/06/03/tariff-hikes-in-uzbekistan-drive-households-to-cut-energy-use#:~:text=The%20results%20showed%20that%20electricity,to%20just%2015%2C000%20in%202024. Accessed: July 2025

Lackó, M. (2000). Hidden economy—an unknown quantity? Comparative analysis of hidden economies in transition countries, 1989–95. *Economics of Transition, 8*(1), 117–149. https://doi.org/10.1111/1468-0351.00038

Medina, L., & Schneider, F. (2018). Shadow economies around the world: What did we learn over the last 20 years? *IMF Working Paper* WP/18/17, 2018. https://www.imf.org/en/Publications/WP/Issues/2018/01/25/Shadow-Economies-Around-the-World-What-Did-We-Learn-Over-the-Last-20-Years-45583. Accessed: July 2025.

MinEnergo. (2024). *Electricity balance report*. Ministry of Energy of Uzbekistan.

OECD. (2002). *Measuring the Non-Observed Economy: A Handbook*. OECD Publishing. https://www.oecd.org/en/publications/measuring-the-non-observed-economy-a-handbook_9789264175358-en.html. Accessed: July 2025.

Schneider F., Buehn, A., & Montenegro, C. E. (2010). Shadow economies all over the world: New estimates for 162 countries from 1999 to 2007. *World Bank Policy Research Working Paper* No. 5356, 2010. https://documents.worldbank.org/en/publication/documents-reports/documentdetail/311991468037132740. Accessed: July 2025.

Schneider, F., & Enste, D. H. (2000). Shadow economies: Size, causes, and consequences. *Journal of Economic Literature, 38*(1), 77–114. https://doi.org/10.1257/jel.38.1.77

Schneider, F., & Enste, D. H. (2002). The Shadow Economy: An International Survey. *Cambridge University Press*. https://doi.org/10.1017/CBO9780511493591

Spot.uz. (2023). What is a shadow economy and how to combat it in Uzbekistan (originally in Russian: *Что такое теневая экономика и как с ней борются в Узбекистане*) April 4, 2023. Online material. https://www.spot.uz/ru/2023/04/04/shadow-economy/. Accessed: July 2025

Statista. (2025). *Total power generation in Uzbekistan from 2016 to 2024* (Online). https://www.statista.com/statistics/1299178/uzbekistan-electricity-generation/. Accessed: Jul. 2025.

Tanzi, V. (1983). The underground economy in the United States: Annual estimates. 1930–80. *IMF Staff Papers, 30*(2), 283–305. https://www.elibrary.imf.org/view/journals/024/1983/002/article-A002-en.xml. Accessed: July 2025.

Tanzi, V. (1999). Uses and abuses of estimates of the underground economy. *Economic Journal, 109*(456), F338–F347. https://doi.org/10.1111/1468-0297.00437

UzDaily.com. (2025). *The size of Uzbekistan's unobserved economy exceeds 505 trillion soum in 2024* (Online). https://www.uzdaily.uz/en/the-size-of-uzbekistans-unobserved-economy-exceeds-505-trillion-soums/. Accessed: July 2025

UzStat. (2024a). *Annual report on the unobserved economy*, 2024 (Online). State Agency of Statistics under the President of Uzbekistan. https://stat.uz. Accessed: July 2025.

UzStat. (2024b). *GDP series (2000–2023)*. State Agency of Statistics under the President of Uzbekistan.

UzStat. (2025). Energy efficiency and fuel balance *2000–2023* (Online). https://stat.uz/en/official-statistics/energy-efficiency-and-fuel-balance. Accessed: July 2025.

World Bank. (2022). *Country partnership framework for the Republic of Uzbekistan for the period of FY2022–2026*. Central Asia Country Management Unit. May 24. https://documents.worldbank.org/pt/publication/documents-reports/documentdetail/558271653576525839/uzbekistan-country-partnership-framework-for-the-period-fy2022-fy2026. Accessed: July 2025.

World Bank. (2024). Uzbekistan energy efficiency indicators. *World Development Indicators* (Online). https://data.worldbank.org. Accessed: July 2025.

Index

E. Bagirzadeh and O. Gokcekus (eds.), *Shadow Economies in Turkic Republics*, https://doi.org/10.1007/978-3-032-12872-0

F

G

S

T

The manufacturer's authorised representative in the EU is Springer Nature Customer Service Centre GmbH, Europaplatz 3, 69115 Heidelberg, Germany. If you have any concerns regarding our products, please contact ProductSafety@springernature.com

Printed and bound by CPI Group (UK) Ltd, Croydon, CR0 4YY
22/09/2026
02220991-0009